A Sense of Control: Virtual communities for people with mobility impairments

CHRISTINE M. TILLEY

Chandos Publishing

Oxford · England

Chandos Publishing (Oxford) Limited
TBAC Business Centre
Avenue 4
Station Lane
Witney
Oxford OX28 4BN
UK
Tel: +44 (0) 1993 848726 Fax: +44 (0) 1865 884448
E-mail: info@chandospublishing.com
www.chandospublishing.com

First published in Great Britain in 2009

ISBN:
978 1 84334 521 3 (paperback)
978 1 84334 522 0 (hardback)
1 84334 521 8 (paperback)
1 84334 522 6 (hardback)

British Library Cataloguing-in-Publication Data.
A catalogue record for this book is available from the British Library.

Typeset in the UK by Concerto.
Printed in the UK and USA.

For
my dear Margaret
with thanks for your love and nurture,
and for all that you are and all that you do.

Contents

List of figures and tables

Figures

Tables

About the author

Dr Christine M. Tilley is an associate of Queensland University of Technology (QUT), Brisbane, Australia. She has lectured at QUT and other tertiary institutions for some two decades, and served as an adviser and board member for numerous library and informational technology committees. Additionally, she was the manager of the QUT Faculty of Information Technology Computer Managed Learning facility; a member of the Preservation Sub-committee, Australian Council of Libraries & Information Services (Queensland branch); a member of the State Committee, Australian Council of Libraries & Information Services (previously Australian Advisory Council of Bibliographic Services); and coordinator of the Early Imprints Project Queensland (EIPQ). She has extensive experience in disability issues, has been active in disability and other community organisations and continues to publish widely in this area. Her research work has included information and communications technology and disability, information literacy, community information use and the EIPQ. Furthermore, she has been an approved Commonwealth valuer (antiquarian and second-hand books, especially early printing, fine printing and illustrated books, Australiana) for the Cultural Gifts Program (Insurance, Family Division and Probate), Department of the Environment, Water, Heritage and the Arts, Canberra, for the past 25 years.

Acknowledgements

Firstly, I acknowledge and thank Professor Christine Bruce, my mentor in academic matters, for sharing her inspiration, wisdom and knowledge over the years. She is an intellectual mentor of the finest kind as well as a friend, and to her go my genuine thanks. Christine is also an excellent role model and her wise counsel and expert guidance in all phases of the planning, research, analysis and writing stages have made this work a reality.

To my other academic mentors, Professor Andrew Hills, Associate Professor Gillian Hallam, Dr Neville Meyers, Professor Donald Schauder and Professor Nicholas Bellamy, director of CONROD, I give my sincere thanks for their encouragement, and also for their practical assistance. I also wish to acknowledge all the members of the QUILT research group who met regularly and offered collegial advice and support throughout the process of the original study – particularly Associate Professor Sylvia Edwards, Michael Middleton and Hilary Hughes.

My friend and ex-colleague Dr Gerard Finn was a source of practical help and inspiration, as were Louise Campbell, Kylie Downs, Gunela Astbrink, my cousin Jan Kiek, Anne Maguire and Drs Faye Thompson, Mary Ditton and Glenice Watson, whose assistance, example and encouragement were essential. In addition to the above persons, my thanks go to other colleagues and friends in the academic, library and support staff of the Queensland University of Technology, Brisbane, Australia, who gave freely their advice as well as their assistance. I also would like to mention Wendy Dent and Judith Anderson, Ray Duplock, High Performance Computing and Research Support Group, Information Technology Services and Laura Venn, assistant to the assistant dean, Teaching and Learning, Faculty of Information Technology. Besides the assistance from the above, many individuals gave advice, help and encouragement in the progress of the work and the

School of Information Systems was particularly helpful with facilities and resources.

I am grateful to Cherry Ekins, a talented editor, who generously read drafts and offered many helpful suggestions for improvement, and to Dr Glyn Jones for publishing this book. Any errors or omissions are mine alone!

However, the whole project could not have been undertaken without the tireless contributions from those knowledgeable people with physical disabilities. I am also indebted to the allied health, information and policy adviser professionals who participated in the interviews and contributed so willingly.

I would like to acknowledge my mother, Margaret Doig Tilley (1911–1992), who contributed in so many ways to my whole being and had a deep appreciation of education, especially for women and persons with disabilities. Without her support, my education would not have occurred. Would that she had lived to see this outcome of her vision and efforts.

List of acronyms

ACA	Australian Communications Authority
ACIF	Australian Communication Industry Forum
ACM-CHI	Association of Computing Machinery-Computer Human Interaction
ADA	Americans with Disabilities Act 1990
ADD	access digital divide
ADD	attention deficit disorder
ADSL	asymmetrical digital subscriber lines
AGIO	Australian Government Information Office
AIDS	acquired immune deficiency syndrome
AIIA	Australian Information Industry Association
ALA	American Library Association
ALIA	Australian Library and Information Association
AMTA	Australian Mobile Telecommunications Association
ANTA	Australian National Training Authority
ASLA	Australian School Library Association
AT	assistive technology
ATAC	Australian Telework Advisory Committee
ATAP	Association of Assistive Technology Act Programs

ATIA	Australian Telecommunications Industry Association
BCC	Brisbane City Council
BITES	basic IT enabling skills
BSL	British sign language
BT	British Telecom
CAUL	Council of Australian University Librarians
CDS	Commonwealth Disability Strategy (Australia)
CHI	computer-human interaction
CMC	computer-mediated communication
CN	community network
CONROD	Centre of National Research on Disability and Rehabilitation Medicine (Australia)
CORDE	National Coordination Office for the Integration of People with Disabilities (Brazil)
CPSR	Computer Professionals for Social Responsibility
CRE	Commission for Racial Equality (UK)
CSG	customer service guarantee
DAB	ACIF Disability Advisory Board
DCITA	Department of Communications, Information Technology and the Arts (Australia)
DD	digital divide
DDA	Disability Discrimination Act (Australia and UK)
DEFIE	Disabled and Elderly People Flexible Integrated Environment system
DEH	disability enquiry helpline (Australia)
DEP	disability equipment programme (Australia)
DIEL	Oftel Advisory Committee on Telecommunications for Disabled and Elderly People

DIRC	Disability Information and Resource Centre (Australia)
DRC	Disability Rights Commission (UK)
DSP	disability support pension
ECD	electronic communication device
ECU	environmental control unit
EE	electronic economy
EIPQ	Early Imprints Project Queensland
EOC	Equal Opportunities Commission (UK)
ESF	European Social Fund
FaCS	Department of Family and Community Services (Australia)
GSM	Global System for Mobile Communication
HCI	human-computer interaction
HECS	Higher Education Contribution Scheme (Australia)
HIV	human immunodeficiency virus
HREOC	Human Rights and Equal Opportunity Commission (Australia)
IBGE	Instituto Brasileiro de Geografia e Estatistica
ICIDH	International Classification System of Impairments, Activities and Participation
ICIDH-2	International Classification of Functioning and Disability
ICT	information and communications technology
IL	information literacy
ILC	Independent Living Centre (Australia)
ISOC-AU	Internet Society of Australia
ISP	internet service provider

IT	information technology
LAN	local area network
MAIC	Motor Accident Insurance Commission
MBA	master of business administration
MS	multiple sclerosis
NII	National Information Infrastructure (USA)
NOIE	National Office for the Information Economy (Australia)
NTIA	National Telecommunications and Information Administration (USA)
ONS	Office for National Statistics (UK)
OPCS	Office of Population Census and Surveys (UK)
OT	occupational therapist/therapy
PC	personal computer
PDCA	Physical Disability Council of Australia
PEALS	Policy, Ethics and Life Sciences Research Institute (UK)
PEN	public electronic network
PDF	portable document format
PIN	personal identification number
PQAQ	Paraplegic and Quadriplegic Association of Queensland
QIMR	Queensland Institute of Medical Research
QUT	Queensland University of Technology
RADIAL	REHADAT Australia Disability Information and Links
RTIF	Regional Telecommunications Infrastructure Fund (Australia)
SCI	spinal-cord injury
SDD	social digital divide

SIACP	Spinal Injuries Ambulatory Care Project (Australia)
SMS	short message service
SPOT	Spinal Outreach Team (Australia)
STD	subscriber trunk dialling
TAD	Technical Aids for the Disabled
TAFE	technical and further education
TCCC	Telstra Consumer Consultative Council (Australia)
TDF	Telstra Disability Forum (Australia)
TEDICORE	Telecommunications Disability Consumer Representation Project (Australia)
TRP	transitional rehabilitation programme (Australia)
TSI	Telecommunications Service Inquiry (Australia)
USO	Universal Service Obligation
VOCD	voice output communication device
W3C	World Wide Web Consortium
WAI	Web Accessibility Initiative
WAP	Wireless Application Protocol
WG	Washington Group on Disability Statistics
WiFi	wireless fidelity
WWDA	Women with Disabilities Australia

Preface

> I am interested in the predicament of disability – the personal experience of impairment, but also social reactions to disabled people – stereotype, humour, incomprehension, hostility. With its frailty, mortality and grace, the body can both bring us together and also set us apart. (Tom Shakespeare[1])

Bourdieu (1992: 40) writes: 'If we are not educated, we cannot think much at all, yet if we are educated we risk being dominated by ready-made thoughts.' After many decades of life, 12 years of schooling and similar in tertiary study, I have accumulated my fair share of 'ready-made thoughts'. However, in this work I have sought to make some of these 'ready-made thoughts' explicit, while still providing a theoretical validity for their presence.

I am a person with severe, long-term physical/mobility impairment as the result of childhood poliomyelitis. The people I talked with in conducting the work reported here identified with my efforts to determine how virtual communities are best facilitated for persons with disabilities, and they recognised the relevance of my question to their respective situations. During some of the interviews, I was aware of the enormous pain it brought to the interviewees to recall the trauma of their accidents and then to recount the nature of their ongoing disability. I began the work knowing there could be some difficult and sad aspects, but not realising the depth of the distress and how it would sometimes affect me.

I am a member of the library community and have worked in libraries and as a library and information studies educator, as well as in the second-hand and rare books trade. I also work as a book and manuscript valuer. Furthermore, as a member of the Board of Management of the Spinal Injuries Association, I have a long-standing involvement with that part of the disability sector. This involvement permitted me to identify and have access to the people who I needed to work with to conduct this investigation.

I would like to believe that my personal experience of deep identification with my interviewees contributed to my sensitivity as I went about this inquiry. Reinharz (1992: 234) says: 'The value in identifying lies in the enhanced understanding one can develop and assistance one can give. The drawback is the pain that comes from identifying with people who are suffering. We may gradually turn away to protect our equilibrium and continue our work.'

This book is organised, written and presented to enhance an understanding of the problem I tackled: what should a virtual community for people with disabilities look like? The processes through which the problem was investigated and analysed, and how I drew conclusions with regard to facilitating virtual communities for persons with long-term, severe physical disabilities, follow in a brief outline of all the chapters presented towards the conclusion of this section.

The literature I discuss in subsequent chapters provides an overview of the relevant recent history of virtual communities. My discussion indicates that certain issues and future directions arise from the global movement in electronic community networking. For example, for virtual communities to function, their resources need to be accessible to all members (Rheingold, 1994a; Schuler, 1997; Schuler, 2000). Resource developers must also face the challenges and implications of this need.

Electronic communities are composed of heterogeneous users with varying skills and access abilities and needs (Bartle, 2004). One of the principles of community networking is that it is an international movement founded on the idea of commonality that 'all citizens' of a local community should have access to low-cost electronic public space. The purpose of this access is to communicate and form communities of practice or interest that may or may not represent local geographic areas. Such citizens include the aged, people with various disabilities and the general public.[2]

Virtual communities have considerable potential to promote participation, social justice, economic betterment, communication, lifelong learning and diverse cultural practices among members of multiple and overlapping communities (Burnett and Buerkle, 2004). However, the success of these online communities depends on the availability of affordable and accessible technology – technology that permits all members of the community to share equally in the benefits of membership. Such communities seek to engage members in a rich environment that people, often ignorant of community member needs, develop. The growth of such communities, therefore, necessitates the transfer of relevant skills and knowledge to virtual community developers. The 'second-level digital divide' compounds this need. Much of the existing literature on the digital divide – the differences between the 'haves' and 'have-nots' regarding access to the internet – limits its scope to a binary classification of technology use by only considering whether someone does, or does not, use the internet (Hargittai, 2002).

People in rural areas, older people, women and people with disabilities have been among those less likely to use information and communications technology (ICT). Many governments are committed to ensuring that all citizens benefit from the information economy (Dube et al., 2005). One priority has been to ensure that barriers to equitable access to the online world are identified and addressed, so that all citizens can benefit from the broad vision of the information economy. However, one aspect of the digital divide that has not received very much attention to date is the manner in which it impacts upon civil and human rights groups which advocate for a more equitable and just society. We need to determine whether these groups, like many of the constituencies they represent, stand on the wrong side of the digital divide. If so, the implications for their work to achieve social justice, or to help shape the new digital society, must be considered. These concerns are as important to people with disabilities as to anyone else.

Who can use this book?

This work will be of value to anyone working with the development of virtual communities for people with physical disabilities. It extends the knowledge and understanding of the allied health and information professionals who provide services to them. It provides a serious stimulus to the IT community and the telecommunications industry to respond to more than the general needs of the markets they serve.

As it is multidisciplinary, the book meets the needs of several markets. It covers the topics of information, ICT, virtual communities, disability and the application of the qualitative research methodology grounded theory. It is aimed at librarians and knowledge managers, researchers and students.

Overview of the book

Chapter 1 introduces the significance of the well-being model through a virtual community for people with disabilities, and gives a brief history of virtual communities and the key elements of the well-being model.

Chapter 2 refines the virtual community definition, then considers the characteristics and functions of virtual communities, the major virtual community pioneers and finally some different models of virtual communities.

Chapter 3 provides an overview of the relevant legislative and government regulatory frameworks, telecommunications initiatives and information policies; and charts, in brief, some progress in these areas.

Chapter 4 considers the nature of information 'poverty', as well as a model of the 'social' information needs of people with long-term physical disabilities. This is done in terms of function, form, clusters, agents, users and mechanisms. It also briefly addresses other relevant 'information' issues for people with disabilities, such as the digital divide and information literacy.

Chapter 5 deconstructs the narratives of persons with long-term physical disabilities in an empirical study. The chapter outlines the cornerstones of a 'best practice' well-being model for a successful virtual community for persons with long-term physical disabilities that emerges from the application of grounded theory to the data derived from the interviews. The various key themes (education of people with disabilities to use ICT; fantasy or virtual-reality activities; information; interest; relationship; and transaction), concepts and barriers to successful participation are identified.

Chapter 6 reports on the narratives of the allied health, information and policy professionals who work with persons with disabilities. The chapter details the emergence and identification of their themes and concepts (education; virtual activities or fantasy; information; interest; community awareness and relationship; and e-economy), as well as the central theme of 'a sense of control', confirming the relevance of the emerging 'well-being model' through a virtual community. They also elaborate some infrastructure barriers to participation for people with disabilities. The chapter concludes by evaluating the methodology on which the study is based.

Chapter 7 details the potential implication of the results and the consolidation of the emergent 'well-being model' from the theory and theoretical framework derived in Chapters 5 and 6. It summarises the research outcomes as the opportunities and challenges of the six types of e-communities and the implications of access and any barriers, and concludes by further refining the emergent model or theoretical framework.

Chapter 8 reviews the significance of the 'well-being model' and its generalisability, and provides six major recommendations and strategies for implementation of the theory. It suggests future directions for virtual communities for people with physical disabilities for the facilitators and stakeholders, and areas for further studies into this topic. How the investigation measures up against the criteria for assessing grounded theory is considered, and how the investigation contributes to the further understanding of virtual communities for people with disabilities is also pursued.

Notes

1. Dr Shakespeare is director of outreach for the Policy, Ethics and Life Sciences Research Institute (PEALS), a Newcastle-based project developing research and debate on the social and ethical implications of the new genetics. The partners are the University of Newcastle, the University of Durham and the International Centre for Life. The chair of the project is Sir Kenneth Calman, formerly chief medical officer, now vice-chancellor of Durham (see www.windmills.u-net.com/home.htm).
2. A new partnership seeking to bring cheap internet access to the aged, veterans and people with disabilities has opted for dial-up rather than broadband (see www.zdnet.com.au/news/communications/0,2000061791,39193112, 00.htm).

Communication, information and well-being for people with disabilities

Central to the advancement of human civilisation is the spirit of open enquiry. (Albert Einstein)

The purpose of this book is to show why we should be concerned about virtual communities for people with physical, or more particularly mobility, impairments. The well-being model through a virtual community (hereafter abbreviated to 'well-being model') introduced here for people with disabilities goes towards advancing the work begun by REHADAT Germany, REHADAT Canada and more recently by the Centre of National Research on Disability and Rehabilitation Medicine (CONROD), Australia. These databases meet many of the informational needs of people with disabilities as determined by this 'well-being model'; however, a socio-political component lacking from the REHADAT and CONROD developments is also necessary, as the 'well-being model' of a virtual community of 'best practice' demonstrates.

The world is changing rapidly, and these changes are representing new opportunities and challenges for our economic, social, family and community life. Global economies, shifting family structures, rapid technological change and new forms of work are just some of these factors. Populations are growing and demographics changing. At the same time, many sectors are positioning themselves to take advantage of new economic, industrial and social opportunities. In this process, governments need to consider their roles as legislators and policy-makers, service funders, service deliverers and employers. They also need to work with other governments, business, the education sector and the community to ensure everyone plays a part.

The well-being model through a virtual community elaborated in the forthcoming chapters provides practical insights into how strategic community investment can support people with disabilities and their families. This may be achieved when regional and community leadership initiatives are provided, along with opportunities for empowerment through community development and capacity building (Turner and Pinkett, 2004). Virtual communities are about engagement, quality of life and support, not just about information. Furthermore, the well-being model examines the role of information technology in building and raising community capacity and social capital in socially and economically disadvantaged communities. It also provides practical insights into community support for people with chronic illness, because unfortunately many people with disabilities form part of the population defined by a chronic illness.

The significance of this work is to be a timely influence on the future 'best practice' for virtual communities for people with long-term, severe physical or mobility disabilities. Virtual community development is surging, and systems are planned or already operational worldwide. These include technical as well as social, political and economic systems. Local virtual or online communities for people with disabilities are burgeoning. The stakeholders – globally, nationally and, more importantly, at the local level – have to be aware of the many difficult challenges ahead.

The first generation of community network developers originated from the industrialised world, and subsequently were joined by innumerable others from all regions of the globe. Schuler (1996b), founding member of the Seattle Community Network, is one of the major prime movers in questioning what these developers are trying to accomplish with these systems. Certain kinds of answers were advanced at the first 'Ties that Bind' Community Networking Conference in 1994 sponsored by Apple Corporation and the Morino Institute. They included rebuilding civil society, securing access to information for disadvantaged or disabled people, community economic development, improving access to healthcare and healthcare information, providing forums for minority and alternative voices, improving communication among civic groups and improving literacy (Morino, 1994). This earlier work, affecting all stakeholders, needs to be reviewed in the context of experience: wider challenges today have different practical and theoretical implications for the future.

- The user interfaces for community networks need improvement; they need to be powerful, yet easy to use.
- The current online systems offer very little for the economically disadvantaged.
- There are some serious threats to community networks, including legislative attempts to promote 'decency' in cyberspace.
- The major focus of network development, both financially and from a media point of view, is on commercialisation and privatisation of networked services – which groups such as the Seattle Community Network always commendably oppose. These aspects of virtual communities affect not only the global stakeholders but also national and even local stakeholders.

The main significance of this multidisciplinary investigation is in the development process for identifying a systematic conceptual framework that facilitates a virtual community for people with severe long-term physical disabilities. The substantive theory that is developed forms a baseline for future studies into this topic, and ultimately enables the generation of a general theory of the appropriate facets of virtual communities for physically disabled people (Tilley et al., 2006). A major challenge is to cultivate broad support to 'institutionalise' virtual communities, so developing national information policies and telecommunications legislation effectively supports this process. It is envisaged that a virtual community for people with long-term physical disabilities would differ from that identified by REHADAT Australia. It meets the needs of a specific group of local stakeholders only, and they are different from the needs identified here. Only thorough research can result in outcomes and reliable strategies for accessing information and implementing this virtual community based on the needs of people with disabilities. CONROD, even in its attempts to implement REHADAT Australia (Disability Information and Links), reinforces the procedures detailed in subsequent chapters. The fact that the exploration is both theory-driven and based on the researched information needs of people with physical disabilities does enrich what has already been achieved. Furthermore, the social significance of this research rests on satisfactorily redefining the concept of 'community' itself within the context of the next generation of 'virtual communities' (Pantry, 1999).

A virtual community involves the use of the new information and communications technology (ICT) for the purposes of local community building and development. Already these kinds of technologies are assisting people with disabilities to access information easier and break down social isolation. This research enhances current understanding of how people with physical disabilities use ICT in their everyday lives. There is, however, a need to appreciate the outcome of this experience, so the future of technology for people with disabilities can be planned. The resultant experience is analysed to provide reliable and effective guidelines that support the virtual community model for people with a physical disability, thereby enabling them to feel empowered not only as citizens but as individuals participating in community development and in information technology environments generally (Mossberger et al., 2007). This research into 'best practice' and informed public policy lends itself naturally to further studies that may lead to significant recommendations in the areas of regional and community leadership initiatives, as well as community development and capacity building. The needs and opportunities for particular kinds of investment offering support to people with a disability and their families would need to be considered, along with any barriers to this investment.

History

The world's first virtual community was started by Lipkin, Felsenstein and Colstad in the early 1970s. It served as a model for facilitating the free exchange of information to communities around the world. Virtual communities now operate in hundreds of locations throughout the USA, as well as in many other countries, such as England and Canada. The Cleveland FreeNet, operating out of Case-Western University, is the largest virtual community in the world, and the Seattle Community Network is renowned for its ethical principles and commitment to values of sustainability (Schuler, 1995, 1996a; Community Network Movement, undated). Many system types exist in the history of community networking, and they demonstrate the motivations, services and approaches that represent the networking process.

During the 1990s a major relevant study into the feasibility of a virtual community for people with physical disabilities in Queensland, Australia, took place. It was undertaken by CONROD Australia (www.conrod.uq.edu.au) – established in 1997 to fund and otherwise facilitate research into all aspects of disability and rehabilitation. This was followed by conducting what is known as the REHADAT Australia National Disability Database Linkage Feasibility Study.

This REHADAT study findings were published in a report divided into two parts (Loos et al., 1998). The first part covered disability information issues, needs and the available resources, and identified information gathering and analysis within the disability sector in Australia. The second part exclusively gave recommendations, which provided a detailed plan for the implementation of REHADAT Australia Disability Information and Links (RADIAL), according to the needs and issues identified in the findings of the first part.

The REHADAT Australia feasibility study was undertaken following an examination of the operation of REHADAT in Germany and Canada. As the final report stated: 'REHADAT Germany is a client focused information system aimed at supporting vocational integration... The simple translation of the German model to Australia is precluded by significant differences between the Australian and German environments, and issues relating to the specific needs and interests of CONROD' (ibid.: 3).

The 1998 CONROD report recognised a strong demand within the Australian disability sector for a nationally accessible internet system linking disability information resources. This finding was well within the interests of CONROD and the memorandum of understanding signed with REHADAT Germany in 1997. As a result, CONROD proposed RADIAL should form as specified in the second part of the report. REHADAT's first task was to address such shortcomings as areas needing greater coverage, the lack of awareness of existing resources and the poor accessibility and questionable reliability of such resources. By May 2004 CONROD had developed and launched a new website as a community service to provide information about everyday life, in an informal way, for people who may have had a serious accident and have recently come out of rehabilitation. This website, Disability Lifestyles (www.disabilitylifestyles.org.au), targets newly rehabilitated people with disabilities.

REHADAT Germany (www.rehadat.de/English.htm) is an international electronic information system for disability management and vocational rehabilitation supporting the integration of disabled persons. The project was commissioned by the Bundesministerium für Arbeit und Soziales (Federal Ministry of Labour and Social Affairs) and established by the Institut der deutschen Wirtschaft Köln (Cologne Institute for Economic Research). REHADAT is a member of the Alliance of Assistive Technology Information Providers. Detailed information about various aspects of vocational rehabilitation is available in English from eight databases designed for use by disabled people as well as by professionals involved in rehabilitation. There is more German-only content.

REHADAT Germany began its development in 1988 and rapidly became available gratis by way of CD or the internet, with an estimated 60,000 regular users nationally. Although REHADAT Germany actively pursued international collaborations, its efforts met with limited success in Europe. However, Canada adopted its version of this information system in 1994, but its progress was slow due to minimal staffing levels. The database structures developed by REHADAT Canada (www.nidmar.ca) varied from the German model. REHADAT Germany was essentially a client-focused information system aimed at supporting the vocational integration of persons with disabilities. The principal users of the system were reportedly rehabilitation practitioners and people with disabilities. There were ten component databases: technical aids, case studies, seminars, research, addresses, literature, law, institutions, sheltered workshops and media (ibid.: 9).

REHADAT Canada, hosted by the National Institute of Disability Management and Research, includes six electronic databases used by rehabilitation professionals in helping their clients find information on disability and work. Its scope is international, although predominantly aimed at Europe and North America. Its language is English. REHADAT Canada holds detailed information about various aspects of the vocational rehabilitation process. The six public access databases (assistive devices, case studies, disability management practices, literature, policies/language and research) provide disability management professionals with a wealth of information to aid in a successful vocational integration process. The databases can be searched by product name, product type, vendor, manufacturer and Canadian products and vendors.

What do we need to take the agenda forward?

Despite the long-standing interest in virtual communities in the Western world, few models of successful virtual communities or models of 'best practice' for persons with long-term, severe mobility disabilities exist. This book proposes a theoretical framework or well-being model through a virtual community for this specific group of people in response to the primary research question posed: how can virtual communities for persons with physical disabilities best be facilitated?

This multidisciplinary qualitative work adopted grounded theory as the research methodology and addressed the strengths and weaknesses of various existing virtual communities. Full examination of this multidisciplinary area showed that while online communities for people with disabilities are becoming more prevalent, 'best practice' in online or virtual communities for such people required more attention (Commonwealth Procurement Guidelines and Best Practice Guidance, 2001). This theoretical well-being model goes some way towards rectifying this deficit.

The research design is based on applying Strauss and Corbin's (1990) grounded theory approach using basic research techniques of semi-structured interviews to obtain the data. There is no assumption of persons with physical disabilities as a homogeneous group; a range of appropriate strategies recognises their diversity. Virtual communities/community networking, communication and information theory literature are reviewed in order to compare accepted theory with theory discovered as a result of the data analysis. The theory in this study emerges directly from the data collected and remains 'grounded in' the data. The literature was reviewed continuously throughout the data collection and analysis phases and the major studies and themes from these literature reviews are considered below.

> It is the interplay between data and literature that is important...
> Using literature in this way is like theoretically sampling it on the basis of interviews then going back and theoretically sampling in reality as based on the literature. Thus, the literature makes one theoretically sensitive to:
>
> 1. conditions that influence the experiences;
>
> 2. strategies for dealing with the experience; and
>
> 3. consequences of what the experience is like. (Ibid.: 53–4)

The following questions have emerged from the literature and provide an overview of the key areas of emphasis; they are reviewed in Chapter 8 in light of the data analysis in Chapters 5–7.

■ What are the information practices of persons with disabilities?

- How does government policy on information provision influence the information needs of persons with disabilities? How do these consumers use this information?

- What other identifiable information needs would enhance the quality of life of persons with disabilities other than social, health and efficacy needs?

- How should ICT address the social, political, informational, health, efficacy and other needs of persons with disabilities?

- How do the real and perceived barriers to persons with disabilities using ICT affect the outcomes?

Telecommunications, information, well-being and disabled people

One body of public health research shows that people who are socially isolated are as much at risk of death as people who smoke. The internet, according to leading American sociologist Putnam (2000), presents rich possibilities for new connections and furthers the concept that information and power mean 'control' over one's life. This control is 'denied' to people with disabilities in the initial stages of their coming to terms with their disability. Sometimes it is lacking even in advanced stages of disability. The concept of power for people with disability comes from their ability to access information as required; it leads them to regain their sense of total well-being: social, intellectual, physical, emotional, vocational and spiritual. Firstly, they must regain this sense of 'control', which may partially be achieved through the ability to access and share information, as detailed in later chapters. This sense of 'control' moves them towards ending social isolation (Tilley et al., 2002).

Social isolation encompasses both physical isolation (a low level of social participation) and emotional isolation (the subjective experience of loneliness). Many individual, social, cultural and environmental factors influence a person's connection with his or her community. These factors, to name a few, include having a disability, needing a carer, ageing, relocation, living in a rural or remote area and being different from most other community members (including culturally and linguistically).

Although many people are socially connected, some factors more commonly impact together on people with disabilities than on other demographic groups. These factors include leaving the workforce, having a physical disability and/or ill health, experiencing the loss of relationships, having few or no transport options and so on. People need to have the opportunity to be socially connected and, if they wish, to participate in community life. The association between communication and interaction with others and mental and physical well-being is now well known in an era when increasing responsibility has been placed on individuals for their own health and wellness (Schott and Hodgetts, 2006).

Marmot's studies (Marmot, 1995; Marmot and Wilkinson, 1999) of British civil servants (known as the Whitehall Studies into the different hierarchies within the British Civil Service), preceded by Cohen and Syme's (1984) research into social support and 'control of destiny', have all contributed significantly towards understanding how psychological and social well-being plays an important role in maintaining physical health. Berkman and Breslow (1983) undertook the first empirical study into the concept of social support and demonstrated that those people who had connections with other people had lower mortality rates. Cohen and Syme's (1984) research led to the conclusion that in order for people to have a sense of well-being, they must use their social support as one of the ways to gain control over their destiny. People look to others who can assist them to negotiate life's challenges with their advice and support. This they also termed 'mastery', describing it as the ability at work to decide how and at what pace to complete work, and at home being able to traverse life's difficulties and resolve daily problems so they do not appear overwhelming. They also advocated the concept of control in everyday life as being a phenomenon that can be taught early in life (as evidenced by the Ypsilante and Headstart Projects). Cohen and Syme (ibid.) developed ways of helping people take control over their destiny, with impressive results.

Marmot (1995), as head of the International Centre for Health and Society at University College London, translated his work on the social determinants of health into ten major components that must be addressed: social gradient; stress; early life; social exclusion (relevant to people with disabilities); work and lack of control; unemployment; social support; addiction; food; and transport.

McEwen (1998) and others in their research into the psycho-neuro-immunology field have demonstrated how loss of control affects cortisone levels and hormone functioning, and how defence systems are compromised by these factors. Douglas, who in 1991 was director of the National Centre for Epidemiology and Population Health, Australian

National University, defined this paradigm shift in thinking from Cohen and Syme's (1984) notions of social support, control and well-being to actual 'health'. He implies that people's ways of responding psychologically to the circumstances of daily life, work and family issues and the way they connect to others in the community can influence health more than whether they smoke, eat badly or do not exercise. Their way of responding psychologically to taking control of their lives can affect their health in its own right, just as a lack of control can be a contributing cause of many chronic diseases. Douglas has been involved in collaboration on a number of projects that take a 'life course approach' to the management of adult chronic disease, and found that intervention and improvement in 'mastery' can lead to improved well-being and community health (Butler et al., 2001; Dixon et al., 2000; Eckersley et al., 2001).

Ryff and Singer (1998: 3), following from their philosophical analyses, propose that the key goods in life, central to positive human health, are primarily having purpose in life and quality connections to others, and secondarily possessing self-regard and mastery. As Ryff and Singer (ibid.: 9) further attest, much social scientific literature probes the role of social relationships and social support in human health.

Nonetheless, it is Baumeister and Leary's (1995: 500) formulation of the 'belongingness motive' which suggests that people need frequent, effectively pleasant or positive interactions with the same individuals. They need such interactions to occur in a framework of long-term, stable, caring and concern, which makes sense in terms of using ICT in virtual interactions for people with mobility disabilities.

This theory equally relates to people with physical disabilities who have experienced a sudden, traumatic change in their lives. The sense of regaining control, or 'mastery', over the problems that may be associated with such disability is not only desirable, but in fact highly necessary (Rodin, 1986; Rodin and Langer, 1977; Rodin et al., 1985). How might this control, well-being or improved health be achieved? Healthcare agencies fall midway between the more proximal influences (such as personal actions and family and friends) and more distal factors (such as community and media or policy influences) (Glasgow and Eakin, 2000). Other significant ways can be through ICT connectivity and information sharing with peers using e-mails and 'chatrooms', and by researching the disability (Burgstahler, 1997). Having a disability can be conducive to loneliness. The isolation can cause stress and depression.

Connectivity introduces the notion of the value of 'social capital': those features of social life – networks and community groups – that enable participants to act together to pursue shared objectives, such as information sharing. Putnam (2000) instigated this concept of 'social capital', referring to community bonds and interpersonal connections. These, he argues, are just as important for the public good as economic well-being. Eva Cox (1995) defined 'social capital' as the store of trust, goodwill and cooperation between people in the workplace, voluntary organisations, the neighbourhood and all levels of government. Cox argued that the degree of accumulated social capital was a measure of the health of communities, societies and nations. It builds a strong, active civil society and encourages a democratic outlook (Portes, 1998). It results in better economic outcomes (Foley and Edwards, 1998; Rotberg, 1999). Although there are strong signs that social capital is diminishing, Cox (1995) is optimistic that, once the problem is recognised, processes and structures can be constructed that will enable people to participate more actively in civil society. ICT enhances these possibilities, particularly for disabled people. Given that the majority of community members are not in relationships with people who have disabilities, and most people in the community expect that the appropriate social services will look after such people, technology has opened the way for freer relationships and friendships. The cycle of dependence on services happens when people do not have friends or social networks. Friendship promotes a feeling of well-being; furthermore, it provides a framework for promoting an ethically decent community. In this way, friendships and the quality of relationships, both in private lives and in the public domain, impact on the world in which people live and help to shape it.

So, as health is a determinant of well-being, control over one's life and social participation in community life are also significant determinants of health and well-being – issues, in terms of ICT, that are pursued further in later chapters (Department of Communications, Information Technology and the Arts, 2005).

Key elements of the well-being model through a virtual community

As part of the process of defining the key terms (below) used in this well-being model through a virtual community, also defining 'information', 'information literacy', 'technological literacy' and the 'digital divide' contributes to a fuller understanding of the potential impact of virtual communities. Chapter 4 considers these latter aspects more thoroughly.

Synergy exists between these terms (as scholars and professional organisations attest), but it is information literacy in the community that is at the heart of the different types of orientations that are activated in the virtual communities described in Chapters 5–7 (Partridge et al., 2008). The term 'literacy' means many things to different people. In recent times, different types of literacies have been proposed and defined, particularly within the range of services and resources available on the internet. Invariably, they are all extensions of the traditional notion of literacy.

'A sense of control'

The phrase 'a sense of control', as used in the title of this book, derives from the central theme that emerged from the open coding analytic process based on grounded theory methodology applied to all the in-depth interviews in this investigation. The people interviewed with long-term, severe physical disabilities desired to regain 'a sense of control' over their lives. Increasingly, they found that this concept of 'a sense of control' was achieved through their use of ICT, and the professionals were as unanimous in their enthusiasm for their clientele using technology as were the disabled people themselves.

What are virtual communities?

A virtual community may be loosely defined as a meeting place for people on the internet. It provides a virtual world designed to facilitate interaction among its inhabitants and collaboration among people who share common interests and needs (Koh and Kim, 2003; Li, 2004; Matei, 2005). Online communities can be open to all or by membership only, and may or may not offer moderator tools. Virtual communities exist in discussion groups, chatrooms, list-servs, list-procs and newsgroups. Schuler (1994: 40) claimed that community networks are 'intended to provide "one-stop shopping" using community-oriented discussions, question-and-answer forums, electronic access to government employees and information, access to social services, e-mail, and in many cases, Internet access'.

Virtual communities have two fundamental components – the physical or technical infrastructure required for connectivity (or, in Preece's terms, the 'usability'), and the social info-structure or process of engaging people in purposeful applications of the physical connectivity (Preece's term again, the 'sociability'). Preece's work on sociability and usability in virtual communities postulates that a primary understanding of a community's needs is essential for developing close dynamic relationships in virtual communities. This understanding contributes to the success of virtual community developers and is also relevant to the findings of this work (Preece, 2000: 27).

In the space of one paragraph, Rheingold (1994b: 58) encapsulates the essence of an online community in a way that is still viable today, when textual communication no longer continues to be the dominant default medium of communication:

> In cyberspace, we chat and argue, engage in intellectual discourse, perform acts of commerce, exchange knowledge, share emotional support, make plans, brainstorm, gossip, feud, fall in love, find friends and lose them, play games and metagames, flirt... We do everything people do when people get together, but we do it with words on computer screens, leaving our bodies behind... our identities commingle and interact electronically, independent of local time or location.

> Community networks are based upon geographical proximity, but participation in a sense of place and community is extended by network communication, such as electronic mail, Internet relay chat, bulletin boards and Web pages. Examples of community networks include municipal governments using the network to involve citizens in political deliberation, or corporations using electronic mail and teleconferencing. Clearly any traditional sense of community is dependent upon frequent personal interaction, but community networks reinforce a sense of membership by making information or communication more accessible. (Lyman, 1999: 6)

While each virtual community is unique, they do share a number of common characteristics that differentiate them from other types of networks. In relation to the use of the word 'community', Lyman (ibid.: 1) asks whether cyberspace can evoke a sense of place, capable of supporting a sense of intellectual community. He says that the term 'virtual community' describes the feelings of social solidarity made possible by interactive network software. He claims that Rheingold and Dibble are the people who made the strongest cases for the existence of virtual communities (ibid.: 6).

The key findings, model and theory for this exploration into how virtual communities can best be facilitated for persons with long-term, severe physical disabilities parallel and extend the general findings elaborated by Beamish (1995) in her work about online communities. They also uphold the five necessary multidisciplinary characteristics that Whittaker et al. (1997: 137) found essential to a virtual community.

Beamish (1995) described community networks as sharing the following three characteristics.

- *A focus on local issues.* In addition to information services, community networks provide forums for discussion of local issues.

- *Access.* The network is concerned to reflect and include all members of the community.

- *Social change/community development.* There is a belief that the system with its communication and information can strengthen and vitalise the community.

How do virtual communities create and sustain a sense of community?

The term 'community' has thus proven to be problematic over the years and can have wide variation in types and definitions. It is sufficient just to elaborate more generally on 'community'. A community suggests a 'place' where people are welcome and welcomed. At the heart of a community is a sense of belonging. A sense of belonging goes hand in hand with a sense of place. A sense of belonging enables people to share a place and brings about feelings of ownership and identity with that particular 'place'. Sharing a place and belonging to a community result in interactions within that community – people having roles to play and participating. Both role and participation depend on confidence. Communities not only own and share a 'place', they also own and share problems, and part of belonging is finding solutions. A community is about people sharing responsibility for each other, and about reciprocity, belonging and participation. These aspects of 'community' make obvious the artificial division between 'real' and 'electronic' communities (Li, 2004).

It is necessary to note the ambiguity of the language about community and how the term is misleading. It is misleading because it implies that collectivities formed in web-based discourse are equivalent to local communities grounded in face-to-face relationships. The reality is that the internet is most effective complementing, and not replacing, face-to-face communication. Calhoun (2004) contributes more to this debate by comparing the general use of the term with its sociological use. Used sociologically, communities are effective only on relatively small scales, and these imply a density of connection. More generally, community is a misleading term for thinking about the internet's role in social solidarity. He argues that heavy reliance on the term 'community' to describe computer-mediated groupings borrows from the warm and fuzzy connotations that the idea of community has in everyday life. Calhoun (ibid.: 244) maintains that this kind of thinking 'obscures one of the most important potential roles for electronic communication, which is enhancing public discourse – a form of discourse that joins strangers and enables large collectivities to make informed choices about their institutions and their future'.

Schuler (1996b) maintains that people use the word 'community' in at least three ways. It may mean a group of people living in a contiguous geographical area, a group of like-minded people or a state of group communion, togetherness and mutual concern. The virtual community breaks these limitations. In his writings on new community networks, Schuler (ibid.: 2–3) uses the term 'community' to mean an integration of the three meanings. However, he also points out that communities rarely have a coherent agenda, shared goals or a political will, and that when communities are aligned together over an issue, it is often crisis-oriented. In fact, he believes that all too often community groups choose to organise against something, and they may have a dark side – one that is exclusive, competitive and fiercely chauvinistic (ibid.: 68–9). Schuler (ibid.: 71) concludes that, for better or worse, communities are embedded in the external world to a large degree, and this knowledge can be used both reactively and proactively in dealing with external forces.

The Academy of the Social Sciences in Australia in its recent research into the structure of social groups and the impact of the mobile telephone in Australia has discriminated between 'communities of practice' and 'communities of interest'. Its definitions of these terms have proven useful for this study.

> 'Communities of Practice' and 'Communities of Interest' are related concepts that focus on social formation, emphasizing shared interests or experience in a given problem, domain or pursuit, a commitment in resolving common issues, and assisting and advising one another in this context. These communities are

often work-based, but also cut across particular places of employment, and particular problems and roles. The related term 'Communities of Use' emphasizes how usage patterns can be understood through research into the crucial role of this technology in bringing people together and emphasizes the new forms of fluid or transient social structures that depend on the facility to communicate quickly and mobilize informally. (Academy of the Social Sciences in Australia, 2004: 7)

Disability

Disability refers to the temporary or long-term reduction of a person's capacity to function (Badley, 1993). The concept of disability encompasses many different dimensions of health and functioning, and the complex interactions with one's environment. The International Classification of Functioning and Disability (ICIDH-2) classifies functioning at the levels of body or body part, whole person and whole person in social context. Accordingly, disablement is losses or abnormalities of bodily function and structure (impairments), limitations of activities (disabilities) or restrictions in participation (formerly called handicaps).

The demand for statistics on human functioning and disability greatly increased following the International Year of Disabled Persons (1981), the adoption of the UN World Programme of Action Concerning Disabled Persons (United Nations, 1982) and the release of the *Standard Rules on the Equalization of Opportunities for Persons with Disabilities* (United Nations, 1993). The World Programme of Action specifically requested the United Nations to develop systems for the regular collection and dissemination of information on disability. A questionnaire on human functioning and disability statistics was subsequently developed based on recommendations and decisions by expert group meetings and the UN Statistical Commission (United Nations, 2003). In March 2006 the UN Statistics Division initiated systematic and regular collection of basic statistics on disability through the existing *Demographic Yearbook* data collection system (United Nations, 2006).[1] Census questions on disability were asked in innumerable countries[2] between 1995 and 2004 (Australian Institute of Health and Welfare, 2000). The work of disseminating information on disability continues, as evidenced by the fifth meeting[3] of the Washington Group on Disability Statistics (WG), held on 21–23 September 2005 in

Rio de Janeiro, Brazil, and hosted by the Instituto Brasileiro de Geografia e Estatistica (IBGE) in collaboration with CORDE (www.cdc.gov/nchs/about/otheract/citygroup/agenda5.htm).

The Australian Bureau of Statistics (2000) recently released the findings of its 1998 survey entitled Disability and Long-Term Health Conditions. The survey concluded that 3.6 million people or 19 per cent of Australians have a disability (long-term health condition or impairment that interferes with their daily living activities). The term 'disability' is variously defined, and since the 1970s the understanding of disability has changed dramatically (Wen and Fortune, 1999). Once perceived as a largely medical problem affecting only a small number of people, it is now regarded as a major social and political issue. The principal source of population data for disability in Australia is the Australian Bureau of Statistics (ABS) disability surveys, which have been conducted in 1981, 1988, 1993 and 1998.[4] The 2006 Census had a specific 'disabilities' question and the data will become available by 2010. Due to the ABS user-pays system, wider access is limited only to published material (Australian Bureau of Statistics, 2004). This does not always provide the depth of information required; for example, very few disability data collected by the ABS contain gender-specific findings.

The definition of disability as used below is consistent with that used by the World Health Organization ([1980] 1997), and includes the following:

- physical,[5] e.g. loss of a limb, paraplegia, quadriplegia;
- intellectual, e.g. Down's syndrome;
- psychiatric, e.g. schizophrenia, depression;
- sensory, e.g. visual impairment, deafness;
- neurological, e.g. acquired brain injury, cerebral palsy, Alzheimer's disease, multiple sclerosis (MS);
- learning difficulties, e.g. dyslexia, attention deficit disorder (ADD);
- physical disfigurement, e.g. burns;
- the presence of disease-causing organisms in the body, e.g. human immunodeficiency virus (HIV)/acquired immune deficiency syndrome (AIDS).

Another broad, non-prescriptive definition of disability that neither marginalises nor excludes particular groups of disabilities is when disability results from disadvantage, discrimination or exclusion of people who have a medical condition(s) that directly or indirectly limits or is used by others to limit their and/or their associates' participation in any aspect of society. The definition of 'medical condition' is one or more of:

- total or partial loss of the person's bodily or mental functions;
- total or partial loss of a part of the body;
- the presence in the body of organisms causing disease or illness;
- the presence in the body of organisms capable of causing disease or illness;
- the body's negative reaction to chemicals and/or other substances whether naturally occurring or artificial;
- malfunction, malformation or disfigurement of a part of the person's body;
- a disorder or malfunction that results in the person learning differently from a person without the disorder or malfunction;
- a disorder, illness or disease that affects a person's thought processes, perception of reality, emotions or judgement, including addiction, or that results in disturbed behaviour.

The definition includes a medical condition that:

- presently exists;
- previously existed but no longer exists;
- may exist in the future;
- is imputed to a person (Badley, 1993; Madden and Hogan, 1996).

Traditionally people with disabilities were defined as 'disabled' because of their specific impairments, such as loss of physical function as the result of illness or injury. More recently the International Classification System of Impairments, Activities and Participation (ICIDH) has proposed a social model of disability that views disability as an inability to participate in activities (World Health Organization, [1980] 1997). Consequently, the focus has shifted from the inadequacies of the individual with impairment to the activity restriction or barriers in society that exclude people from participation. This has resulted in a number of legislative initiatives being enacted to assist people with disabilities to enter the workforce and access the technology they require to carry out various tasks.

The 'social model of disability'[6] argues that although individuals have various impairments, the degree and nature of the disablement they experience are a result of the arrangements society makes to support their social, economic and cultural participation. Such insight has critical implications for professional disciplines from engineering to law, from nursing to architecture, from ICT to business and commerce. Social isolation (as well as physical, social and attitudinal barriers) creates much of the suffering that arises from having a disability. It also comes from the devaluation of any human condition which is not reflective of the societal worship of youth, agility and physical beauty. Inadequate support services, dehumanising institutions, high levels of unemployment and exclusion from regular education are some of the results of this societal devaluation. Besides these, wars, environmental degradation, hunger, deprivation and, paradoxically, many aspects of the consumerist lifestyle cause much disability. Nevertheless, amid their difficult circumstances and given the right support, many people with significant disabilities experience their lives as profoundly as anyone else does. Such a phenomenon of good life satisfaction is also widely reported in research literature, even by respirator-dependent people with high levels of paralysis.

It is also reasonable to link the notions and definitions of community with disability and create a composite meaning from the two terms instead of using each in isolation. If individuals are to develop their capacity to live, learn, work and participate in all aspects of living in the community, sometimes they must be supported to achieve these skills. This comes only through a delicate balance of both paid and unpaid support. Similarly, the community is encouraged to develop its capacity to welcome and support people – even people with severe disabilities who have high support needs and have not always had the same opportunities as others to participate in community life in meaningful, productive ways. Often people simply need social or attitudinal barriers dismantled to enable them to make their way in the community. In both direct and indirect ways, supporting people to contribute and participate makes good economic sense, and it produces communities that are stronger and all the more constructive.

In society today, people with disabilities are increasingly demanding equal access to the full range of community resources, information and opportunities. Disability *per se* is no longer accepted as being a barrier to gaining an education, taking part in civil and political life, enjoying a fulfilling social life, raising a family, being involved in the community or engaging in paid and unpaid work. On the contrary, the community now actively supports the participation of people with disabilities. Businesses and community organisations are expected to make reasonable efforts to ensure that people with disabilities can use their goods and services. Governments, too, are expected to facilitate the participation and inclusion of people with disabilities and are rightly held to a higher level of accountability by the community in this regard. Credit for some of these attitudinal changes must go to Wolfensberger (1975, 1983) and his theory of social role valorisation that the community has embraced along with disability discrimination legislation. In Australia, the Disability Discrimination Act (DDA) is a law passed by the Federal Parliament on 15 October 1992 which came into force on 1 March 1993. The Australian DDA quite closely resembles the British Disability Discrimination Act 1995. The British Disability Discrimination Act 2005 builds on and extends earlier disability discrimination legislation, principally the 1995 Act.

'Information', 'information literacy', 'technological literacy' and the 'digital divide'

While 'information literacy' and the 'digital divide' are fulsomely considered in Chapter 4, 'information'[7] may be briefly defined as an item of knowledge and 'technological literacy' may be defined as the ability to use the appropriate technology responsibly to communicate, solve problems and access, manage, integrate, evaluate and create information to improve learning (Technology Literacy Assessment Work Group, 2003).

*　　*　　*

These are the five main components that comprise the well-being model through a virtual community for people with mobility impairments and form this basic well-being paradigm.

Notes

1. This website (http://unstats.un.org/unsd/demographic/sconcerns/disability/) is a statistical reference and guide to the standards, methods and available data on human functioning and disability.
2. American Samoa, Argentina, Aruba, Australia, Bahamas, Belgium, Belize, Benin, Bermuda, Botswana, Brazil, Bulgaria, Canada, Cape Verde, Chile, Cook Islands, Costa Rica, Côte d'Ivoire, Croatia, Dominican Republic,

Egypt, Estonia, Fiji, Gambia, Guam, Guernsey, Guinea, Guyana, Haiti, Honduras, Hungary, India, Islamic Republic of Iran, Iraq, Ireland, Isle of Man, Jamaica, Jordan, Lithuania, Malaysia, Maldives, Malta, Marshall Islands, Mauritius, Mexico, Mozambique, Namibia, Nepal, New Zealand, Northern Mariana Islands, Occupied Palestinian Territory, Oman, Pakistan, Panama, Peru, Philippines, Poland, Portugal, Puerto Rico, Republic of Korea, St Lucia, Samoa, Sierra Leone, Solomon Islands, South Africa, Sri Lanka, Swaziland, Syrian Arab Republic, Trinidad and Tobago, Turkey, Turks and Caicos Islands, Uganda, United Kingdom of Great Britain and Northern Ireland, United Republic of Tanzania, United States of America, United States Virgin Islands, Venezuela, Yemen, Zambia and Zimbabwe.

3. Objectives for the fifth meeting were to:

- present work on continued development of the general disability measure;
- present work on the written protocols and plans for implementing the general disability measure, including lessons learned from regional workshops;
- present work on the development of extended measurement sets and the associated papers;
- discuss methodological issues related to proxy and non-response and continue discussion of full population coverage;
- discuss strategic issues.

4. The Office of Population Census and Surveys (OPCS) is the UK government department responsible for the compilation of statistics on local and national populations. It also conducts demographic surveys of births, marriages and deaths. The OPCS carries out a Census every ten years and the statistics obtained are used by other government departments and local authorities to plan public services. The most recent British Census was conducted on 29 April 2001. In 2001 almost a quarter (23 per cent) of the population in Wales reported having a limiting long-term illness or disability which restricted their daily activities. Rates increased with age, especially as respondents were instructed specifically to 'Include problems due to old age'. Plans are being made to hold the next Census in 2011. On 13 May 2007 the Office for National Statistics (ONS) conducted the first major field-test for the next Census. The purpose of conducting the voluntary test was to assess a wide range of different aspects in planning, testing and evaluating the Census operation and feed these into the design of the 2011 Census. The National Center for Health Statistics (US Department of Health and Human Services) website is a rich source of information about America's health (www.cdc.gov/nchs/). As the nation's principal health statistics agency, it compiles statistical information to guide actions and policies to improve the health of the people. This is a unique public resource for health information – a critical element of public health and health policy.

5. The ABS (www.abs.gov.au/) estimates the number of people with a disability who require mobility aids as 533,600 – manual wheelchairs 132,500; power wheelchairs 19,100; scooters 13,500; walking frames 103,200; crutches 21,400; walking sticks 208,900; sonar canes 35,000.

6. The 'social model of disability' posits that the problem of disability lies not within persons with disabilities, but as a social construct in the environment that fails to accommodate them and in the negative attitudes of people without disabilities (Oliver, 1990).

7. 'Information' is the result of processing, manipulating and organising data in a way that adds to the knowledge of the receiver. In other words, it is the context in which data are taken. This term has many meanings depending on the context. For example, it is often related to such concepts as meaning, knowledge, communication, truth, representation and mental stimulus. Often used very broadly to encompass all ideas, facts and imaginative works or instructions; any sort of knowledge or supposition that can be communicated. Can also be used to mean a single data element. Whole volumes have been written in the effort to define it satisfactorily.

Virtual communities' research – the perspective

> When people seek to express their sense of community, they seek an ideal speech situation – that is, one free from power and constraint in making a choice. (Habermas, 1991)

Developing online communities presents a compelling prospect, not only for internet entrepreneurs but also for computer users with the widest variety of home countries, interests, backgrounds and motives for banding together. But what truly makes a 'community'? How are community relationships built, nurtured and supported when the process bridges both technical and social properties (Thurlow et al., 2004)? The theorist literature answers these questions; it provides the main drivers in understanding the organising principles behind the virtual community literature. Over the past two decades, online communities have been operational and have become very focused. They now give their reasons for existence as support, commerce or learning, whereas in the beginning online communities seemed to want to be all things to all people. Consideration must now centre on the role of those most able to influence community participation: the essential element of virtual communities for people with physical disabilities (Seymour and Lupton, 2004).

Furthermore, this chapter not only explores the theory and practices of online communities, but also the contributions of three researchers who have emerged as major pioneers and ongoing contributors to the virtual community literature. It considers Rheingold's popularisation of the topic in 1994, and the paradigm shift Schuler presented in 1996 and Preece put forward in 2000. The social issues and technological ramifications have deeply concerned all three of these researchers. Their perceptions of virtual communities have moved from mere speculation about their 'futurist' potential to change people. They have a more pragmatic approach; they accept virtual communities, explore their design and investigate how that affects sociability. These three issues are particularly relevant to the findings of this study. The contributions of Rheingold, Schuler and Preece to the ongoing virtual community debate will also be examined in terms of how they compare with the themes emerging from Beamish's (1995) study, 'Communities on-line: community-based computer networks'. Further, their contributions will be considered in the context of the core attributes identified by the 1997 ACM-CHI (Association of Computing Machinery-Computer Human Interaction) conference on human factors in computer systems. The conference, held in Atlanta, Georgia, discussed the theory and practice of physical and network communities.

Refining the virtual community definition

Ongoing significant debate has failed to define exactly what constitutes a virtual community (Preece and Maloney-Krichmar, 2003; Preece et al., 2003). However, for the purposes of this study Chapter 1 established a definition which this chapter further discusses (Jones, 1997: 3–4; Jones and Rafaeli, 2000: 215). A virtual community must be distinguished from the medium or platform in which its users or agents interact (Lechner and Schmid, quoted in Jones and Rafaeli, ibid.). Jones and Rafaeli favour the definition of a virtual community as social relationships forged in cyberspace through repeated contact within a specified boundary or place (for example a chatroom) that is symbolically delineated by a topic of interest (Fernback and Thompson, quoted in Jones and Rafaeli, ibid.). Jones and Rafaeli argue that the value of Fernback and Thompson's definition is that it allows for a distinction between a virtual community, its computer-mediated space or virtual-settlement and its population. Furthermore, they maintain its virtue lies in its recognition of the emergent properties of a virtual community's components, which they refer to as social relationships (ibid.).

In discussions about electronic and virtual communities, 'community' can variously refer to a moral or normative community, a community of practice, an intentional community or a proximate community. There are deficiencies in definitions of an ideal-type community, as well as the artificial nature of a division between real and electronic communities (Komito, 1998: 97). De Cindio (2004: 199–200) provides an outline of the attempts made to provide a definition of the concept for a community network (CN). She maintains that while all the characterisations are accurate, the most adequate and powerful way of representing CNs is as enabling environments that promote 'citizen participation in community affairs' (Schuler, 2000). De Cindio (2004) defines CNs as the appropriate socio-technical environment for enabling citizens to develop their own projects that shape the network society.

One of the main difficulties stems from how people come from various perspectives to define 'community' in a way that satisfies a multidisciplinary range of interests. The sociologists have defined and redefined this concept over the years (Wellman, 1982). Wellman (2001: 228) says: 'I define "community" as networks of interpersonal ties that provide sociability, social support, information, a sense of belonging and social identity.' However, finally, sociologists have come to focus on the strength and type of relationships among people as the most useful criteria for 'community' (Wellman, 1997, 1999: xiv–xv; Haythornthwaite and Wellman, 1998). The e-commerce entrepreneurs, on the other hand, have devalued the notion of 'community' in that they have settled for a much broader view of the term. For them, any chatline, bulletin board or communications software is conceived as an online community. The researchers and virtual community advocates argue that an online community is infinitely more than just a stream of messages. This study has tried to remain cognisant of this diversity of perspectives with respect to the definition of concepts on which it is based. Additionally, it has tried to keep in mind Wellman's (1999: 37) conclusion that a community is a network – nebulous, far-flung and sparsely knit, but real and supportive, exchanging sociability, information, social support and a sense of belonging.

Lyman (1998) believes that the idea of the virtual community frames human understanding of digital networks as modes of communication, and this provides the basis for new kinds of social relations and civic life that may now be possible in cyberspace. He also points out the ironic use of the word 'community' in relation to computer-mediated communications, given that one frequent criticism of urban life in a technological society is the absence of community. He argues the importance of the community metaphor in providing a tacit theory of economic justice. By this he means that the web may be perceived as a gift exchange economy, one in which millions of authors are giving away intellectual property for the sake of developing a sense of community. Nonetheless, he observes that the word 'community' provides a useful metaphor, because it defines the need for community as a social goal. He points out that two very interesting findings emerge from virtual communities. The first is that there are distinctive new kinds of social groups, which are strongest when they complement their network communication with face-to-face meetings. The second finding revolves around the debate about whether or not social science concepts and methodologies must be changed for these new social formations to be detected and analysed (ibid.: 6–7).

Characteristics and functions of virtual communities

Although unique, each virtual community or community network shares four common characteristics that differentiate them from other types of networks (Odasz, 1994, 1995b, 1995c). The use of electronic communication extends and amplifies this existing social concept. Firstly, community networks provide access to public space in cyberspace. Secondly, they recognise the equal importance of communication and information provision. Thirdly, their local focus leads to wide variations in the types and definitions of communities that exist. Fourthly, community networks seem to work best when they cover comprehensively all aspects of life. Their developers also often have a strong sense of community responsibility. For example, the Seattle Community Network (www.scn.org/) developed a set of principles that are a series of commitments to help guide the continual development and management of the system for both the organisers and the participating individuals and organisations (Community Network Movement, undated; Odasz, 1995a).

Beamish (1995) described community networks as sharing three essential sociological characteristics: a focus on local issues; access; and social change and community development (see Chapter 1). The 1997 ACM-CHI conference identified five necessary multidisciplinary characteristics of virtual communities.

- Members have a shared goal, interest, need or activity that provides the primary reason for belonging to the community.

- Members engage in repeated, active participation; often intense interactions, strong emotional ties and shared activities occur among participants.

- Members have access to shared resources, and policies determine the access to those resources.

- Reciprocity of information, support and services among members is important.
- There is a shared context of social conventions, language and protocols (Whittaker et al., 1997: 137).

While wide agreement exists about the capability of virtual communities to provide both information and interpersonal interactions, the degree to which they can be seen as specifically information-oriented social spaces has been open to some question. Burnett (2000) proposes a typology of activities that can be used to describe the ways in which participants in virtual communities behave in terms of their use of information and their information seeking in those communities. He expects that different communities, in part because of their focus on different topics and areas of interest, will differ significantly in the behaviours of their participants. His typology provides a mechanism for assessing the characteristics of virtual communities in terms of their support for information exchange, and this enhances understanding of virtual communities as information environments.

The ability of virtual communities to provide personal support for their participants has been well documented. In fact, communities have been formed expressly to provide such support for well-defined groups of users, such as parents of children with special needs (Mickelson, cited in Burnett, ibid.) and people with particular health problems (Preece, cited in Burnett, ibid.). Even in virtual communities that are not explicitly designed as support groups, interpersonal relationships commonly develop (Parks and Floyd, cited in Burnett, ibid.). Such relationships can be both intimate and supportive, even though they may be, in some cases, closely tied to the specific subject domains of the communities in which they appear (Rosson, cited in Burnett, ibid.; Wellman and Gulia, 1999). According to Burnett (2000), little specific research has been conducted into the types of interactions that may be used to provide this emotional support, or whether they are linked with information exchange within virtual communities. However, Preece (cited in Burnett, ibid.) asserts that emotional support and information sharing are likely to be closely linked in such situations.

Major virtual community pioneers

Sproull and Kiesler's *Connections: New Ways of Working in the Networked Organization*, published in 1991, can be identified as one of the earliest seminal works. Its excellent foundation linked empowerment with the implications of working online. Several more recent theorists are now seen as the main 'drivers' behind virtual communities. Rheingold (1994b), author of *The Virtual Community: Homesteading on the Electronic Frontier*, was another early cyberspace expert and the first to write about the phenomenon of social communication in cyberspace. He was consultant to the US Congress Office of Technology and Assessment on the subject of communication systems for an information age. Rheingold is among the most widely known experts on virtual communities. He later created a web-zine and web-conference-based virtual community called Electric Minds. Today, Rheingold is president of Rheingold Associates, a group of 40 consultants who help not-for-profit organisations and Fortune 500 companies construct their own virtual communities. He defines as virtual communities those cultural aggregations that emerge when enough people bump into each other often enough in cyberspace (ibid.: 57). He refines this definition further to describe a virtual community as a group of people who may or may not meet one another face to face, and who exchange words and ideas through the mediation of computer bulletin boards and networks (ibid.: 58). A virtual community emerges from the net when enough people carry on those public discussions long enough, with sufficient human feeling, to form webs of personal relationships in cyberspace (ibid.: 5). Rheingold was labelled as a technological determinist, because he held that there was a predictable relationship between technology and people's behaviour (Jones, 1997: 3).

Rheingold (1994b: 12–13, 15) is convinced that CMC (computer-mediated communication), by way of a virtual community, has the potential to change lives on three different, but strongly inter-influential, social levels:

- as individual human beings;
- at the level of person-to-person interaction (that is, as communities);
- at the political level, which derives from the middle, social level (that is, as democracies or virtual cities).

Therefore, he postulates that advocates of communities need to try to understand the nature of CMC, cyberspace and virtual communities in every important context – politically, economically, socially, cognitively – if the way communications technologies are transforming human communities is to be understood. While he is very positive about virtual communities, he does warn people to be aware of the downside of connectivity. It could equally serve as a means to put virtual communities under surveillance and lead to communications technology multinationals dominating them.

Schuler, chairman of Computer Professionals for Social Responsibility (CPSR) and author of another seminal, socially aware work, *New Community Networks – Wired for Change* (Schuler, 1996b), views community networks as a resource that should be built by the community. But he sees their role as combining aspects of old and new, because he credits history as being an important part of community. Specifically, his text addresses the philosophy, goals and processes involved in developing the Seattle Community Network – one of the first and most innovative free networking projects (of which he was a founding member). However, Silver (2004: 313–22) reminds us that the environment for this system has changed dramatically. Schuler (1996b) gives case studies from the Santa Monica Public Electronic Network (PEN) project, Community Memory in Berkeley, the Cleveland FreeNet and the Big Sky Telegraph system in rural Montana, as well as details of issues critical for the success of these community-based networks. Schuler (ibid.: xi) says of community networks:

> They must rest on the solid foundations of principles and values and be flexible and adaptable, intelligent, and creative. They must be inclusive. Everyone must be allowed to participate. They will have to engage both governments and business because they both exist to provide services for people. These institutions must be accountable to the people, and not the reverse.

Schuler has made a unique contribution to the literature on social uses of technology. He addresses both the social and the political needs of communities. He believes that CMC can and should be used for community building. He looks for ways that technology, and specifically community networks, can help support what he sees as some core values (and the attributes of the core values) for virtual communities: democracy, education, health, equality, information exchange and communication. His text, *New Community Networks*, describes the stages in the life cycle of a community network. He addresses how to evaluate the network, ensuring its long-term impact and sustainability, and the critical question of funding. Schuler makes a point of referring to Godwin's nine principles for designing virtual communities to indicate how these principles play a role in, but are not identical to, those needed for 'community networks' (which as he knows were designed around geographical communities) (ibid.: 257–8).

One of the more significant aspects of Schuler's work for this study is his contention that voluntary association is the key to the development of the new community and virtual communities. He argues that voluntary associations have an additional role to play in the revitalisation of democratic participation – that of a mediating institution linking together two other institutions, which in this case are communities and their government. As Schuler sees the role, ideally the mediating institution can articulate needs and wants, promote discussion and awareness on an issue and present a more coherent, more compelling and more feasible case than community members individually could develop. As he points out, because the aims of voluntary associations coincide significantly with the aims of the new community movement, a special effort should be made to develop support of voluntary associations by means of virtual communities. Strengthening voluntary associations should strengthen the community network movement and vice versa (ibid.: 138–9).

Figello (1998), managing director of WELL, an active member of the WELL community and author of *Hosting Web Communities*, shares his proven experience and vision for planning, developing and maintaining a successful web community. Cohill and Kavanaugh (1997), authors of *Community Networks: Lessons from Blacksburg, Virginia*, are also vociferous exponents of virtual communities. The town of Blacksburg, Virginia, is regarded as America's first truly 'electronic village', despite its five-year evolution. The concept was originally embraced in 1991, and rapidly more than half the population were connected to the internet to order groceries, voice their views on a new bond issue and expose online a multitude of opinions on everything. They have recorded how living in a 'connected town' has impacted on the decisions and responsibilities of civic leaders, educators, parents and business professionals. From the start, the Blacksburg Electronic Village (www.bev.net) was promoted as a people project, not a technology project (ibid.: 235). Casalegno and Kavanaugh (1998) undertook a study of the Blacksburg Electronic Village, based on a 1993–1997 focus group and electronic questionnaire data. Their study showed how an electronic community can resemble a geographic community, and that local information is of the greatest interest to users. Silver (2004: 303–13) questions whether the inhabitants can now free themselves from the bonds of the history they have helped write.

Rheingold and Schuler were the front-runners in visioning and implementing online communities through the 1990s. Although Preece has not been directly involved with developing a specific online community, she has written extensively on usability and human-computer interaction (HCI) and has now contributed the text *On-line Communities: Designing Usability, Supporting Sociability* (Preece, 2000). It correlates the key themes of sociability and usability to create the link between knowledge about human behaviour and appropriate social planning, policies and software design that will carry virtual communities well into the new millennium. Usability has been identified repeatedly as an important component of HCI design (Preece, 1993; Preece et al., 1994; Shneiderman, 1998; Preece et al., 2001). Usability is primarily concerned with developing computer systems to support rapid learning, high skill retention and minimal error rates. Such systems support high productivity and are consistent, controllable and predictable, which makes them pleasant and effective to use (Shneiderman, 1998). The implications for online communities are that users are able to communicate with each other, find information and navigate the community software with ease (Preece, 2000: 8).

Preece (ibid.: 10), likewise, has found the term 'virtual community' a slippery one to define; she prefers a working definition of an online community that consists of four essential components: people, purpose, policies and computer systems. She finds this working definition sufficiently general to apply to a range of different communities, because most definitions treat 'community' only as an entity rather than a process. Communities develop and continuously evolve, and it is only the software supporting them that is designed and not the community itself. Preece's general or working definition also includes physical communities that have become networked (Schuler, 1996b: Lazar and Preece, 1998; Diaper and Stanton, 2004), and communities supported by a single bulletin board, list-server or chat software. However, it is the first three components of Preece's (2000) definition that relate to the complexities and unpredictability that comprise human behaviour and link back into her notion of sociability (Carroll, 2001; Hirose, 2001). For Preece, sociability is concerned with planning and developing social policies that are understandable and acceptable to members as ways to support the community's purpose (Preece, 2000: 26). Understanding a community's needs is essential for developing communities with good sociability and usability. Preece has represented these close dynamic relationships in a way that is very useful to a virtual community developer and attractive in terms of the findings and analysis in this study (Preece et al., 1994; Preece, 2000: 27).

Different models of virtual communities

'Smart communities' is the response or model from the USA and Canada, while 'learning cities' is the British model used to support communities in meeting the challenges of communications technology and the knowledge age. To date, the British model has primarily informed Australian virtual communities. However, Australia can learn much from these two different interpretations of the concept. A study of the two models and their similarities and differences could have far-reaching implications for the development of virtual communities everywhere. On both sides of the Atlantic Ocean, virtual communities have sought new ways to extract economic advantage and increase social cohesion, using partnerships and lifelong learning as fundamental to community success. Technology underpins these goals. However, in the USA 'smart communities' have evolved with the focus on technology; while Britain has created 'learning cities' that have lifelong learning as their central focus (Crawley, 2002; Longworth, 2002; Renninger, 2002).

Innumerable models of vital virtual communities can be found throughout the world (Venkatesh et al., 2004). To summarise their direction, initially they were taken up by some governments but were not as widely embraced as they might have been. Eventually they captured the attention of researchers in tertiary educational institutions. However, it is the three major North American pioneering figures behind 'smart communities' who have defined the key issues, made the significant early contributions outlined above and provided the direction for other models. They were armed with knowledge and guided by a clear, human-centred vision of online communities and a commitment to civil discourse. Their strengths have primarily come from their concerted attempts to document fully their philosophical positions and achievements. Rheingold (1994b: 276) was alert to the fact that virtual communities could help citizens revitalise democracy, or could become an attractively packaged substitute for democratic discourse. Furthermore, he raised the concern that the most insidious attack on people's rights to a reasonable degree of privacy might come not from a political dictatorship, but from the marketplace (ibid.: 292). He also articulated three different kinds of social criticisms of technology that are relevant to consideration of claims of virtual communities as a means of enhancing democracy:

- electronic communications media have pre-empted public discussions in their 'commodification of the public sphere';

- high-bandwidth interactive networks in conjunction with other technology could equally be used for surveillance, control and disinformation as for useful information;

- information technologies have already changed 'reality' into electronic simulation, or what the hyper-realists call a 'society of the spectacle' or 'disinfotainment' (ibid.: 279–81, 297).

Rheingold sought to balance the dilemma of believing in the democratising potential of virtual communities and the technological criticisms. He believed people must constantly question the reality of their online cultures and remind others of the powerful illusory capabilities of electronic communication. People need to look closely at new technologies and question how they might assist in building stronger, more humane communities. If they take such steps, according to him, they are likely to prevent disaster. According to Schuler (1996b: 353), as far as evaluating virtual communities is concerned, Gygi's (1995) two main types of evaluation and the five dimensions[1] she suggested for comparing systems and models have infinite validity.

What happens in virtual communities is largely up to citizens themselves. Preece's (2000) model of 'designing usability and supporting sociability' with 'lifelong learning as the central focus' (as Britain has created in its 'learning cities') seems to offer a powerful, although complex, future model. Models of 'good practice' for successful, vital virtual communities abound, as do definitions of what constitutes a successful virtual community; however, it took CONROD Australia's Disability Lifestyles portal to present the first significant virtual community specifically for people with disabilities to emulate. Developing a model of a virtual community for people with mobility impairments, as undertaken in this investigation, also has the potential to extend the work done so far in the area of virtual communities.

Notes

1. In her report on the evaluation of community networks, Gygi (1995) describes two main types of evaluation: the comparative analysis of computer network systems in which individual systems (or generic computer network models) are compared; and the individual project assessment in which an individual community network system is evaluated according to the goals or criteria that the organisation or community itself has designated as important. Gygi also suggested five dimensions for comparing community network systems and models: services, capacity, accessibility, ownership and financing.

Governments' policies, legislative and telecommunications regulatory frameworks and information policy

> Information highways, digital libraries and virtual communities – these are the metaphors that shape public dialogue about social justice in an information society, shaping intellectual property law and information policy for a digital age. (Lyman, 1998: 1)

This chapter provides an overview of the telecommunications legislative and regulatory frameworks and government policy; charts, in brief, some progress in telecommunications industry self-regulation and the issue of universal service; and finally explores some recent government information policies and implications for people with disabilities.

Types of relevant legislation and government initiatives

Britain and Australia share a common telecommunications heritage – a government-owned monopoly building the telephone network and providing telephone services to business and residential customers. However, in both countries, over the past couple of decades some of the government monopolistic service systems have devolved to various business enterprises that compete in the carriage and delivery of telecommunications services (Jolley, 2003). Goggin and Newell (2003: 40), in their analysis of the global context of telecommunications, found:

> Strenuous efforts have been put into designing telecommunications as a responsibility of privately owned and operated companies

operating across world and domestic markets. Most Western countries have restructured their telecommunications industries, allowing great competition – through a series of U.S. court decisions and finally the 1996 U.S. Communications Act, the 1997 Australian Telecommunications Act, the 1993 Canadian Telecommunications Act [Rideout, 2003], British reforms since the mid-1980s, successive European directives, and the World Trade Organization February 1997 agreement on basic telecommunications.

People with disabilities are primarily affected by two types of legislation: the various Telecommunications Acts, and the various Disability Discrimination Acts.

The UK Telecommunications Act (1984) has been superseded by Oftel, the British regulator for the telecommunications industry (www.ofcom.org.uk), the Office of Communications (Ofcom) and the Electronic Telecommunications Act (2000), as well as the Privacy and Electronic Communications (EC Directive) Regulations 2003. Oftel has played an important leadership role through its Advisory Committee on Telecommunications for Disabled and Elderly People (DIEL), a specialist advisory body that is influential with both government and industry. Ofcom has statutory duties, as set down in the Communications Act 2003, and regulatory principles it will seek to follow in fulfilling those duties. It is the independent regulator and competition authority for the British communications industries, with responsibilities across television, radio and telecommunications. Ofcom complies with the UK data protection and freedom of information legislation as well as with rules on accessibility and diversity, for example in improving disability equality.

The USA had a specific Technology-Related Assistance Act (1988) that addressed some of the accessibility aspects of universal service. However, it was the Americans with Disabilities Act (ADA) (1990), dealing with the rights of people with disabilities, that was significant. But even so, it was limited in its coverage of telecommunications issues. The US disability movement demanded a new definition of universal service, telecommunications and people with disabilities. This was ultimately addressed, at least to some extent, in the Telecommunications Act (1996).

The Australian Disability Discrimination Act (1992) has aimed to eliminate discrimination against people with disabilities – specifically in the provision of goods, services and facilities (see Chapter 1). This law is administered by the Human Rights and Equal Opportunity Commission (HREOC). The UK Disability Discrimination Act (2005) builds on and extends earlier British disability discrimination legislation, principally the 1995 DDA. The UK Special Educational Needs and Disability Act (2001) had concerns about inequitable access to telecommunications equipment and services for people with disabilities. This has been an issue both in Britain and Australia. There was widespread speculation about new legislation being introduced in the UK to ensure that websites are accessible to disabled users. In fact, many countries have already introduced some kind of law about this. The UK DDA does not mention websites; however, the Code of Practice for the Act explicitly mentions websites and can be downloaded in its entirety from the UK Disability Rights Commission (DRC) website. The DRC closed its doors on 30 September 2007 after more than seven years of working towards equality for disabled people. The climate has changed and discrimination against disabled people has increasingly been seen as unacceptable. On 1 October 2007 the three equality commissions – the Commission for Racial Equality (CRE), the DRC and the Equal Opportunities Commission (EOC) – merged into the new Equality and Human Rights Commission. The websites of these commissions have also been incorporated into the new commission's website (www.equalityhumanrights.com).

It is the Telecommunications Acts (1991, 1997[1]) that regulate the telecommunications industry in Australia – that is, the carriers and carriage service providers. The Telecommunications (Consumer Protection and Service Standards) Act (1999) aims to promote the interests of consumers and achieve open, equitable and pro-competitive service access across the country. In Australia, accessibility for people with disabilities was not recognised in legislation until the 1992 DDA with its limited implications for telecommunications. The Australian Communications Authority administered telecommunications legislation and regulations and monitored performance. The Australian Communications Industry Forum is an industry-owned and managed self-regulatory body to develop industry codes and standards. The Telecommunications Industry Ombudsman resolves complaints from small businesses and residential consumers. There are specific legislative consumer protection measures – they include the Universal Service Obligation, the Digital Data Service Obligation and the Customer Service Guarantee (Bourk, 2000). Telstra is Australia's current universal service provider and, like British Telecom, has made efforts to make services and equipment accessible to people with disabilities. British

Telecom has a long-standing record of tailoring its services to the needs of older and disabled customers, providing support and information through a dedicated Age and Disability Action Unit and website.

In Australia, based on the European COST 219[2] Telecommunications Charter, the Telecommunications Disability Consumer Representation Project (TEDICORE) (http://tedicore.ipb. icemedia.com.au) has taken on this vital advocacy role. The Commonwealth government supports TEDICORE[3] through the Grants to Fund Telecommunications Consumer Representations programme of the Department of Communications, Information Technology and the Arts (DCITA). TEDICORE, as an advocacy group, represents the interests of disabled telecommunications consumers and has promoted equity and accessibility to the products and services offered by the telecommunications industry since 1998. It provides a forum for discussion of pertinent issues, actively participates in regulatory bodies such as the Australian Communications Industry Forum (ACIF) and the Australian Communications Authority (ACA), and gives people with disabilities a further opportunity to raise concerns in public, government and industry forums. TEDICORE aims to develop partnerships with a range of organisations to research, develop and implement examples of products and services that underpin the principles of universal design. TEDICORE can funnel many logistically and technically complex issues from government and industry directly to people with disabilities. The project aims to provide further support for people with disabilities to raise concerns that can be effectively heard and dealt with by government and industry (Astbrink, 2002).

TEDICORE's recent significant activities have included the following:

- assessing the disability equipment programmes of Telstra and other carriers;
- writing a submission to the ACA regarding harsh restrictions that current compliance testing puts on entry of 'low-volume' assistive equipment;
- working towards reducing barriers to importation of assistive equipment;
- providing input to website specifications and compliance with ACIF standards through the Australian Telecommunications Industry Association (ATIA);
- working on the ACIF Disability Advisory Board (DAB) guidelines for codes and standards that are important for people with disabilities;

- working towards encouraging universal design for equipment;
- responding to enquiries about Global System for Mobile Communication (GSM) phones and e-commerce;
- compiling a document on 'best practice' in the conduct of telecommunications business with respect to people with disabilities (Astbrink, 2004).

The best practice guidelines were developed to highlight the many areas that still need to be addressed. They were formulated as a set of recommendations, listed under key principles adapted from the European COST 219 Telecommunications Charter. The recommendations reflect issues such as legislation and regulation, telecommunications equipment, universal design, accessible network services, public procurement, a range of internet access issues, pricing, consumer consultation processes and the promotion of accessible products and services (Goggin and Newell, 2003: 55–6).

Since Australia's telecommunications infrastructure is made up of a variety of networks where service providers are using each other's networks to provide their communication and information services, access rules are needed to ensure that systems work with each other. The Telecommunications Act provides these rules, which means that the service providers interconnect with each other on fair terms. The Act also ensures that the prescribed carriage service, standard telephone services and payphones are available to all Australians no matter where they are located. Nonetheless, the Telecommunications Service Inquiry (TSI) found limited resources and inadequate training arrangements have prevented people with disabilities from taking advantage of services and equipment to meet their needs. This same inquiry also found low levels of awareness about services available to people with special requirements, such as those with medical priorities or those on low incomes (Besley et al., 2000: 57).

In March 2000 the Australian government announced its intention to introduce two pilot projects in regional areas to test new arrangements for contestability in delivering the Universal Service Obligation (USO). This initiative, a key element of the government's commitment to introduce competition in the delivery of the USO to regional Australia, provides opportunities for improved service quality and greater choice for regional consumers. The USO ensures that all Australians are guaranteed reasonable access to a telephone service. Under these arrangements, telecommunications companies compete for industry-funded subsidies for the provision of USO services. A telecommunications company (other than Telstra) wishing to enter a contestable market must seek approval from, and be qualified by, the ACA to operate as a competing universal service provider. The ACA monitored these projects; the outcomes were conveyed through a discussion paper based on the ACA's understanding of the government's policy related to USO contestability and the legislation introduced in Parliament in June 2000. This consultation process with industry and consumers developed guidelines for service providers which applied to take part in the pilot projects. It is heartening to note that five of the 17 issues brought to the attention of industry and consumers concern information provision for all customers, including those with a disability, and the ACA is cognisant of the DDA 1992 (Australian Communications Authority, 2000: 11–13, 15, 19).

The Australian government has taken some steps to ensure that people with disabilities have adequate access to online information and communication services; for example, the industry self-regulatory body, the ACIF, established the consultative Disability Advisory Board. However, despite the important initiatives described above, Australia, like Britain and the USA, has relied on its disability legislation rather than being proactive in its telecommunications regulation.

Telecommunications initiatives and progress

British Telecom (BT) has been hailed for its Broadband for All initiative, which seeks to extend the use of broadband technology to customers disadvantaged by the digital divide. BT research suggests that as many as 23 million adults might be digitally excluded by 2025 unless more can be done to encourage use of the internet. This is seen to be increasingly important as more services are provided online, resulting in people without access to this new technology being disadvantaged in their day-to-day living. BT's response has been to use its new Age and Disability Action website launched in March 2006 (www.btplc.com/age_disability) to include an online step-by-step guide for older and disabled customers in understanding and ordering broadband, with specific examples of its benefits. The site offers high levels of accessibility and is also available in British sign language (BSL). BT is the only FTSE100 company to provide information in BSL on a website. To reach older and disabled customers who do not currently have online access, BT has produced a supplementary booklet designed to help people overcome their fear of computers and the internet, highlighting the advantages of the internet and demonstrating how life-enhancing it can be, using case studies from older and disabled customers who have successfully joined the digital age.

Evidence suggests that telecommunications progress has been relatively quick in Australia in recent years compared with the previous quarter-century (Goggin and Newell, 2004, 2000b: 148–58; Newell, 1998). Telstra, as the national primary USO provider[4] since the 1980s, has an obligation to ensure that standard telephone services are reasonably accessible to all people in Australia on an equitable basis, irrespective of where a person resides or undertakes business. After the Telecommunications Service Inquiry in 2000, also called the Besley Inquiry, the Minister for Communications, Information Technology and the Arts announced detailed initiatives to address each of the TSI's 17 recommendations, claiming that the first 15 initiatives had been fully implemented, including recommendation 13 regarding reviews of USO contestability (Besley et al., 2000: 5–7). This obligation to provide equipment to people with disabilities is enshrined in legislation – even though telecommunications were explicitly left out of areas named as being important and worthy of disability standards in the 1992 DDA. The Australian DDA applies to the provision of goods and services, including telecommunications goods and services. Obligations also exist under telecommunications legislation (Jolley, 2003). The USO in the Telecommunications (Consumer Protection and Service Standards) Act (1999) requires the universal service provider(s) to supply equipment to people with disabilities. However, the Telecommunication Act 1997 specifies that the universal service provision must include the functional requirements of people with disabilities. The traditional definition of 'universal service' has been tied to the universal availability of telecommunications, with some thought given to affordability. One of the neglected components has been universal accessibility, and people with disabilities have been poorly served under this perception of universal service (Newell, 1998). In fact, in Australia universal service did not become an explicitly legislated goal of telecommunications until 1975 (Goggin and Newell, 2000a: 129).

Telstra (Australia's prime telecommunication company) does not claim for equipment provision under the USO levy scheme. The USO needs to be applied to all carriers or suppliers, and it needs to be strengthened (Australian Communications Authority, 2000, 2001). The DDA does not cover the public procurement of accessible IT and telecommunications equipment, although countries such as the USA have legislated that the government will only purchase accessible IT and telecommunications products. Other countries such as Japan, Ireland and Sweden are working on guidelines and policies to incorporate accessibility in their public procurement programmes. This has already had an impact on the development of accessible products by major corporations. In Australia the Commonwealth Disability Strategy (CDS) concerns itself with deficiencies in accessibility – such as the height of payphones for people with physical disabilities (Australian Communications Industry Forum, 2001). New Zealand has already addressed this issue, as all phones are at an accessible height and incorporate universal design features (Connell et al., 1997).

In June 1998 Telstra established a dedicated Disability Services Unit, responsible for formulating policy and overseeing the direction of disability activities within Telstra. Nevertheless, it took many years for it to provide a link on its website to its disability equipment programme (DEP) and its actual disability services. Then in 2003 Telstra closed its Aged and Disabilities Centres in all Australian capital cities due to what it cited as 'lack of demand'. The service was relocated into various commercial Telstra outlets and external agencies. It is the only telecommunications carrier/carriage service provider in Australia with a range of products and services that cater for the diverse needs of people with a disability, and it has provided specialised equipment since 1981. The Disability Services Unit launched the online version of the disability product catalogue in July 2002, featuring products available through Telstra's DEP, which supplies eligible customers with a range of specialised telephone equipment at the same cost as standard telephone rental. A DEP is specifically designed for persons with disabilities and not for the general consumer market. Product information is organised into categories such as hearing, speech, vision, mobility and dexterity, as well as rental telephones. The online resource complements the existing hard-copy and CD-ROM versions of the catalogue and was developed by Telstra's Disability Services Unit as part of its ongoing commitment to providing customer information in accessible formats. The disability equipment products page complies with international standards for online accessibility. This means that the design aspects give people with disabilities access to all the information and/or functions that are available. Optus, one of the other carriage service providers, has incorporated W3C standards into its website, and has also developed a DEP.

Telstra was one of the first major corporations in Australia to develop a Disability Action Plan, and it lodged its first plan with the Human Rights and Equal Opportunity Commission in 1996. This Disability Action Plan is designed to uphold the principles underlying the DDA 1992: that people with a disability have the same fundamental rights as the rest of the community (Telstra Disability Services, 1998, 2002). Developed in consultation with consumer and disability organisations, the plan provides a framework for improving the accessibility of Telstra products, services and facilities. Telstra publicly lodged its fourth Disability Action Plan with the HREOC on 26 July 2007, setting new objectives to improve access to next-generation technologies for people with a disability. Optus (2001) also has a Disability Action Plan, and some other minor carriers like AAPT, Vodafone and Orange have grappled with the need for such a document, as has the Australian Mobile Telecommunications Association (AMTA).

Telstra, like BT, has a consultation process in place that is formalised through the Telstra Consumer Consultative Council (TCCC) (www.telstra.com.au/tccc/index.htm). The group has been meeting since the early 1990s and provides an ongoing opportunity for consumers and Telstra representatives to engage in telecommunications issues, products and services, with a mutually acceptable outcome. Consumer representation comes from a broad cross-section of the Australian community and includes representatives from disability organisations. The council meets nationally and also runs a consumer forum (established March 1999) in each state and territory.

Despite Telstra[5] having a special Priority Repair Service for people with disabilities or life-threatening conditions, problems occur. Two major disasters challenged this service in 2002, and Telstra was forced by public opinion to engage PriceWaterhouseCoopers to undertake an extensive and comprehensive review of the service. In response to its findings, Telstra boosted its funding to fast-track equipment repair services and improve reliability of repairs for people registered with the Priority Repair Service. Furthermore, Telstra is now obliged to report on its progress in this area to the ACA on a quarterly basis. Additionally, it undertook a public awareness campaign around this issue in consultation with the Telstra Disability Forum (TDF) state and territory consumer representatives.

In an effort to address special needs, TSI recommendation 13 (Besley et al., 2000: 181) tellingly highlights the fact that funding for consumer representation is available through the Commonwealth of Australia. The report also points to disabled people's ability to participate effectively in future industry processes regarding equipment design and standards. The disabled community's low level of awareness of the availability and use of special needs equipment was identified and flagged as an issue. It was recommended that additional funding should be provided to address these current deficiencies through existing grants programmes. The federal government response to the 17 recommendations made by the TSI was released on 24 May 2001 (Australian Communications Authority, 2001). The response specified that it is a priority of the government that people with disabilities and consumers in regional, rural and remote Australia have adequate representation – a priority that had been stated earlier (Australian Regional Telecommunications Infrastructure Fund Secretariat, 1998).

The Besley Report was followed by the Regional Telecommunications Inquiry (that produced the Estens Report) in August 2002 to assess the adequacy of telecommunications services in regional, rural and remote Australia, and to advise on a number of other policy issues. Among the findings and recommendations were items relating to fixed telephones and payphones, mobile phone services, internet services, higher-bandwidth internet services, legislated consumer safeguards, Telstra's local presence, sharing of future benefits and other key service issues (Estens et al., 2002). Women with Disabilities Australia (WWDA) presented one of 606 public submissions advising the government that improvements in these areas must be completed before the government changes its relationship with Telstra. The criterion of a demonstration of ongoing improvement with various initiatives within a reasonable timeframe is not sufficient: the initiatives should be complete. Furthermore, WWDA argued that adequate safeguards had been ignored and needed to be put in place to guarantee essential telecommunications services for people with disabilities (Women with Disabilities Australia, 2002: 14).

If the future is to be equitable, or one based on social justice of access, equity, participation and rights for disabled people, the choices are in their own hands as far as telecommunications, communication and information are concerned (Astbrink and Newell, 2002a, 2002b, 2002c). People with disabilities must continue to be vocal advocates for their own cause. It is not for the government to provide all the telecommunications services and products for such people, but it is its place to facilitate accessible services and products and for people with disabilities then to determine their own futures (Cullen and Robinson, 1997).

Goggin and Newell's (2000a, 2000b) work is a constant reminder of the dismal circumstances of 'disabling' telecommunication technologies in Australia prior to the disability rights groups taking the initiative, and how rethinking universal service through disability can lead to inclusive policies that benefit everybody.

Information policies

Lyman (1998) argues that in the information society, intellectual property provides the capital that drives a global national economy, although this contradicts the notion of the creation of a more just society through free access to information. If these emerging concepts in communication and information are to be relevant to people with physical disabilities, the information technology must be accessible as well as affordable, and people with disabilities must become information literate.

Lyman (ibid.: 3) says that 'the information highway is a very powerful and useful metaphor, for it reminds us that computer networks are a means of transportation, one that instantly carries a new kind of economic commodity – called information – around the world'. He also reminds us that the Clinton administration in the USA popularised the idea of an information highway as part of its *National Information Infrastructure: Agenda for Action* (Computer Professionals for Social Responsibility, 1993). This policy was followed by the influential report *The Global Information Infrastructure: Agenda for Cooperation* (US National Telecommunications and Information Administration, 1995a). Electronic commerce, or e-commerce, superseded the information superhighway terminology, and the report *A Framework for Global Electronic Commerce* followed (US Department of Commerce, 1997). It is encouraging to note also the report *Access to the Information Superhighway and Emerging Information Technologies by People with Disabilities* (US NCD, 1996). The USA has continued to forge ahead with technological and social access to computing, information and communication technologies (Kling, 1998).

Europe, in the 1990s, also explored the economic potential and implementation possibilities afforded by information policies, provision of universal service and the global information society, and predicted the risk of the digital divide as a result of the new technologies (Schiller, 2005).

In Australia, an initial focus is to look at the recent legislative framework and government policy on information and technologies, as well as considering briefly the implications of international information policies. A specific emphasis is on how these policies have impacted on community information and the 'information superhighway', and how they have influenced one another (Australian Bureau of Statistics, 2005). Together, these factors become a balancing act between government policy (National Office for the Information Economy, 1998b, 1999), legislation (for example, the DDA 1992; Telecommunications Act 1997; Telecommunications (Consumer Protection and Service Standards) Act 1999; Telecommunications (Equipment for the Disabled) Regulations 1998; and AS/ACIF SO40: 2001 Requirements for Customer Equipment for Use with the Standard Telephone Service – Features for Special Needs of Persons with Disabilities), industry partners (for example, IBM.com; Telstra.com) and consumers (for example, isdac.com; WWDA).

In Australia, one of roles of the Department of Communications, Information Technology and the Arts is to promote community organisations in their use of the information highway. Grants from the National Office for the Information Economy (NOIE) were provided for this purpose. WWDA, for example, submitted a funding proposal to the DCITA in 1998 to complete a project on women with disabilities and telecommunications. Members had expressed concerns that they did not have equal access to telecommunications services, including internet training and access.

The Attorney General in 2000 gave the Human Rights and Equal Opportunity Commission (www.humanrights.gov.au) a brief to investigate the implications of the new technologies in e-commerce for older Australians and Australians with disability, and for the provision of government and other services. Furthermore, the HREOC has been required to outline these people's specific needs in accessing services that use these technologies. The HREOC recommended the World Wide Web Consortium's (W3C) Web Content Accessibility Guidelines (www.w3.org/WAI) and AusInfo's Guidelines for Commonwealth Information Published in Electronic Formats for their sound advice on integrating accessibility into electronic publishing, believing that these would satisfy the access requirements of the DDA 1992.[6] Successful access to information and use of information technology by people with disabilities is referred to as 'accessibility' (Hakkinen and Velasco, 2004).

Progress in access has not been limited to telecommunications but has extended to include the appearance of information for consumers. It is not simply a matter of providing information, but also providing it in an accessible format (World Wide Web Consortium, undated; Zimmerman et al., 1997). The director of the Australian Interactive Multimedia Industry Association argued that it is not just the disabled who benefit from a new generation of simple and accessible websites: people who are suffering from download and graphic fatigue, those with low-end technology and those in STD remote locations gratefully thank designers and developers who put accessibility first (Spender, 2000). The W3C has established the Web Accessibility Initiative (WAI) standard that provides advice on requirements and means of compliance for users with disabilities (Waddell, 1998). The Australian government has adopted this international standard in its legislation.

The information economy literature provides an insight into those aspects that contribute positively towards well-being for people with disabilities and connect them with other people during and after rehabilitation. This has social justice implications for disabled people, and draws on other literature from diverse cultures and disciplines, such as medicine, psychology, disability and telecommunications. The results, so far, of this literature overview have been encouraging, in that Australians with disabilities are being taken into account in the purpose, scope, implementation and evaluation of ICT in the national economy (Department of Communications, Information Technology and the Arts, 2003).

The NOIE (www.noie.gov.au) produced the Australian government's information policy, 'Towards an Australian strategy for the information economy: a preliminary statement of the government's policy approach and a basis for business and community consultation' (National Office for the Information Economy, 1998a) and 'A strategic framework for the information economy: identifying priorities for action' (National Office for the Information Economy, 1998b). The NOIE was renamed in 2004 as the Australian Government Information Office (AGIO). The draft framework principles referenced several existing government policies, programmes and initiatives. The government's mission in this framework was 'to ensure that the lives, work and well-being of Australians are enriched, jobs are created, and the national wealth is enhanced, through the participation of all Australians in the growing information economy' (ibid.). The referenced government policies, programmes and initiatives included the Telecommunications Act 1997, the Networking the Nation programme,[7] 'Investing for Growth', 'Getting Business On-line', the New Silk Road programme, the 'Information Industries Action Agenda Report' and the 'National Scoping Study on the Telemedicine Industry in Australia'.

Networking the Nation, a five-year $320 million Regional Telecommunications Infrastructure Fund (RTIF) programme, was to ensure that regional, rural and remote areas outside capital cities were participating in the opportunities to be derived from telecommunications services. The aim of Networking the Nation was to fund projects that would:

- improve telecommunication services and infrastructure;
- increase access to and use of services available via telecommunication networks;
- reduce differences in access to facilities and services.

Some of the obvious social justice benefits that people with disabilities could derive from Networking the Nation would be a reduction in isolation and increased opportunities for social development.

The National Scoping Study on the Telemedicine Industry in Australia was the third and final government initiative that impacted on the strategic framework. Telemedicine was the name given to the delivery of health services and information through the use of telecommunications. In 1998 the government released a report entitled *Fragmentation to Integration: National Scoping Study on the Telemedicine Industry in Australia* (Mitchell, 1998). The report highlighted the relatively small size of the telemedicine industry in Australia, and also its rapid growth compared with other countries. Telemedicine, because of its integration with information technology, promised to add value to the Australian economy and provide another way of improving healthcare. Only in the second half of 2000 did the Minister for Communications, Information Technology and the Arts open Australia's first laboratory for the online transfer of medical information and health records in text and images.

As indicated, following extensive consultation the draft Australian information economy policy was released in January 1999 as a strategy document and first progress report, entitled 'A strategic framework for the information economy, overview: key priorities for action' (National Office for the Information Economy, 1999). The framework outlined ten strategic priorities for Australia's participation in the information economy. Each of the priorities has direct implications for persons with physical disabilities, but three priorities in particular impacted upon a virtual community for people with long-term, severe physical disabilities. In 2000 the second progress report was released (Department of Communications, Information Technology and the Arts, 2000), then 'Advancing Australia – the information economy progress report 2002'

(Department of Communications, Information Technology and the Arts, 2002), and finally on 13 July 2004 the 'Strategic framework for the information economy 2004–2006: opportunities and challenges for the information age' (Department of Communications, Information Technology and the Arts, 2004).

The information economy promises new and dynamic ways to learn, live, create, work, communicate, buy and sell as a result of new information technologies. All countries need to embrace these new technologies to create the 'knowledge economy' that will allow new ways of doing business, help overcome geographical distances and establish a place in the global marketplace. Businesses from both private and public sectors potentially benefit from the information economy: they rely on information flows and are information consumers. If the information economy can provide online technologies that will deliver information efficiently and effectively, then businesses prosper. Online services allow better access for businesses to markets and market information, provide efficient and effective distribution and marketing of services and products, and thus lead to strong, viable communities.

Notes

1. The Telecommunications Act 1997 was formulated to allow telecommunication networks to interconnect with each other and to provide safeguards against anti-competitive behaviours.
2. COST 219, entitled Future Telecommunications and Tele-Informatics Facilities for Disabled and Elderly People, started in 1986.
3. The TEDICORE project is run under the auspices of Blind Citizens Australia, with funding under s. 593 of the Telecommunications Act 1997, and represents the interests of telecommunications consumers with disabilities.
4. The Universal Service Obligation (USO) is the obligation under the Telecommunications (Consumer Protection and Service Standards) Act 1999 to ensure that standard telephone service, payphones and prescribed carriage services are reasonably accessible to all Australians on an equitable basis, wherever they reside or carry on a business (Department of Communications, Information Technology and the Arts, 2000: 249). The concept of universal service can be portrayed in many different ways. An influential report by the Consumers' Telecommunications Network stated that there are five elements to universal service: universal geographical availability; universal accessibility; universal affordability; universal technological standard; and universal telecommunications and participation in society (Wilson and Goggin, cited in Roe, 2001: 164).
5. For the dedicated Telstra policy coverage, visit Telstra's website: www.nowwearetalking.com.au.

6. These guidelines explain how to make web content accessible to people with disabilities. The guidelines are intended for all web content developers (page authors and site designers) and for developers of authoring tools. The primary goal of these guidelines is to promote accessibility. However, following them will also make web content more available to all users, whatever agent they are using (e.g. desktop browser, voice browser, mobile phone, automobile-based personal computer, etc.) or constraints they may be operating under (e.g. noisy surroundings, under- or over-illuminated rooms, a hands-free environment, etc.). Following the guidelines will also help people find information on the web more quickly. These guidelines do not discourage content developers from using images, video, etc., but rather explain how to make multimedia content more accessible to a wide audience (Web Content Accessibility Guidelines 1.0: www.w3.org/TR/WAI-WEBCONTENT/).

7. The Minister for Communications, Information Technology and the Arts, Senator Helen Coonan, released an evaluation in 2006 of the $320 million Networking the Nation programme, showing it helped connect Australians in rural, regional and remote areas by funding more than 720 communications projects (www.minister.dcita.gov.au/media/media_releases/networking_the_nation_evaluation__connecting_more_australians2).

Information needs research for people with disabilities

Value, like beauty, is in the eye of the beholder. (Feeney and Grieves, 1994: 16)

In 2004 the Commonwealth Department of Family and Community Services (FaCS), Canberra, commissioned the TNS Social Research Group, Sydney, to conduct research into the online information needs and uses of people with disabilities and their carers. The report produced was for internal use only. The study of users and their needs has preoccupied many information scholars; but the work of Elfreda Chatman, known for her studies on the information needs and information-seeking behaviour of the poor and the elderly, is considered in some detail in this chapter because of its perceived direct relevance. Moore's model of the social information needs of people with disabilities is examined as a means of achieving a deeper understanding of what particular information needs are most relevant to disabled persons. People with disabilities are usually economically poor as well as information poor or deprived, and the poor seek information differently to other demographic sectors of the community. The primary research question implied that persons with long-term physical disabilities are technologically literate and, to some degree, information literate.

Any examination of these issues starts with an evaluation of information. In most circumstances, greater value of information is allied with greater use, but in the case of disablement this is not always so. Equity requires the empowerment of small numbers of people with a particular disability comparable to the empowerment of more prominent groups. The evaluation of both the information and the access to it is absolutely crucial in these circumstances.

Information literacy research

What is information literacy (IL)? The American Library Association (ALA) defines information literacy as a set of abilities requiring individuals to 'recognize when information is needed and have the ability to locate, evaluate, and use effectively the needed information'. The ALA (1989) also states that 'information literacy is a survival skill in the Information Age'. But information literacy is much more: 'Information literacy forms the basis for lifelong learning. It is common to all disciplines, to all learning environments, and to all levels of education. It enables learners to master content and extend their investigations, become more self-directed, and assume greater control over their own learning' (ibid.). The Council of Australian University Librarians (CAUL) adopted the Australian School Library Association (ASLA) Statement on Information Literacy in 1994 (Council of Australian University Librarians, 2001). The Australian Library and Information Association (ALIA) adopted its policy statement on information literacy for all Australians in 2001 and amended it in 2003 (Australian Library and Information Association, 2003). Information literacy promotes the free flow of information and ideas in the interest of all people and a thriving culture, economy and democracy. ALIA believes that a vibrant national and global culture, economy and democracy will be advanced best by persons who recognise their information needs. They also need to be able to identify, locate, access, evaluate and apply that information.

The process begins with recognising a need for information and its role in transforming communities (International Meeting of Information Literacy Experts, 2003: 3). Then the information must be accessed, evaluated, organised and manipulated in whatever format (print index, online database, internet, etc.) it appears. The interviewees in this study were intuitively aware of their need for information, and for the information and technological literacy deemed desirable by the UNESCO (2005) thematic debate on information literacy. Furthermore, people need the ability to refine data to information and use it to solve needs. Such application, combining judgement, decision-making and common sense, can be used functionally, aesthetically, academically or scientifically.

As information literacy informs a variety of viewpoints, such as the library and information community and the education, ICT and media communities, an understanding of how internet search engines and libraries are organised is necessary. Familiarity with the resources they provide and knowledge of commonly used research techniques are an essential prelude to the process of information literacy. The skills required to evaluate the information content critically and an understanding of the technological infrastructure on which information transmission is based, including its social, political and cultural context and impact, are also essential to a person being information literate. Bruce (2000: 97) argues 'My own research leads me to conclude that information literacy is an appreciation of the complex of ways of interacting with information. It is a way of thinking and reasoning about aspects of subject matter.'

Bruce (1997) believes that IL is still in its infancy, and that the concept may be construed as representing people's ways of experiencing information use (ibid.; Bruce, 1999). IL is a relatively recent field of research originally conceived in the 1970s and subsequently attracting the attention of the education and information professions (ibid., 1999). These professions have developed along with IL as an academic field of enquiry the related concept of 'lifelong learning'. In fact, lifelong learning is now a global policy priority, adopted and promoted by the OECD and European Union, among others (for example, the World Bank and British virtual communities). This policy is linked closely to the need for both initial and ongoing vocationally oriented education and training, given the rapid shifts in the nature of work, technology, including ICT, and changes associated with globalisation. Equity-related policy in Australia is directed in the first instance to indigenous Australians and people with disabilities. The no longer extant Australian National Training Authority (ANTA) released a support document for the new national strategy for vocational education and training (2004–2010) that had implications for shaping the future for everybody, including traditionally marginalised groups (Australian National Training Authority, 2004).

According to West (2002), results suggest that engaging the non-user in the knowledge economy relies on more than the provision of technology. Rather it encompasses issues at both macro and micro levels. For the individual, it means addressing personal motivation to engage in lifelong learning with appropriate awareness-raising and teaching methodologies. At a macro level, technology needs to be developed and provided in a manner that adheres to universal design principles. Since the internet is predominantly text based, people with physical and intellectual disabilities often face difficulties in accessing material. Williamson et al. (2002) have developed websites with a variety of designs and models that make the internet less threatening and more accessible to their target groups – people with physical and intellectual disabilities.

Since the mid-1990s the meaning of the terms 'information literacy' and 'digital divide' have been largely absorbed into both professional vocabulary and the language of popular culture. Now researchers believe that if they can successfully define and measure the digital divide, this understanding can form the basis of new principles and strategies to overcome the divide and deliver digital opportunity and digital justice in global, metropolitan and especially urban community contexts (McDonald and Denning, 2002; Servon, 2002). As discussed in Chapter 3, an information-enabled society proposes an environment where connections between people can be enhanced, isolation can be reduced and supportive relationships can be established. These improvements in social support are known to have a positive impact on health and empowerment of individuals and the community in which they live. We need to examine the literature indicating that information literacy is a critical success factor in bridging the digital divide.

Lifelong learning implies a diversity of learners, communities, cultures, languages, communications, needs, goals or purposes, motivations, learning styles, literacies, learning facilitators, information sources and conceptions about lifelong learning and information literacy. It does not necessarily imply universality or ubiquity. This study proposes that in its diversity lifelong learning has relevance for people with disabilities and the different orientations they seek in virtual communities.

The IL discourse has focused on sets of skills or competencies and the measurement of those competencies, hence its link with lifelong learning and education. While undoubtedly measurement of such competencies is important, especially in tertiary education – the setting of most IL research to date – the importance of IL is now being acknowledged in the broader community and the workplace (Bruce, 2000; Edwards et al., 2004; Hughes et al., 2005; Partridge et al., 2008). Of the two recent models proposed – a relational model (Bruce, 1999) and a constructivist model (Cheuk, 1998) – it is the relational model that has gained international acceptance. The model identifies critical features associated with variation in people's experience. However, it was developed within a higher educational framework and has yet fully to establish its relevance in the community and corporate sectors.

Bruce (1997: 36–7) explains why information literacy has been vested in sets of competencies as the result of trying to fit our thinking about IL into frameworks based on world views of dualism, behaviourism, information processing, constructivism and economic rationalism. Bruce

Table 4.1 The seven faces of information literacy

The information technology conception	IL seen as using IT for information retrieval and communication
The information sources conception	IL seen as finding information
The information conception	IL seen as executing a process
The information control conception	IL seen as controlling information
The knowledge construction conception	IL seen as building up a personal knowledge base in a new area of interest
The knowledge extension conception	IL seen as working with knowledge and personal perspectives adopted in such a way that novel insights are gained
The wisdom conception	IL seen as using information wisely for the benefit of others

Source: adapted from Bruce (1997: 154)

proposes an alternative IL paradigm and its associated research based on the benefits of a relational or interpretive approach. Her model describes the critical differences in the understandings of the phenomenon of IL itself, which means IL research is no longer hampered by limited and limiting definitions. In fact, she discriminates between the seven different conceptions of IL as understood by experienced information users and those in higher education. She represents these conceptions of the different ways of experiencing IL diagrammatically within a phenomenographic framework, summarised in Table 4.1 (ibid.: 154). Each category is distinguished by a particular way of focusing on the world that correlates with a particular meaning associated with IL. The categories represent people's subjective experience of different parts of the phenomenon that are logically related.

Given there are these varying conceptions of information literacy in higher education, it follows that there are likely to be comparable varying conceptions and understandings of the IL needs in virtual communities for people with physical disabilities. These are seen in the first phase of the analysis in Chapter 6 of this study. Ultimately, IL for persons in higher education, the community or the workplace concerns the strategic use of information associated with variations in people's disablement. The challenge for persons with disabilities is in embracing lifelong learning, the digital divide and information literacy in order to be able to participate fully in the emerging information society (Williamson et al., 2002).

Overview of the digital divide literature

> Logically, the more a group uses technology, the more information that group is aware of and has available to help meet various information needs. Thus, information-poor groups can change the aforementioned societal indicators for the better, and become more socially empowered and economically competitive, by seeking membership into groups [becoming part of groups] that utilise and benefit from the advancements of modern information technology. (Hoffman and Novak, 1998: 390)

The existing research into the concept of the digital divide (DD) takes primarily a socio-economic perspective and suggests that the primary factors influencing the development and growth of the DD are income, employment and education (Civille, 1995; Compaine, 2001; Smith, 1995). The US Department of Commerce's National Telecommunications and Information Administration (NTIA) published three reports entitled 'Falling through the net' (US National Telecommunications and Information Administration, 1995b, 1999, 2000), detailing who had internet access and who did not. However, it was not until the third report that it specifically investigated internet access and computer use among people with disabilities (ibid., 2000). At the core of US telecommunications policy is the goal of 'universal service' – the idea that all Americans should have access to affordable telephone service (Benton Foundation, 1998; US National Telecommunications and Information Administration, 1995b: 2).

As personal computer prices fall and internet services to households are increasingly less expensive, the socio-economic view of the DD is less convincing (Lenhart et al., 2003). Harper (2000: 4) proposes the existence of two digital divides: an access digital divide (ADD) and a social digital divide (SDD). The ADD is based on cost factors and is frequently discussed in terms of the presence of computers and internet access in the household. The SDD is 'a product of differences that are based on perception, culture and interpersonal relationships that contribute to the gap in computer and Internet penetration'. Harper (ibid.: 5) advocates that the 'issues surrounding the digital divide must be redefined away from the hardware and towards humanity', and recommends that the scholarly community starts to build research that explores the socio-psychological and cultural differences that contribute to the SDD. Both digital divides may affect persons with disabilities (Waddell, 1999; Guo et al., 2005).

One of the key and common forces in framing national policy to create the 'information society' is that nations need globally connected communities with residents who have the skills to compete in the global economy. The other side of this coin is the interest shown in information literacy and the social impact of the digital divide – that is, between the people who have access to the internet and IT, the 'haves', and people who do not have access to the technology, the 'have-nots'. Lack of access inhibits the growth of, or erodes, social capital – the capacity of communities to enact and express their worth (Winter, 2000). Interest in narrowing the DD and providing local communities with opportunities for online access to the information society, knowledge economy and ICT age is growing as social inclusion versus exclusion in the knowledge and information-enabled society becomes apparent (Warschauer, 2003; Rideout and Reddick, 2005).

To bridge the digital divide in Australia would require a shared effort between three sectors – federal government, business and the community sector. The aim would be to ensure equitable access to technology and staff able to impart the necessary skills and knowledge to enable people to use the technology with confidence. Target groups include older Australians, people on low incomes, those with a low level of formal education and people in remote areas (and any or all of these categories may include people with physical disabilities) (Hoffman and Novak, 1998). The Australian government has introduced a programme called BITES (http://bites.dest.gov.au) which provides foundation skills in information technology to mature job seekers (45 years and over) who have no post-school IT qualification and are part of the labour force, but on low incomes. The skills it provides enable participants to operate personal computers at a basic level in the workforce. BITES is the acronym for 'basic IT enabling skills for older workers'. Given that the Welfare to Work legislation (passed in 2005) is now a Commonwealth Act (www.comlaw.gov.au/ComLaw/Legislation/Act1nsf/0/1E82138 F7F5CDBABC A2570DB0082AF88/$file/154-2005.pdf), more programmes like BITES may become available.

Community digital divide projects currently being run by the Smith Family, the Inspire Foundation and Work Ventures in Australia have already had considerable success in this area and have the potential to do much more. These projects, and others of their ilk, require a willingness and commitment by all three sectors to work together for a common purpose, leadership and the ability to turn a vision into reality. The collaboration by the Smith Family and Cisco Systems on the Ignite website is an excellent example of what can be achieved. Ignite aims to increase the educational opportunities of 9–15-year-old students on the Smith Family's education support programme 'Learning for Life'. Ignite provides password-protected access to educational resources such as virtual tutoring and links to educational sites, a bulletin board, 'chat' facilities and e-mail access in a youth-friendly setting.

Another important player in the digital divide or digital opportunity environment in Australia has been the Australian Information Industry Association (AIIA). It has created opportunities for its members to work collaboratively with the federal government and the community to address equity and access issues in the information economy.

There are many international sites working to reducing the digital divide; the majority are US based. The majority of the Australian DD websites are federal government sites; however, a major category of DD sites are those run by not-for-profit organisations or community groups, such as the extensive 'info-exchange' sites. There are relatively few commercial sites – Recruit-net, a company whose business is specifically bridging the DD, is one of the few.

Although there are many sites relating to DD issues in existence, most are of little relevance as they are locality specific. The overseas sites (the US ones in particular) are useful for obtaining general information on broad DD issues. However, in general the sites do not make reference to practical DD bridging activities outside their country. A similar situation occurs with Australian sites, as region-specific ones bear little relevance for those out of that region. Rural and Peninsula Disability Support (Victoria) and Tasmanian Communities On-line are well-structured and informative sites, but of no application outside the region at which they are aimed. They could provide good models in devising other sites for people in different regions. The most practical DD sites are those that have search facilities where users can locate their nearest DD bridging facility (such as an internet access point). This is generally limited to internet access, and in many cases basic IT skills are assumed.

There are many DD sites that provide information about access locations for public internet facilities. However, none of those viewed included basic information about accessibility (such as by wheelchair). There is obviously room for improvement. Information on the sites could be structured to be of infinitely more use to people with disabilities. Informative e-mails to webmasters could directly encourage them to include practical information on their sites for people with disabilities. The development of networks with similar sites, through the inclusion of links and information pages, is specially to be commended. It creates a greater ease of access for users.

Light (2001: 242) argues that the notion of a digital divide is:

> a paradigmatic example of a technological solution redefining a problem. Inequality became access to technology. These initiatives relied on the shaky causal inference that closing one gap would close another. I invite you to fast-forward a generation and substitute the words 'digital divide' and 'Internet access' for 'low performance' and 'calculators'... Will the conceptualisation of inequality in the information society as a 'digital divide,' focused on computer equipment and computer skill, achieve anything more than a short-term technological fix? Can we reasonably expect the inequalities that correlate with a lack of access to technology to disappear?

Furthermore, she argues that policy-makers who take a long and broad view can identify in advance what might otherwise seem like unintended consequences. For her both the 'digital divide' and the legal concept of 'reasonable accommodation' from the US Rehabilitation Act 1973, which set the standard for bringing people with disabilities into the mainstream, present examples where new technologies are only beginning to exert their effects. Light's answer to this unfortunate dilemma is to put in place a set of public policies attentive to the predictably complex and even contradictory consequences of technological innovations. This would avoid the mistakes of the past, when hopes that new technologies would reduce gaps between haves and have-nots were not often realised (ibid.: 244).

The recent technological developments have changed the methods of access to information and interpersonal communication in the context of the 'information society'. The ACTS AVANTI ACO42 project 'Adaptive and Adaptable Interactions for Multimedia Telecommunications Applications' (1995–1998) aimed to enable the integration of people with disabilities into this emerging information environment, with main reference to issues related to the access of information. This project was based on the universal design approach, and on the concepts of adaptability and adaptivity of information contents and user-to-terminal interfaces. This is particularly critical for people with disabilities and builds on the results of other European research and development activities. There were two field trials set up in the context of the AVANTI project, to test the applications dealing with access to information related to the accessibility of sites of interest (for example, transportation, hotels, public buildings and so on) and of importance for the autonomous mobility of people with disabilities. This information was integrated into general databases for tourists and presented when requested by the user (Emiliani, 1997: 2).

Information needs and the poor

In recent years, scholars such as Brenda Dervin and Elfreda Chatman have studied the 'information poor' while focusing their attentions on the information user. Dervin seeks to comprehend information poverty in terms of information behaviour and needs from the perspective of the message receivers, as opposed to the message senders, and Shannon's theory on information with senders and receivers.[1] The 'sense-making' model developed by Dervin (1992: 61) provides a framework for information professionals in studying the 'making of sense that people do in their everyday experiences'. Chatman's studies take Dervin's theoretical approach to the next step, in that she links the 'interplay between conceptualisation and empirical testing' in the 'impoverished life-world of outsiders' (Chatman, 1996: 197). She tests existing methods and theories through observation and experimentation, and adopts an applied and empirical approach towards her theory, building and understanding information-seeking behaviour within the full context of a life. Many of her findings reveal inconsistencies in theories, and she explores various methodological issues by expanding on the concept of a 'small world' (Chatman, 2000). Chatman is the information scholar whose studies into information poverty and the information poor are the most relevant and directly applicable to persons with disabilities.

Chatman (1988) chose 'opinion leadership theory' as her second study, and the results indicate that if opinion leaders are identified, they play a major role in the interpretation of new information. Alienation theory and gratification theory are two additional conceptual information frameworks that Chatman employs in her studies, with similar research outcomes that confirm previous studies. The difference in results lies in the focus. Her alienation theory study concludes that information behaviour and most life events for the poor are consistent with characteristics such as meaninglessness and powerlessness, but, significantly, not normlessness (Chatman, 1991). Subsequent studies substantiated her finding that social norms are very significant factors governing information behaviour. Gratification theory, on the other hand, suggests that the poor seek immediate gratification because of their social construct and that the meaninglessness is due to facts inherent in one's social milieu. Her results suggest that in this world, things of most value are those that centre on immediate reality, and her perceptions are validated by Moore's (2000) survey of the 'social' information needs of persons with disabilities. Chatman (1991: 447) argues that information that is related to life events is concrete in its utility value, but is translated into terminology that is easily understood and provides the key elements in the design of a system of information delivery.

Dawson and Chatman (2001) explore the application of the theoretical framework of 'reference group theory' to information behaviour research. Contemporary research indicates that all barriers contribute to some degree in varying cultural information-seeking patterns (Metoyer-Duran, 1993). Information professionals are demanding and developing new information systems based on the information-seeking habits and knowledge domains of the numerous and different user populations they serve. Pendleton and Chatman (1998: 748) argue that the cultural worlds of individuals play a major role in forming 'standards' for the individuals' information-seeking behaviour. 'Very little is known about non-users, but they are known as a "social type". They, too, share a world view about us and the manner in which they may or may not approach us for needed information.' They maintain that it is 'impossible to respond to information needs if we do not have a clear understanding of the situations that generated those needs' (ibid.: 733). They posit that the four conceptual schemes of social norms, world view, social types and information behaviour can help information professionals develop their understanding of the information needs of ordinary people. Again, this conceptual scheme is consistent with Moore's (2000) survey of the 'social' information needs of persons with disabilities.

Childers (1975: 32) describes the 'information poor' as those persons facing at least one of three major barriers. These he presents as low level of 'processing' skill (by this he means reading and communicating), deficient in the information shared by the larger society and having a 'pervasive sense of helplessness'. He believes that the least disadvantaged 'only' contend with economic poverty and the most disadvantaged have multiple indicators to deal with and are 'resigned to those conditions of life'. This 'culture of information poverty' concept is not new. It was explored earlier by Lewis (1969) as the 'culture of poverty'. However, both Lewis and Childers are guilty of 'blaming the victim'. Today, Childers is castigated in that he did not identify the lack of opportunities for access to information as being a fundamental element in information poverty.

Chatman is always willing to build on previous theorists, and finds Wilson's (1983, quoted in Chatman, 1991: 440) distinction between first- and second-level knowledge useful. Wilson believes that first-level knowledge is 'knowledge of things' derived from first-hand experience that exists in one's local sphere, and is regarded as the most credible source of information. The second-level knowledge is 'knowledge about that which does not yet exist in one's immediate awareness of things'. While Chatman is influenced by Dervin's work, her studies apply to many of the same demographics as Childers (1975) and she is influenced also by the sociologists Merton and Zuckerman (1972) and Whyte (1981). From Merton and Zuckerman, Chatman adopts the concept of insiders and outsiders in information-seeking behaviour, and from Whyte she appropriates the world of social norms. She also applies his observation that two social groups which inhabit the same society may exhibit distinctly separate norms to her studies on information-seeking behaviour (Whyte, quoted in Chatman, 1996: 197). These concepts are the core of all her studies and analysis over the past two decades.

Chatman and Pendleton (1995), in 'Knowledge gap, information-seeking and the poor', determined how the poor use media sources for information gathering. Television and newspapers are viewed by the poor as a means of distraction, not as ways of obtaining information. Chatman and Pendleton conclude from this study that there is a knowledge gap between the poor and the non-poor. The study also notes that this gap is in second-level knowledge, and the poor are oblivious to this knowledge gap. Chatman (1996) uses the aged in a retirement village in 'The impoverished life-world of outsiders' to contrast the information world of insiders and outsiders. The four concepts that Chatman discovers to characterise the needs of the information poor are secretive, deceptive, opposed to risk-taking and only seeking information of immediate ('situational') relevance. She concludes that the information poor and the retired are not necessarily economically poor, essentially share the concept that they are outsiders and view themselves and are viewed by others as marginalised. Their small world consists only of themselves. Each person is an alone insider and everyone else is an outsider (ibid.: 204–5).

Julien (1999) demonstrates that most information behaviour studies are of users of professional information services – or insiders in Chatman's terms. Apart from Chatman, there has been minimal interest by scholars in studying the behaviour and needs of people who are not part of an institution or occupation-centred information environment. This is despite the fact that most of the population have been non-users (West, 2002). Economic success and well-being today are increasingly dependent on effective access to and use of relevant information. The discourse in today's 'information age' is typified by terms such as 'digital divide' and 'knowledge gap', rather than Chatman's terminology of 'information poverty'. Gaziano (1997: 253) highlights the increasing number of 'knowledge gap' studies completed during the 1990s, and then draws comparisons with the increasing socio-economic inequality. Britz and Blignaut (2001: 63) define information poverty 'as an instrumental form of poverty affecting all other spheres of life'. The importance of all these studies is that the concepts are applicable to many other marginalised groups, not just the poor.

Chatman's three main theories or concepts in her studies are:

- the theory of information poverty (Chatman, 1996: 197–8);
- the concept of the small world (Pendleton and Chatman, 1998);
- the theory of life in the round – closely related to her theory of normative behaviour (Chatman, 1999).

Her studies show that poor people have a smaller world view, and that world view has implications concerning how the poor seek information. The small world view, coupled with the idea that future planning is not worthwhile, discourages the poor from seeking information from outside sources. Often first-hand knowledge from direct contact with another person is preferred to second-hand information from formal channels. Generally, nearly all of Chatman's studies try to determine the users' world perspective and the particular channels of information that are preferred by the poor. Since the 1990s, information acquisition has been perceived as active and individual, and Chatman begins constructing her theories by identifying information needs and acquisition as primarily 'social'. The significant construct becomes the 'digital divide' and the thrust is towards people owning personal computers and being networked. With these changes, it becomes accepted that information not only has a value, but also carries a cost. The poor and marginalised do recognise the importance and potential of ICT in today's world. The people with disabilities interviewed in Chapter 5 are representative of this section of the community.

A model of social information needs for people with disabilities

The Australian Library and Information Association (2002) adopts in principle the right of people with a disability to equitable access to information through all library and information services, and promotes the observation of current Commonwealth, state and territory disability discrimination legislation.

Social information is the information that people use in the course of their daily lives – essential to people with disabilities (Westbrook, 2001). It stands to reason that information required to meet the needs of persons with disabilities might be termed 'social' information. Oliver (1990) has seen fit to classify the fourth disability type identified as the 'social model of disability'. 'Social' information, according to Moore (2000), a researcher who has studied the information-seeking behaviour of persons with disabilities in Britain, is complex, but can be thought of as having six different dimensions. Each dimension provides a basis for analysis in terms of the information needs that are met for persons with disabilities. The six dimensions of 'social' information identified by Moore (ibid.: 6) are function, form, clusters, agents, users and mechanisms.

Function – why do people need information?

People with physical disabilities need all the information that non-disabled people need (Browne and Edwards, 1992). People need social information to support them in the two roles they play as members of society – as citizens and as consumers (Moore and Steele, 1991). People need access to information that will enable them to play their full part as active citizens, making democratic choices, holding organisations of all kinds accountable and exercising their rights and responsibilities as members of society. This includes information, for example, about their condition and the aids, equipment and services that are available, as well as self-help groups, rights and entitlements.

People need access to information as consumers, otherwise they lack the power to choose and, through their choices, to influence ways in which society is organised and goods and services are provided. In addition to the information needs that they share with everyone else, persons with physical disabilities need information that is relevant to their position as disabled people. In fact, there is overwhelming evidence attesting to the gap between the need for and the provision of information to persons with disabilities as consumers of information (Tinker et al., 1993). Not only is information specifically tailored to their needs not available, but often there is minimal provision for having access to it. In a consumer society, the inability to exercise consumer choice, through either lack of resources or lack of information, is a measure of social exclusion. The research literature, including this study, suggests that persons with disabilities lack both resources and information and, as a consequence of these deficits, invariably experience exclusion.

Form – what kind of information do people need?

People seek, process and absorb many different kinds of information. Mostly we absorb information by continuous scanning of the environment. We accept information from family and friends, workplace, books and newspapers, the broadcast media, educational institutions and our daily encounters with every possible source. The extent to which we interact with our total environment, then, will become the extent of our social inclusion.

At a basic level, people want answers to questions such as how they can apply for a social welfare benefit, or where they can find a particular piece of equipment and possibly assistance with advocacy. The information they seek will have a direct, individual value for them. People with severe physical disabilities can encounter the frustration of not being able to retain such information – except in their memory. Clearly, the services that provide these answers need to be easily accessible, authoritative and capable of explaining and providing the information, but they need an awareness of the support services for disabled people's specific needs. The 'packaging', therefore, becomes of utmost importance. The right information alone is seldom enough. One of the functions of social information is to reduce the overall amount of information available, represent and repackage it so people can absorb it and use it to become more proactive in their behaviour.

Women with Disabilities Australia has developed an accessible information and referral portal (www.wwda.org.au). This project builds on a type of community information service established in Adelaide for women in 1978 (Beattie, 1989). The portal enhances WWDA's capacity to respond better in meeting the needs and concerns of women with disabilities. It does this by developing internal information systems that enable WWDA to provide effective information, advice and referral to these women, their associates and the broader community. Specifically, WWDA researches and develops an accessible information and referral portal of relevant services, agencies and organisations at national, state/territory, regional and local levels. WWDA has also developed a data collection system that records incoming requests for information from women with disabilities. These data inform WWDA's systemic advocacy work and enhance its capacity to act as a two-way conduit between the government and the community on social policy issues as they affect women with disabilities. The information and referral portal is available on WWDA's website and is developed to conform to international standards of web accessibility for people with disabilities. The portal is linked to the website (www.women.gov.au) developed by the Commonwealth Office of the Status of Women (Women with Disabilities Australia, 2004b, 2004a: 17).

Clusters – what do people need information about? What is the specific subject matter of social information?

There are different groups of people who need information in connection with physical disabilities. Furthermore, the actual information needed varies from group to group. According to Moore (2000: 41), the extent to which there is a core of needed information for all is not clear. A useful approach to this problem is adopting the 'hierarchies of need' derived by Maslow (1943). Starting with the most basic needs, Maslow listed five different levels:

- physiological needs (food, water, warmth and protection) – these are the strongest needs, because without their being met, the person would die;
- safety needs;

- love, affection and belonging/social needs;
- esteem needs;
- autonomy/self-actualisation needs.

Each of these levels calls for certain clusters of information to clarify, inspire and initiate action. The cluster of information associated with social welfare benefits, for example, is an important contributor to the satisfaction of physiological needs. The cluster of information associated with the condition of a person with a long-term physical disability may facilitate its treatment and likely outcome. Maslow's hierarchy certainly informs the general structure of social information needs, and also identifies the information needs of specific groups of users.

With the physiological needs met, it becomes imperative for that advantage to be supplemented strongly by safety. Supporting services, aids and equipment are of crucial importance at all stages of disablement. Information about such options is vital. The need for love, affection and a sense of belonging allows an escape from an overpowering and depressing sense of loneliness and isolation. Where family and friends are limited, information on alternative social groups and networks is critical.

The two higher levels of needs – self-esteem and self-actualisation – are largely dependent on the fulfilment of the earlier levels. Information provision alone, however, hardly satisfies their realisation – even in the general population, let alone for persons with disabilities. However, their realisation would undoubtedly generate additional information and communication needs. In other words, the information need would be as a consequence of the realisation of psychological needs as opposed to the means of satisfying the needs. Thus the majority of persons with physical or mobility disabilities are more concerned with obtaining the information they require in order to satisfy Maslow's first three basic levels of need. While the two higher levels are for the most part still just an aspiration, the interviewees in this study demonstrate the way forward in this particular regard.

How people with physical disabilities currently interact with information must be understood in order for their future information services and environments to be appropriately designed. This changing interaction may be seen by comparing the 1997, 1999, 2001 and 2003 Paraplegic and Quadriplegic Association of Queensland (PQAQ) member surveys. The personnel responsible for the 1997 member survey reported:

> The advent of technology in the form of computers and the Internet does not appear to have made any significant in-roads into the lifestyles of members of the Association at this time. When asked their views of using the Internet to access *Paraview* or to purchase the PQ Lifestyles range of products, most respondents declined to support the service or to use such technology. (Paraplegic and Quadriplegic Association of Queensland, 1997: 4)

The following findings that profile 'information' aspects of the membership in 1999 are to be noted.

- Forty-three per cent of respondents reported 'information' as being the highest unmet need in their area. For example, they required information covering recreation activities, travel, holiday accommodation, sexuality and relationships. They required health information dealing with such problems as respiratory difficulties, sleep apnoea, pressure-sore prevention and management, post-polio syndrome, transverse myelitis, pain management and incontinence, along with information on appropriate products.

- Less than 20 per cent of members use internet facilities as a means of accessing *Paraview* (the association's newsletter) and ordering products. If information is listed on the internet, 31 per cent use it as a reference and 15 per cent preferred e-mail to normal post. This largely negative response is attributed to lack of access to either a computer or the internet. Many listed the cost of the technology as a prohibiting factor (Paraplegic and Quadriplegic Association of Queensland, 1999).

It is worth noting that the 2001 PQAQ member survey was both available online and distributed by conventional methods. Thirty per cent of the responses were returned online from public libraries. A mere two years after the 1999 survey, almost 90 per cent of respondents reported that they had access to both the internet and e-mail, which represented a significant increase on the 20 per cent of users reported in 1997. However, by the 2003 member survey only 51 per cent of respondents had access to both the internet and e-mail (Paraplegic and Quadriplegic Association of Queensland, 2003). This reduction in access to and use of ICT might link to the fact that more respondents (38.8 per cent) indicated now receiving the disability support pension, compared to only 32 per cent of respondents who indicated having employment of some kind.

The 2001 survey focused on demographics, member satisfaction, unmet needs and *Paraview*, and produced a similar profile to the survey undertaken in 1999, with the following exceptions (as well as a changing disability profile of members).

- Some 88.8 per cent of respondents had access to both the internet and e-mail. Proportionally more male respondents than females had access to both internet and e-mail. Those with quadriplegia were more likely to have access to both internet and e-mail than other disability types.

- Respondents indicated that the highest benefit the association provided to members was information, in the form of news, articles and disability-related information. Equipment loans, social support and contact, personal care and a higher standard of living generally followed 'information' as perceived benefits (Paraplegic and Quadriplegic Association of Queensland, 2001).

The increase in numbers of PQAQ respondents who used ICT for accessing information in the two-year interval between 1999 and 2001 was fourfold. Presumably, this manifest change in skill and attitude can be attributed to two major training facilities: the public libraries, which have taken an important training role in teaching people about the new technologies, and the BridgIT project (www.qrwn.org.au/). The name BridgIT was derived from 'bridging the gap in information technology'; it began in January 1999 and was funded in Australia as a Networking the Nation project until June 2003. The brief was to conduct internet and e-mail training and assist those just connected or about to be connected to get over those first hurdles of using the internet in isolation. BridgIT offered personalised basic internet training and modem and software installation to individuals and small groups in ten rural and remote areas of Queensland by having centrally based trainers living and working in these areas. Post-training support was also available and was teleworked from the trainer's home base via phone, fax and/or e-mail. The support offered via e-mail, in particular, was deemed an important stage in the person's learning how to use these technologies efficiently.

Tester (1992), in her report into the information needs of elderly people, argued that these needs could be associated with major life events such as retirement or moving into residential care. Moore (2000) points out that there are two flaws in the life events approach to defining clusters of social information needs: firstly, many social information needs fall outside any scheme of life events; and secondly, each person approaches a life event differently because of different backgrounds and circumstances. Moore recommends that a useful alternative approach is to identify 'families of need' or clusters of information needs. He believes it is possible to identify eight main clusters of information need: the disability condition; its treatment and likely outcome; social welfare benefits and money; general health; aids and equipment; housing and accommodation; mobility, services and facilities; and employment, education and training (ibid.: 10–12, 44–50). There are other types of information that people with disabilities might pursue, such as information about transport and shopping, leisure opportunities and religious and cultural information.

On 15 March 2002 the Disability Information and Resource Centre (DIRC) in Adelaide launched EnableNet (www.enable.net.au), a disability information portal on the internet. It is the DIRC's vision to be a national and international example of excellence and a model for disability information dissemination (Meier, 2002). EnableNet is an integral part of this vision. EnableNet was conceived to further the electronic information services of the DIRC that began with the Common Ground bulletin board in 1992. Common Ground, as its name suggests, offered people with a disability and those with an interest in disability a place to meet and communicate on a common platform; a 'place' where everybody was equal. It is envisaged that EnableNet will not only continue but will also foster the sense of community that developed through Common Ground.

EnableNet has been described as being about empowering people with a disability, and, although different, has certain similarities to WWDA's new development of an accessible information and referral portal with regard to 'cluster information' about disability, women, housing, legal matters and so on. One of the ways EnableNet achieves this empowerment is through providing relevant information in an easily accessible format. There is a great amount of disability-related information on the internet, but not all of it is easy to locate. EnableNet offers 'one-stop shop' accessibility to thousands of disability-related websites, indexed using the EnableNet disability subject thesaurus. The thesaurus takes a subject from its primary or first-level subject heading (such as disabilities, diseases and disorders) to a second level (headings such as physical disabilities, sensory disabilities and psychiatric disabilities), and then third and even fourth levels if appropriate. So physical disabilities can be browsed for body system disorders such as musculo-skeletal disorders which in turn includes fourth-level headings like osteoporosis.

Visitors to EnableNet will find links to websites under a particular subject heading and also titles of books and videos held in the DIRC library, as well as factsheets to answer frequently asked questions on a condition. EnableNet is about more than information: it is about developing a sense of community. This is achieved by providing chatrooms, message areas and a place for fun and games. These functions are only available to EnableNet members, but membership is free and open to anyone with an interest in disability. The 'news and events' section has media releases and details of Australian and international disability-related conferences, workshops and seminars. The 'other services' section provides links to selected online shopping, ticket purchasing and telephone directories. EnableNet serves not only as a website available globally, but as a dial-up intranet (with personal e-mail account) to people in receipt of a disability support pension (DSP) who reside in South Australia. Eligible people will not need to pay for internet access through an internet service provider. They will, however, only have access to websites to which EnableNet provides a link, which may prove to be restrictive given people with disabilities have the same diverse information needs as any other person, plus some specific information needs.

Information about conditions, treatment and likely outcomes is required particularly when a disability first occurs or is first diagnosed. There is research evidence to suggest that at times of stress, people forget much of the information that is conveyed to them orally (Kempson, 1987). Hence, for example, the value of the Queensland-based websites Disability Forum (www.disabilityforum.org.au) and Disability Lifestyles (www.disabilitylifestyles.org.au). Disability Lifestyles is an online information and communication service (see Chapter 7) that provides a portal to seven key areas for those recently disabled (especially because of road accidents). Training, employment, recreation, transport, accommodation, personal support and relationships are all covered. Each one of these areas provides links to a variety of other relevant websites. The primary aim of the Disability Lifestyles website is to establish an attractive online environment for people who are usually young and completing their rehabilitation. It has been made available because these young people with disabilities may not have taken in all the information they were given initially after a traumatic accident that left them with a severe spinal injury. There are other useful relevant websites, such as WWDA, EnableNet and the Physical Disability Council of Australia (www.pdca.org.au). These sites are all information-oriented, interest-oriented and relationship-oriented, and can provide more necessary information about a condition, its treatment and likely outcomes to people with severe long-term physical disabilities who are ready to assimilate this information. They also provide emotional support (Burnett, 2000).

In addition to the need for information about their condition, its treatment and likely outcome, persons with physical disabilities have the same wide range of health information needs as the rest of the population. Historically, the emphasis has been on information about illness, its treatment and living with chronic conditions, providing information about medicines, continence and so on, as well as free calls to pharmaceutical organisations about, for example, living better with osteoporosis. More recently, however, this interest has been broadened to include information about prevention, well-being and healthy living. Nonetheless, there are still national information helplines available for people seeking assistance. Information about aids and equipment for persons with physical disabilities is also covered.

As mentioned previously, persons with disabilities are among the poorest in society and invariably have a pressing need for information about social welfare benefits and money. It is therefore reasonable that information about benefits and money should be readily available. Additionally, the person may need support to complete a claim for a benefit. Housing and accommodation information needs for persons with disabilities can also be pressing, especially when the person must move from independent living to sheltered accommodation or residential care. Similarly, information about services and facilities available to disabled people is required if they are to feel well informed about option choices.

It was the Australian government's stated intention in 2006 to remove as many disabled people as possible from the disability support pension and enable them to enter the workforce. Consequently, persons with disabilities need to be well informed about employment, education and training. Success in education or training ultimately may mean employment and the full satisfaction of Maslow's (1943) most basic social and psychological needs. This, in turn, can produce self-esteem and self-actualisation.

Agents – who initiates the information activity?

Three different agents account for the model of social information: the users or seekers of information, the information providers and the intermediaries who process the presented information – such as the professionals interviewed in Chapter 6.

The intermediaries have it in their power to add value by structuring data in consistent formats so that they are easier to use. If their information is to be credible, it also must be based on authority, an important determinant of its trustworthiness.

Providers need to be absolutely aware that persons with physical disabilities need access to information services that are designed to meet their specific needs. EnableNet, Disability Forum and Disability Lifestyles are all excellent examples of providers with specially designed information services. Physically disabled people, like the elderly, also need ready access to other information and advice services, such as those provided by government, that are available within the community. These insights are not new (Webb, 1988: 12; Williamson and Stayner, 1980: 195). In some cases these information services are accessible, but in other cases people with physical disabilities face barriers that need to be overcome.

Users – how do needs differ between different groups of people?

Not only are individuals inherently different, but they invariably belong to different social groupings and will usually belong to more than one group. Accordingly, they will demand different patterns of information to meet their differing roles. In the case of persons with physical disabilities, the research literature suggests that the main factors affecting the range and nature of needs are age, degree of impairment, time since onset of disability, ethnic origin and incidence of other disabilities (Williamson et al., 1999). There are other significant groups that share common information needs with the persons with physical disabilities: carers (Lamb and Layzell, 1995), family and friends and professionals involved with disabled people, who need to be well-informed, and increasingly the elderly (Phillips, 1996). Older people reflect the same range of impairments, personal circumstances and requirements of levels of support as the population with disabilities (Street, 1998). In the research literature the elderly are often portrayed as passive, making few demands, expecting little and receiving less (Lloyd and Thornton, 1998). At the other end of the age range, children also constitute a vulnerable group, and it is parents who are the highly motivated information seekers and users on behalf of their children.

Mechanisms – which mechanisms can be used to meet the information needs of persons with physical disabilities?

The traditional way of recording and storing information has been to write it down. Now information technology assists in printing and the distribution of the written word recorded in digital form for easy, cheap transmission and output in a variety of different formats. Traditionally, libraries have provided enormous stores of information; public libraries have provided community-based information and materials for leisure purposes, and increasingly have tried to make specific provision to meet the needs of persons with disabilities. Leaflets, an important part of community-based information, have always been a significant source of information. Epstein (1980), in her seminal work on information needs, highlighted the fact that the usefulness of a leaflet depended largely on it being available in the right place at the right time.

Although libraries have found it costly to store and transmit information, traditionally they have tried to deal with these difficulties by using inter-library loan services and providing computer-based and personal reading services. By comparison with the transmission and communication capabilities of broadcast and digital media, all past devices appear slow, cumbersome and very expensive. Broadcast media have been the most powerful means of communication in society since the late twentieth century. The importance of broadcast media is largely because they constitute the primary means that persons with physical disabilities have of scanning the information environment. Again, future technological development, such as digital television with many more channels, is likely to improve matters further. In fact, it is not inconceivable that an organisation like the PQAQ (now know as Spinal Injuries Inc.) may choose to operate a channel designed to meet the specific information needs of its community. However, it would need to be mindful of Chatman and Pendleton's (1995) insight into television and newspapers being viewed by the poor and marginalised as a means of distraction, not necessarily as ways of obtaining information.

The great advantage of information being stored in the World Wide Web lies in the transmission capability of the internet and the fact that the information is digital and can be output in different accessible formats. There are, of course, potential barriers to people with disabilities in that computers, digital equipment and software are expensive, and there is also an initial investment required in training and familiarisation with the technology. Notwithstanding these constraints, the long-term benefits of ICT to disabled people are considerable. This is not to discount the telephone in its own right as a powerful means of communicating information, additionally overcoming problems of distance. As telephone and internet-based services become interchangeable, it will become easier for persons with mobility disabilities to obtain information and transact all kinds of business without needing to leave their homes.

There is a clear need for information to be customised to meet the particular needs of individuals, and many research studies reinforce the importance of people in the process of customising information to satisfy the information needs of people with disabilities (Coopers & Lybrand, 1988). Furthermore, this has the added benefit of dissipating some of their feelings of social exclusion (Zarb et al., 1998). General practitioners and medical specialists are important elements in the chain of customised information, as are self-help groups. The 'value' of customised information means one can locate it when it is needed, frequently reinforced by complementary information. The reinforcement need is seen most explicitly in the situation of oral information provided by medical specialists, but the principle applies generally. Few people have the kinds of information needs that can be satisfied by means of a single message or communication. The value of dedicated portals is that they are an ongoing source of authoritative information.

In an information-intensive society, we all need ready access to a wide range of information in order to function effectively (Nicholas, 1996). Australia's long-term economic development is dependent on its ability to use information to make decisions that enable growth, progress and productivity. The library profession sees itself as contributing to an informed society by acquiring, organising, archiving, retrieving, using, synthesising and analysing information and thereby empowering users so they are information literate in their decision-making processes (Australian Library and Information Association, 1996a, 1996b).

Lack of access to information is increasingly seen as one of the defining characteristics of social exclusion. People with disabilities face more challenges than many others do when trying to meet their information needs. Not only do they have additional needs that are particular to their disabilities, but they also may be constrained in the formats and delivery mechanisms they can use in order to access the information needed as citizens and consumers. Since the advent of ICT, concerted efforts have had to be made to reduce the impact of the DD and factor in IL so that people with disabilities can access the information that everybody expects to be delivered to them as a matter of course. According to the six propositions of Pendleton and Chatman's (1998) theory of information poverty, many persons with disabilities live in a state of information deprivation where they lack access to the information they need to satisfy their most basic physiological, psychological and social needs. However one views the issue, there is the potential for a significant, yawning gap to exist between information need and information provision, which translates into unmet need. As well as addressing this unmet information need within the context of ICT and virtual communities, it is desirable to establish benchmarks and standards to guide the service providers in their efforts to meet the information needs of persons with disabilities. In the same way that the development of library services once benefited greatly from the formulation and application of information performance standards, so too would the information service providers and their clients benefit.

The definition and breadth of literacy have changed over time. In the past couple of decades we have added a new literacy – technological literacy – an understanding of which is now necessary before coming to terms with the DD and IL. There will always be people of every age and background who are keen to learn and engage with a changing society. For these people the provision of technology and training in an appropriate manner will be enough to enable them. However, there are a large number of people for whom this is not the case, and older people and people with disabilities are found to be among those most at risk in terms of IL and the DD. In other words, the larger and more intractable problem rests in the socio-cultural gap between insiders and outsiders identified repeatedly in Chatman's work.

People with disabilities are over-represented in low socio-economic groups compared to the population in general. This affects their ability to access ICT and further disadvantages them in a range of activities that are now conducted over the internet. Many e-commerce activities – for example, bill paying and banking – offer discounts for business conducted online. Lack of internet access further penalises people who are already under financial strain. In addition, this lack of access deprives people with disabilities of the social interaction afforded by e-mail contact with family, friends, disability support groups and other special-interest groups. Many people with disabilities are on the wrong side of the DD, where lack of access to computers, the internet and IT training precludes them from participating in the information society. There are many initiatives under way, both internationally and Australia-wide, which seek to bridge this gap. The impetus for their development comes from community, non-government and government organisations, and in those areas it is imperative that awareness is fully cultivated. Developing a model of a virtual community for people with mobility impairments as undertaken here also has the potential to extend the work done so far in the areas of IL, the DD, virtual communities, telecommunications and their information needs.

Notes

1. The pioneer of information theory, Shannon developed a theory of how much information can be sent per unit of time in a system with a given, limited amount of transmission power. As originally conceived, the model contained five elements all arranged in linear order: an information source, a transmitter, a channel of transmission, a receiver and a destination. Messages (electronic messages, initially) were supposed to travel along this path, to be changed into electric energy by the transmitter and reconstituted into intelligible language by the receiver (Cole, 1997).

5

Deconstructing the narratives of people with disabilities – towards a well-being model for a successful virtual community

The deconstruction, analysis and findings from the narratives of people with severe long-term physical disabilities presented in this chapter were based on in-depth interviews (Kvale, 1996). This chapter situates the study in the environment of disablement and attends to the development of the primary categories necessary to the process of grounded theory. The interviews centred around one question: 'What can you tell me about your experience with virtual communities and how you use ICT (information and communications technology) both personally and professionally?' Subjects were interviewed according to grounded theory principles, and the series of interviews continued until 'theoretical saturation' of content occurred. This study required 12 interviews before no new content was emerging. Later interviews, dealt with in the next chapter, were conducted with allied health, information and policy professionals – this allowed comparison with these earlier interviews.

This chapter deals with phase 1 of the grounded theory analysis:

- the emergence and identification of themes and concepts;
- the phenomenon of 'a sense of control' and its centrality to the emerging model;
- the six cornerstones for a virtual community for people with disabilities – including the scope of each key concept, the opportunities and the barriers emanating from each category.

Thus, the basis for the emerging theory, theoretical framework or model is established.

The 12 original owners of the experiences who were interviewed were as follows (pseudonyms used):

- a social worker (Jane: Interviewee 1);

- a database manager (Dan: Interviewee 2);

- a chartered chemist (Bob: Interviewee 3);

- a solicitor (Jack: Interviewee 4);

- a programme officer for the BCC (Joe: Interviewee 5);

- a representative of the Physical Disability Council of Australia (PDCA) (Sally: Interviewee 6);

- a facilitator for the Spinal Injuries Association member network (Simon: Interviewee 7);

- a director of an advocacy organisation (Keith: Interviewee 8);

- a psychologist (Marcie: Interviewee 9);

- a membership promoter for a charitable organisation (Tom: Interviewee 10);

- a senior reservoir engineer/petrophysicist (Sam: Interviewee 11);

- a designer and moderator of the Disability Forum website (Val: Interviewee 12).

They were all people with mobility impairments who had interactive technology access and some background in using technology. In profile, their ages ranged from 24 to 60 years with a mean age of 44. Four females and eight males were interviewed. Eight people had suffered traumatic spinal injuries resulting in quadriplegia and two were paraplegic, while one person had had poliomyelitis and another had a muscle-wasting condition. Two people were extremely severely affected physically as a result of their injuries. Six people would be regarded as very affected (six of the eight persons with quadriplegia), while the remaining four were not as severely affected. In fact, the greater the severity of the injury and consequent disability, the greater the potential dependence of that person on technology for their 'independence' and the resumption of their 'sense of control' over their lives. The educational attainment of this diverse group of persons with severe long-term physical disabilities was as wide-ranging as most of their other distinguishing criteria – two had secondary education, three TAFE education and seven tertiary education, with six of these having higher degrees. The range of disability onset was 13–51 years, the average onset time of disability was 27.5 years ago and they would be categorised as persons with long-term disabilities. Consequently, this group of people have primarily dealt with all the rehabilitation, personal care and basic lifestyle survival issues that would invariably preoccupy newly disabled people, such as those served by the Disability Lifestyles website.

Emergence and identification of themes and concepts

According to the grounded theory research methodology, phenomena are the central ideas in the data, represented as concepts. Concepts are the building blocks of the theory. Categories are concepts that stand for phenomena; for example, in this study the major theme that emerged was 'a sense of control', which initially surprised the author. On reflection, it made eminent sense. Properties are the characteristics of a category, the delineation of which defines it and gives it meaning; for example, for the category 'transaction' the properties were 'e-commerce' and 'employment'. Dimensions are the ranges along which general properties of a category vary, giving specification to a category and variation to the theory. For example, some of the dimensions of the category 'transaction' were 'investments', 'shopping', 'ordering' and 'bill paying'. Subcategories are the concepts that pertain to a category, giving it further clarification and specification – in this case they were 'teleworking' and 'telemarketing' (Strauss and Corbin, 1998: 101).

As indicated above, the central theme or idea that emerged from the open coding analysis of the in-depth interviews was that these persons with severe long-term physical disabilities desired to regain 'a sense of control' over their lives. Increasingly, they found that this concept of 'a sense of control' could be achieved by their use of ICT. The significant categories that emerged from these interviews were the importance of education; the seeking of 'fantasy'; the need and use of information; interest; relationship; and transactions. These six categories are the building blocks or cornerstones of the theoretical model or conceptual framework for a virtual community that would be useful to the users – persons with long-term, severe physical disabilities – and the facilitators of such a community. The categories are developed further in the final section of this chapter.

Another very important phenomenon, or concept, to emerge from the interview data was the notion of 'access' and 'barriers' (which, in fact, are the two sides of one coin) to the success of a virtual community for people with long-term physical disabilities. The characteristics or properties of the 'barrier' category included economic and social costs, as well as other physical and technological aspects of connectivity. It is the diversity and range of costs and the physical, social and technological aspects identified by interviewees that limit their successful use of ICT. These are termed 'dimensions' in grounded theory. They give further specification to 'barriers' as a subcategory and oppose 'access' in the emergent theoretical framework for a virtual community for people with long-term physical disabilities. Crucial subcategories also emerged from the analysis of interview data, including the necessity of a climate of 'access' by way of information and technology literacy to allow full usefulness for users and facilitators of virtual communities. Again, from this study, specific terms or properties such as 'capacity building', 'moral purpose', 'peer support' and 'e-commerce' give further meaning to the phenomena, concepts and categories that emerged so readily from the rich interview data. Words such as 'digital divide', 'confidence', 'information exchange', 'well-being', 'motivation', 'skills' and so forth are the dimensions that add clarification and specification to the properties. All these aspects of grounded theory methodology will be developed more substantially in the final section of this chapter.

Strauss and Corbin (ibid.) acknowledge that developing theory is a complex activity. According to them, theorising is work that entails not only conceiving or intuiting ideas (concepts), but also formulating them into logical, systematic and explanatory schemes. They argue that at the heart of theorising lies the interplay of making inductions (deriving concepts and their properties and dimensions from data) and deductions. Deductions are hypothesising about the relationships between concepts; the relationships are also derived from data, but data that have been abstracted by the analyst from the raw data.

It is thus argued that the concept/phenomenon of 'a sense of control' and the six categories outlined above meet the criteria of a model, framework and theory for a virtual community for people with mobility impairments. The phenomenon and categories as they emerged from the interviews form more than a taxonomy. Together with the opposing aspects of 'access' and 'barriers', they provide a configuration or structure that is a simplified description of this virtual community system (shown in full in Figure 7.1).

The well-being model for a virtual community for persons with severe long-term physical disabilities that emerged was a meld of six types of electronic communities. The types of e-communities or sets of well-developed discrete categories (e.g. themes and concepts) that the data from this study revealed, depending on the types of consumer needs they met, were:

- education;
- fantasy-oriented;
- information-oriented;
- interest-oriented;
- relationship-oriented;
- transaction-oriented.

For the model/theory to be truly generalisable and transformational, all six types of virtual communities as typified by the categories need to be established as potential portals to be developed for disabled people. It is also possible that the well-being model for a virtual community for persons with long-term, severe physical disabilities in fact meets several, if not all, of the above needs, purposes or orientations simultaneously. In the end, it must be emphasised that if any one of these types of e-communities was ignored, the full virtual community experience would not be available to disabled people.

This is not to suggest that a substantive theory (developed from the study of one small area of investigation and one specific population) has the explanatory power of a larger, more general theory. It cannot, because it does not build in the variation or include the broad propositions of a more general theory. However, the real merit of a substantive theory lies in its ability to speak specifically for the populations from which it was derived and apply back to them. Naturally, the more systematic and widespread the theoretical sampling, the more conditions and variations will be discovered and built into the theory and therefore the greater its explanatory power (and precision) (Strauss and Corbin, 1998: 267).

Table 5.1 presents the material from the analysis of findings in Chapters 5 and 6, analysed and sorted to show the relationships between categories, properties, dimensions and subcategories according to the grounded theory methodology.

Table 5.1   Grounded theory relationships

Phenomenon: 'a sense of control'			
Categories	Properties	Dimensions	Subcategories
Education	e-learning, capacity building, information literacy, technological literacy	digital divide, confidence, information exchange, wellbeing, motivation, skills	empowerment, engagement, equality, lifelong learning, shared vision
Fantasy	virtual activities, virtual living, virtual reality	access, anonymity, communication, interaction, participation	double-edged sword of technology, barrier-free, recreation
Information	e-searching, equality, virtual communities	discussion groups, education, entertainment, legislation, leisure	access, choice
Interest	disability rights, leadership, moral purpose, social justice	access, equity, independence, mobility, participation, values-driven	assistive technology, civil society, inclusion, self-determination, vision, voice
Relationship	community role, virtual community, virtual family, peer support, systemic advocacy	collective experience, shared knowledge, self-esteem, valued role	acceptance, identity, privacy, social networks
Transaction	e-commerce, employment	investments, shopping, ordering, bill paying	teleworking, telemarketing

'A sense of control' and its centrality in the emerging well-being model

The central and all-pervasive theme that emerged from all interviews in this study into a virtual community for people with physical disabilities, either overtly or implicitly, was that the use of ICT invariably provided 'a sense of control'. However, as some interviewees were hasty to point out, the use of ICT by persons with disabilities may prove to be a 'double-edged sword'. This involves consideration of how the use of ICT by these people may be damaging as well as empowering or informative. Anti-discrimination legislation has promoted various levels of inclusion (especially in access to places of employment) for disabled people. ICT usage by persons with disabilities reduces their isolation by connecting them to the virtual 'world' and is thus empowering, but may in fact promote exclusion from the real world by disconnecting them physically from an employment environment and consequently prove to be disempowering. This notion is discussed in more depth later in this chapter, when telecommuting is considered. Additionally, disabled people feel themselves to be under constant threat of disenfranchisement from the new ICT, unless, for example, universal design is part of national systems of regulation and legislation for technology (Wilson and Goggin, 1993).

Although it is common knowledge that people with disabilities benefit from access to and use of technology, initially the vehemence with which the majority of these interviewees expressed the positive role technology had in their lives was surprising. One person, Val (Interviewee 12), said: 'Technology has allowed me to become a more whole human being... I just hope that "technology" can keep up with my demands.' As mentioned earlier, the greater the severity of the injury or disease and subsequent disability, the greater the potential dependence of that person on technology for their 'independence' and resumption of their 'sense of control' over their lives.

The two most obvious, overt themes that emerge from Jack (Interviewee 4) are the need for a sense of control in and over his life and the need for independence and self-reliance where possible. ICT has met these needs to some extent for him.

> Control is a big issue for someone whose life depends on someone coming in the morning and helping me getting up and coming back at night and helping me go to bed, and you rely on it and otherwise getting used to it. Control is an underlying issue for me and I know that if things health-wise aren't going well, that's outside of my control. I do anything that puts order back into my life, so the internet is another, I suppose, little aspect of that which gives me that control to move things and give away things without relying on someone else. Whether it's paying a bill, transferring funds, online broking; I can't tell you if I'm better off, I just know that I'm doing it myself and there is some comfort in that.

While all the interviewees without exception hailed the technology as helping them regain a sense of control over their lives, Jack and Val spelled out their need for control most frequently, in most detail and most overtly. Jane (Interviewee 1), who learnt to use the technology through one of her personal care assistants, was also very positive about its value in her life – from knowledge expansion to improved self-esteem. One example of knowledge expansion she quoted was how she learnt to set up a proprietary limited company when she had an Adult Lifestyle Support funding package for personal care assistance. Keith (Interviewee 8), too, finds that the technology can start to make people with disabilities more independent, more autonomous and likely to have greater control over activities.

Tom (Interviewee 10) recalls that 50 years ago disabled people did not aspire to high achievement, because society did not embrace people with disabilities and did not believe they had a future. He has a vision of medical advances preventing and curing paraplegia and quadriplegia. In the meantime, he hopes adequate funding will be implemented. In fact, his current perception of the future for persons with severe physical disabilities is for them all to gain or regain 'a sense of control' and independence over their lives using environmental controls and employment through telecommuting. Tom was not concerned about the 'double-edged sword' issues; his focus was exclusively on technological empowerment.

People want to be able to exert some control over the outcome of even unavoidable events (Bar-tal, 1994; Brenders, 1987). Most theories and research into the relationship between control and stress are based on the assumption that having control is stress-reducing. This is not always the case. Beliefs about control, whether shaped more by personal factors or by situational contingencies, play a major role in determining the degree to which a person feels threatened or challenged in a stressful situation (Ferguson et al., 1994; Folkman, 1984).

A large body of evidence suggests that 'organisms' can learn they are powerless to affect their own destinies. Undoubtedly experiencing the effects of full body paralysis after a traumatic spinal injury to a young, healthy, active person must serve to reinforce feelings of powerlessness for some considerable time in a very slow and frequently only partial rehabilitation process.

Miller and Seligman (1975) reported a series of experiments demonstrating that animals can learn that their own behaviour has no effect on an environmental event – known as 'learned helplessness' (Abramson et al., 1980). It is this phenomenon of which Jack in particular and the other interviewees seem to be cognisant, and that Bandura (1997), in his social cognitive theory, also explains in terms of self-efficacy. Bandura's theory is that those with high self-efficacy expectations – the belief that one can achieve what one sets out to do – are healthier, more effective and generally more successful than those with low self-efficacy expectations. It is for this reason (if they want to regain 'a sense of control') that severely disabled people feel the need to try to find ways to overcome aspects of lack of choice. Peterson et al. (1993) maintained that 'learned helplessness' can create certain deficits:

- motivational, in that the helpless person makes no effort to take the steps necessary to change the outcome;
- cognitive, in that helpless people fail to learn new responses that could help them to avoid the adverse outcomes;
- emotional, in that learned helplessness can produce mild or severe depression.

It is to the credit of all the interviewees, but especially Jack, that they battle with 'learned helplessness' inflicted on them unwillingly by their severe physical disabilities and make attempts to regain 'a sense of control' over their lives and self-reliance in whatever few areas are still feasible for them.

This learned helplessness model has been criticised on a number of grounds, including its failure to address individual differences and its inattention to the duration of the helplessness – sometimes for several years after a person has suffered a traumatic spinal injury. The research into helplessness theory maintains that a misattribution about adverse (or the non-occurrence of positive) events is critical. These events must occur for the processes to operate. The tendencies to misattribute negative events will be strongest when the person is under stress. In a reformulated model, such factors have been acknowledged as critical determinants of how chronic and pervasive the feelings of helplessness will be. Consequently, three attributional dimensions are now regarded as significant in producing helplessness (and certainly could be seen to be important in all interviewees' lives, but especially Jack's life and thinking).

- Internality-externality, or 'locus of control' (Rotter, 1966). One can attribute helplessness externally (that is, 'no one can do anything about this problem'). Internal attributions are more likely to produce greater helplessness.

- Stable attributions (that is, 'these problems will plague me whatever I do') produce more helplessness than unstable ones (for example, 'this job isn't for me').

- Globality – the extent to which the helplessness is confined to one sphere of life or extends to many spheres. If it extends to many spheres of influence, it may produce feelings of more pervasive helplessness than non-global attributions.

By implication, then, internal, global and stable perceived causes of helplessness produce the most pervasive decrements in motivation, cognition and emotion – presumably and sadly all issues for Jack, in particular, to deal with on a daily basis.

If the definition of stress (when the demands of the environment are perceived to be greater than the individual's resources) is accepted, then 'helplessness' is central to stress. Consequently, one may start to have some insight into the ongoing tension between control and stress in the life of every person with disabilities interviewed. Specifically, the helplessness phase (presumably at the beginning of rehabilitation), in which efforts repeatedly range from impossible to unsuccessful, is analogous to ongoing stress. Likewise, the fact that uncontrollable events in their lives would produce more stress than controllable events clearly implicates control, or the loss of it, in their experience of stress.

The reformulated model of learned helplessness explains why uncontrollable events are more stressful than controllable ones. If, for example, Jack attributed his lack of impact to stable, unmodifiable factors, he would come to believe that no amount of personal effort on his part could remedy his situation – as he said, 'it won't help you get around'. Accordingly, his inner resources would clearly be inadequate to meet the stressful situation, a condition that would produce a subjective feeling of stress. The reformulated model is also useful for understanding the beneficial effects of control, thus enhancing intervention in times of stress. As noted previously, stress effects are less pronounced when individuals are given some response that enables them to control, or believe they can control, the stressor, as many interviewees indicated.

The helplessness argument would maintain that when a person is encouraged to feel that he or she has control over a stressful event, they are more likely to change their attributions of the cause of the stress. Jack's belief that he can bring about some desired outcomes is restored because he has taken control of his own stock investments, even if he has no control over what time he can go to bed. Therefore the cognitive, motivational and behavioural deficits associated with helplessness are reversed: '[even though] it won't help you get around, [I am still more] independent and self-reliant than I was prior to using ICT'.

Sam (Interviewee 11) repeatedly makes the point:

> There's no way that I would be able to do my current job without computer skills. Because I was there from the start, as the technology came out, I was able to absorb that a bit at the time. Whereas someone coming out of the blue now would be bombarded with e-mail and chat groups, servers and any number of different ways of accessing things and their new disability. It's probably the case for a lot of people in wheelchairs. Their initial training and free access is essential. So much work these days is done with computers that it's a very easy way for people to go into their chosen fields and fit within the workplace... It allows you to go out and to go along the career path that perhaps you wouldn't think was possible. Perhaps you wanted to do so before your accident and felt that you couldn't post-accident, which was certainly my initial thought... It gives one a greater sense of control of your life and more satisfaction.

Val pointed out how the more access one has to advanced technology, the more one wants and expects. 'Technology gives you a sense of control, a sense of freedom and totally 100 per cent independence which is something I think a lot of people crave for, because I'm, I've always been independent and I just, I would go whole hog if I could afford to, I would have everything as controllable as I would like.' In 1983 she moved into a house accommodating five disabled people. She needed an alarm to the nursing staff bedroom during the night, and was absolutely thrilled to be loaned the prototype for an environmental control unit which allows five appliances to be plugged into the rear of the unit. She activated the unit by pressing a slippery cushion pad with her head while in bed. She now could turn on and off her television, a light and an alarm to the staff room. Val exercised her first independence and control over her environment post-accident.

Val has replaced the original environmental control unit with a Gewa Prog (www.tecsol.com.au/PROG.htm) that she can connect to her computer and television, to convert it a large monitor when she is confined to bed. Her computer is on a wheeled table, so she can use it in different rooms. The ability to connect the Gewa Prog to her computer has other positive impacts in her life. She controls the Gewa Prog by voice using her voice-recognition programme (Appleton et al., 2004). If she feels too hot, she can turn on her air-conditioner or fan – just by voice control. She can turn on the television to see what is on while she is waiting for the computer to download a programme from the internet. She can record a programme on her VCR while working on the computer. She can turn on background music if she feels like it, or listen to a CD or tape. She can do all this on her own without having to call for assistance or have remote controls set up on separate tables.

> The freedom and control it has given me is quite remarkable. For example, I do not sleep a lot of a night-time. Once upon a time I used to just lie and stare into the dark. I can turn on a radio *or* listen to a [taped] book *or* watch a bit of TV. In the future, I am hoping to be able to use the computer in the wee hours of the morning also. I have another friend who is also a 'backyard mechanic' who is looking into microphones for me. At the moment, in order to use my voice-recognition program I have to wear a headset. The headset will not stay still of a night-time and the microphone goes out of reach of my voice.

Keith, like Val, finds technology makes people with disabilities more independent and autonomous, and likely to broaden their activities. Dan (Interviewee 2), however, emphasised how he is fearful of these systems failing him and described the measures he has taken to ensure this will not occur. The cost of new technology is an ongoing difficulty for him. Also, he is continually trying to keep abreast of new technological breakthroughs of relevance to his workplace, in particular. He is aware technology is evolving so rapidly and he worries about disabled people falling behind. Some further themes that emerged from his interview concerned technology reliability, service difficulties, how new versions of software and hardware were not always compatible with his disability and his fears that future technology standards might disenfranchise people with disabilities. He believed that adaptive technology should be simple to use; however, it was often hard to discover its availability (he requires Dragon Dictate plus a headset microphone). 'If you can't manage it, what's the good of having it?'

Cornerstones of a virtual community for people with disabilities

Many additional, positive themes are shared by interviewees pertaining to other aspects of the online experience. They made comments like 'the world comes into your own home', 'it breaks down isolation by connecting you with other persons of similar interests' (but, as already indicated, this can be a double-edged sword because it is done virtually rather than in reality) and 'you can share information and experiences'. They also observed other important aspects, such as 'It replaces bulletin boards – but is private' and 'You can research health, aids and equipment, access and transport information.' 'It has the potential to change the paradigm and concept of work – particularly for persons with disabilities, because of the flexibility.' Furthermore, 'You can maintain your independence, for example, by undertaking banking, shopping, paying bills, trading stock and so on – [but] it won't help you get around' (the all-important concern for Jack).

Chapter 2 discussed the CONROD website, Disability Lifestyles, described as an online information and communication service designed specifically to help people restart their lives after being disabled or seriously injured in accidents. It was launched in May 2004 and aims to be a bridge between rehabilitation and active participation in the community for people who have suffered severe injuries. This community project has provided a portal to seven key areas: training, employment, recreation, transport, accommodation, personal support and relationships – compared with education, fantasy, information, interest, relationship and transaction identified in this study. Each of the Disability Lifestyles areas provides links to a variety of relevant websites. The primary aim of this project was to establish an online environment for the provision and sharing of information about everyday life, in an informal and friendly manner, for people who are completing or have recently completed rehabilitation.

As the average onset time of disability was 27.5 years ago for the population interviewed in this study, this group of people have primarily dealt with the majority of rehabilitation, personal care and basic lifestyle survival issues that invariably preoccupy newly disabled people (Verbrugge and Jette, 1994). This shift in emphasis of need over the passage of time for persons with disabilities is consistent with Maslow's (1943) 'hierarchy of needs' theory. While there is some overlap with people who are restarting their lives after being disabled or seriously injured in accidents, people with long-term disability tend to focus on other key quality-of-life aspects. These include education and fantasy or virtual-reality activities in this study. Furthermore, assistive technology, health, travel and accommodation, interest (in terms of disability rights or a moral purpose), relationship (meaning a community role or peer support) and transaction (banking, bill paying, the stock market and teleworking) are all key areas (elaborated earlier in this chapter). Nonetheless, even though 'a sense of control' was the central and significant theme, or preoccupation, that kept recurring in every interview, it was these other six categories and related concepts that informed the detail of the interviews. These six categories may be regarded as the cornerstones for a virtual community for people with long-term, severe physical disabilities. Consequently, each of these categories will now be considered in depth and contextualised by the deconstruction and analysis of interviewees' narratives.

Education category (educating people with disabilities to use ICT)

As noted in Chapter 4, people with disabilities are one of the groups who are seen to be on the wrong side of a digital divide, where lack of access to ICT and IT training precludes them from participating in the information society. Moreover, the lack of access to ICT deprives people with disabilities of the social interaction afforded by e-mail contact with family, friends, disability support groups and other special-interest groups. Other disadvantaged groups traditionally include people in low socio-economic strata, people with disabilities, women, seniors, youth (homeless youth, students), Aboriginals and Torres Strait Islanders and people from other cultures (Kimble and Hildreth, 2005). There are many initiatives now under way both internationally and Australia-wide which seek to bridge the DD. The impetus for their development comes from community, non-government and government organisations. People with disabilities are one of the groups who are seen to need to become information literate. Information literacy (Chapter 4) has been seen diversely as using information technology, as combining information and technological skills, as acquiring mental models of information systems, as a process, as a mix of skills, attitudes and knowledge, as the ability to learn and as a method of experiencing information use (Doyle, 1992).

Scope

For the category 'education', the scope of the key concepts within it is defined by the properties (e-learning, capacity building, information literacy, technological literacy), the dimensions (digital divide, confidence, information exchange, well-being, motivation, skills) and the subcategories (empowerment, engagement, equality, lifelong learning and shared vision), which are apparent in the following discussion on opportunities emanating from the interviews.

Opportunities

One of the opportunities emerging from these interviews is that this group of people with disabilities are fortunate enough not to be part of one of the disadvantaged groups of people who are seen to be on the wrong side of a digital divide, nor are they completely information illiterate. Val calls herself a 'technology junkie' and has access to and is comfortable with ICT, and in fact uses many gadgets to make life more comfortable. She maintains that 'if it wasn't for technology, I think I'd be dead nowadays, because if I hadn't died of boredom, I'd have died of something else – because you have to have something stimulating to keep you going all the time. And some of the challenges I've found has been figuring out how this bloody technology works...'

She also pointed out how the more access one has to advanced technology, the more one wants and expects, and she will welcome 'smart housing' for people with disabilities. She finds her webcam and digital camera essential now for maintaining her health and medical well-being. She can send digital photographs to her medical practitioner for diagnosis without necessarily having direct contact with medical personnel.

Jack is highly ICT literate, having used technology since he recommenced his tertiary law studies in 1988. His second tertiary degree as an external student was undertaken a decade later, and introduced him to a range of ICT experiences. He particularly began to appreciate the internet for information searching – not for 'cold' (general) searching, which he found to be rather a 'hit and miss' affair, but instead for building on already half-known knowledge. He describes himself as using ICT for 'functional reasons' – 'not as time fillers' – as he says: 'I log on with a purpose in mind.'

Marcie (Interviewee 9) first experienced the internet in 1997 as a student when she was introduced to web browsing, e-mail, chatrooms and so forth. Not only has the e-mail facility proved to be useful socially, but it was invaluable in completing her master's in clinical psychology in 2003. It provides a fast, time- and energy-saving contact with her supervisor at a large teaching hospital. She is mainly self-taught and received *ad hoc* help from friends and other students. As a tertiary student, Marcie paid for the hardware and dial-up connection, but the university provided ICT access gratis. However, as an employed person she was aware of costs, and anticipated seeking a bundled telecommunications deal.

> I've had a mobile phone for about five years and initially got it for security reasons, just being alone at home if something goes wrong... I always take it with me when I'm driving [alone]. It's been very handy in a lot of cases, especially if I've gone somewhere and the disabled park is taken or I can't park and I can at least let the person know upstairs that I'm here, but there's nowhere for me to park.'

Sam is very computer literate, and this ability has proved to be very empowering for him after his severe spinal injury as a young doctoral candidate. After completing a post-accident education qualification, he worked for nine months as a temporary university research fellow. During this time he was involved in research into 'use of computers by people with disabilities', 'speech-recognition systems' and 'at-risk children'. This research resulted in publication in refereed academic journals. He also taught courses on webpage design and internet research skills. He has worked in the oil and gas industry as a senior reservoir engineer and petrophysicist for a large multinational company since 1997. Sam is justifiably proud of some of his other public achievements. He says: 'I'm lucky in that I am able to get back into the workforce and have got a wide circle of friends outside the disability area. Other people have not been so lucky.'

Resuming employment was an imperative for Sam. He began work as a systems administrator in the organisation in which he is currently employed as a geologist, and branched out from there – he believes it was only possible because of the technology.

> I think that it just means that people, regardless of whether they're in chairs or not in chairs, are at the same level as everybody else competing on the basis of their computer skills, not on the physical

skills in a job situation. If this is the case, when they are going for the same position, really from an employer point of view, it makes no difference. They'd rather have the person who can do the job best and can handle the computer best and more jobs are going to become computer-based over the next few years. As long as you can use a computer, I really feel that from an employer's point of view, it would make no difference.

Jane described her increasing reliance on the internet, e-mail and technology, and suggested that in order for future digital divide projects to be equitable for people with disabilities, teaching should be undertaken on a one-to-one basis. In fact, she was emphatic about the importance of learning to use ICT for people with disabilities, as well as the creative adaptation of technology to specific needs – in her case it was only body positioning, but trialling this in public was embarrassing for her. Furthermore, she suggested 'welfare-supported telecommunications' (such as is available for accommodation). She believes that, by this means, the cost, affordability and availability issues might prove to be less of a barrier to a virtual community for people with long-term physical disabilities and this concept might become part of future disability action plans. This interviewee was also supportive of the virtual community concept, because of the opportunities she perceived for people with disabilities to share experiences and diminish their sense of isolation. However, she was committed to seeing ground rules established for people when online. She felt this would be even more essential for a group of people interacting online. One of her suggestions was, for example, listening and respect for each other's different opinions. If this was achievable, she believed that it would be sufficiently empowering as to drive disability policy, and then the technology could be used to establish focus groups and so forth.

To try to define 'internet empowerment' is difficult, but relevant to people with disabilities when they have bridged the DD. Is the empowerment primarily attitudinal, or is it a measurable combination of online access, vision, motivation, skills, equipment and community application that produces a specific percentage of citizens involved at a requisite level of ability (Chamberlin, 1997)? Odasz (undated), who has worked with marginalised groups, claims that measurements define success. You cannot prove that you have empowered people without a measure of the empowerment. Success or failure will rest on the ability to prove that communities are:

- motivated and engaged in active ongoing learning;
- delivering measurable benefits and skills to a known number of citizens;
- sharing a vision and consensus on where applications of this technology need to be headed – that is, defined processes for producing local content development, local collaborative capacity, peer mentoring, online learning and earning, job creation and so on (ibid.: 1–2).

Bob (Interviewee 3) is attracted to people and organisations that are 'values-driven' and focused on positive outcomes for people with disability, 'particularly those that harness our knowledge, experience and wisdom to tackle the issues that affect our lives. Our voice on issues that affect us!' He has given the concept of 'community' deep thought. He would like not only the virtual community but all communities to be connected, and he'd like to see the whole notion of 'community' defined differently and more inclusively. As discussed in Chapter 1, our contemporary understanding of 'community' continues to be a vexed one. In fact, Lyman (1998: 2) argues that 'modern life in an urban industrial society is marked by the absence of community'.

The terms 'capacity building' and 'community development' are used in many fields. The literature on capacity building within developing countries describes it as an 'approach to development' that builds 'independence'. Capacity building increases the range of people, organisations and communities that are able to address problems, and in particular problems that arise out of social inequity and social exclusion. Furthermore, it can be a 'means to an end', enabling others to develop and sustain particular programmes, or an 'end' in itself, where the purpose is to enable others to have greater capacity to problem-solve together.

Community development occurs when a community uses a process by which people get together, communicate, identify priority needs, plan and take action to resolve problems and achieve outcomes that are desired by the community. Community development involves deliberate efforts to foster socio-cultural change on the human community level – change of a kind seen as valuable or progressive, usually including an improved quality of life through increases in resources, skills, facilities, technology, social competence and social power. It is an incremental process through which individuals, families and communities gain the power, insight and resources to make decisions and take action regarding their well-being. The primary goal of community development is to create a better overall quality of life for everyone in the community. It is used to describe any process that increases the capacity of communities to identify their own solutions to their own needs and priorities. It describes a contribution to the community's or group's improved capacity to act on its concerns, and not on the group's actual achievement of goals relating to those concerns. It involves a commitment to the principles of participation, empowerment, equity and social justice and to working with oppressed and marginalised communities (Ife, 2001). Such a holistic way of thinking, as exemplified by Simon's case, can put economic development back into perspective: seeing it as necessary for a strong community, but in itself being far from sufficient.

So, it is appropriate to attribute 'capacity building' to the activities that occupy much of Simon's (Interviewee 7) time. In addition to his involvement in the two things that really do preoccupy him most, the Spinal Injuries Association and a regional disability advisory group, he has become the disability representative on the regional neighbourhood centre's management board. Further, he is an independent advocate for persons with severe disabilities who have moved into the regional centre after the closure of an institution for disabled people. Also, he has recently been elected to the management committee of a leisure accessible club as their regional representative. The club was formed to give people with a disability, including any person with mobility difficulty, the opportunity to pursue recreational activities. He is in regular ICT contact with the president and secretary. Effective capacity building is very strongly dependent on the efforts, motivation and enthusiasm of the individuals involved. Furthermore, it is very much dependent on the presence of values, attitudes and behaviours that are supportive of partnership working, integrated service delivery and the broad objectives of the capacity-building and social capital process.

Simon's interview outlined practical insights into how strategic community investment in regional, rural and remote communities can support people with a disability and their families, because it provides regional and community leadership initiatives as well as opportunities for empowerment to be found in community development and capacity building. Simon himself found he had acquired confidence and administrative skills beyond his pre-accident training and expectations as he began to take control of his life again. He is able to exert himself in his local community and in the disability rights area. Technology changes how communities function, how decisions are made and who has a voice. He initially found the severity of his disablement disempowering, but given that his more recent virtual community experiences with various different local groups and organisations were about 'engagement', quality of life and support, not just about information, he seems to have changed his perceptions.

Fantasy category (or virtual-reality activities)

People with disabilities, in particular, may be drawn to virtual-reality 'activities' (see www.dreamfit.com.au) as a 'substitute' for real activities because of limitations imposed by severe mobility problems (Alm et al., 1998). They may create new environments, personalities, stories and role-play. Many of the interviewees also refer to the virtual-reality concept as the 'double-edged sword' of access versus isolation. According to a recent Harris poll, one of the most serious consequences of a disability is its tendency to increase social isolation and reduce community participation. This is not because people with disabilities do not want to be more involved or to participate more. The problem is that many such people do not feel their participation is welcomed by community organisations (Taylor, 2000a).

Scope

For the category 'fantasy', the scope of the key concepts within it is defined by the properties (virtual activities, virtual community and family, virtual living and reality), the dimensions (access, anonymity, communicate, interact, participate) and the subcategories ('double-edged sword' of technology, barrier-free and recreation), which are apparent in the discussion on opportunities emanating from the interviews.

Opportunities

The investigator commented in a chatroom that she was doing research into virtual communities for persons with physical disabilities and would like ideas about the following: 'What is your secret wish? Assume that the telecommunications and information technology industry is going to grant one wish to the disability sector. What should it be? It could be hardware or software... Any wish, no matter how way-out. Just as long as it relates to telephones, computers, the internet and so on. I would like some background and for you [the respondent] to be explicit about how this would benefit you or others in a similar situation.' One response was: 'I'd like to try cyber sex with one of those full body suits. I'd also give cyber sky-diving a go, deep-sea diving, mountain climbing, body surfing – the lot. Stuff I can't do in real life. Virtual reality would bring my wildest fantasies to life.'

Marcie, a clinical psychologist as well as a person with disabilities, realises that learning to communicate via the internet can remove barriers and dispel isolation for some people with disabilities (even if only using the internet to play cards). However, like other interviewees, she was aware of the negative aspects of the technology:

> One of my concerns would be that people wouldn't go out possibly as much and that could be a bit of a danger. But I think the internet is good where it saves some energy and time, but hopefully it doesn't stop people getting out and interacting with real humans... I sometimes think we have clients that are depressed and they are withdrawing from people anyway; one of things we do is we encourage them to force themselves to get out there and be around people. So I would hope that the internet doesn't help people to withdraw even more. But on the whole, I see the internet as being 90 per cent excellent in terms of what it can provide for us and that 10 per cent is only a possibility that people will do this – so, on the whole, I think it's really good. It makes life easier and opens up a whole new world for people that otherwise wouldn't see that.

Marcie finds the technology most suitable for communicating with friends and family and for meeting new people (with the added bonus of the person getting to know her before being potentially overwhelmed by any visual barriers associated with her disability). She also defines it as:

> a social thing to get on the net and chat to people, even if it's just mucking around and talking about what's been on the news or something like that. It's actually social interaction and that can be achieved through not even leaving your house and having to get taxis or get dressed, or anything like that. I think that's a very important aspect of it, that probably I underestimate sometimes.

Nonetheless, Marcie is aware that 'you have to be careful that you don't suddenly become reliant on just the computer screen... that you actually manage your world outside of that computer screen'.

Joe (Interviewee 5) alluded to the other positive aspects of the anonymity of being online:

> If you're firing e-mails around or leaving comments online, you become part of that great cyber conversation that's going on all around the world. You're included in it, there is no barrier, once you've actually got online and you can make that keyboard work, and you overcome any hardware problems, any software problems, any ISP problems, you're there. You're part of a community online and that is so empowering to people, and their morale goes through the roof. All of a sudden, I'm somebody. I'm not an outcast, they can't see that I'm using a wheelchair or that I've got a harelip or this, that or the other.

Jack, who relocated recently, continues to e-mail his previous friends periodically (phoning is too expensive), but does not feel that he has 'replaced that [social group] with technology. I don't find that a very appealing or stimulating thing to do.' He likes to balance technology with face to face, and would much prefer to use the telephone or meet people – chatrooms are not for him (and not just because he is unable to use a keyboard with sufficient speed). He said rather sadly: 'I don't really think in wider terms how that brings the community closer to me or me closer to the community.' Val, on the other hand, thought that she would develop a website so all her family, relatives and friends could keep in touch virtually. She could not access chatrooms, 'because the conversation in chatrooms is fast and furious and Dragon Naturally Speaking makes too many errors'.

Bob is very comfortable with the use of search engines in his information seeking, and sees himself more as an informational user of the internet rather than using it for virtual living, even though he is extremely disabled. 'My street is not very friendly... you've got all boxes in isolation. No transport, no community infrastructure, no support. So I guess I would love to think that a virtual community is what I would want to live in.'

Keith said:

> I find the use of the internet for those personal, professional and social good things, but again it's the stuff that I think sometimes you can get very trapped in, particularly if you're surfing and you wanted to waste some time. You waste too much time in that and there's a potential for it to become all too absorbing sometimes. It

can be at the expense of other relationships. So again it's like everything, you've got to be conscious of the impact it's having upon you.

However, in his community role in the advocacy organisation, he uses the internet for several purposes, such as live discussion groups via hotmail, whereby he either chats directly one to one or has a net-meeting or brief conversations with his virtual friends and acquaintances about social justice issues – all for the price of one connection. Sam never uses chatrooms or computer games and would prefer to use the telephone for most of his communication needs when they are not achieved face to face. However, he does use e-mail to keep in contact with his fairly wide network of friends interstate and overseas. Apart from professionally, Sally uses ICT personally all the time: e-mail and telephone to keep in contact with her many close, but dispersed, family members – in fact, they operate their own virtual family. This is a discussion list in order to keep every family member in touch and informed. When confronted with a problem, Sally's response is to use technology to its maximum extent. 'It's just you've got to reframe your thinking – that's all.'

After Tom retired from the international IT company, he became involved very quickly with the Skill Share project to help find employment for the long-term unemployed. The vision was to place IT in rural homes to enable people isolated from workplaces to gain employment working from home, 'using the potential that is imprisoned within them'.

> Through using the internet, voice-recognition systems, environmental systems etc. I saw that it had great potential to enable people with quadriplegia to participate. They could manage all their household functions, using the environmental system where everything was integrated into it, and use their spare time to join a virtual community and even paid part-time employment. So simply by using their voice they could open and shut windows, open and close doors, turn the air-conditioning on, the washing machine, and all these sorts of things. So, their mobility requirements would be extremely limited.

Dan emphasises the importance of computer technology in all areas of his life. His computer is turned on before he rises in the morning and is often turned off very late at night. 'I'm a real computer user... I *use* technology.' In many ways he is very dependent on this technology, particularly in his work, but also socially. As he is a self-employed programmer, he has everything to optimise his functioning in this realm. For his social life, as with many computer users, he accesses friendships with more ease through this technology.

Information category

People with disabilities, apart from their general information needs, have other more specific information needs related to their disability, mobility and access issues, as elaborated in Chapter 4. They use virtual forums, specific websites and virtual communities that are already in existence when they are looking for information about aspects of health and disability, travel and accessible accommodation, and assistive technology (AT) (Brownsell and Bradley, 2003). However, just as people need a broad spectrum of literacy skills in order to use ICT effectively, they must also recognise the need for quality content and IL.

Scope

For the category 'information', the scope of the key concepts within it is defined by the properties (e-searching, equality, virtual communities), the dimensions (discussion groups, education, entertainment, legislation, leisure) and the subcategories (access and choice), which are apparent in the discussion on opportunities arising from the interviews.

Opportunities

Another Harris poll examined how the internet had a very positive impact on the lives of adults with disabilities who are online, and how this impact is much greater than it is among adults without disabilities. As the number of adults with disabilities online continues to increase, the internet has helped to improve the quality of their lives greatly, allowing them to be better informed, more connected to the world around them and get in touch with people who have similar interests and experiences. The data from the survey were statistically weighted to be representative of all adults, with and without disabilities, who were online, whether from home, work, school, library or another location. People with disabilities are less likely to be online than people without disabilities (43 per cent compared with 57 per cent). In particular, they are much less likely to be online from work (16 compared with 30 per cent), because fewer of them are employed (Taylor, 2000b).

Jack, for example, has used internet and phone banking facilities since 1993 because of the independence they afford him. He uses the internet regularly for information searching. He checks his investments daily. He uses it for searching for accessible accommodation when he travels – also for shopping; however, he was using phone and/or fax to the supermarket as his current mode for meeting this need. He found the internet invaluable for background research into appliances prior to purchase. The manufacturer's own web specifications were more reliable than any salesman. Also, he checked out health sites regularly. In this regard, the information he found about recent surgery gave him 'peace of mind'.

As far as information searching is concerned, Sally (Interviewee 6), a disability organisation's executive officer, is currently researching material for a submission to the United Nations on a 'Bill of Rights' for people with disabilities. She is also researching material for a submission on welfare reform regarding working-age income support for people with disabilities; and she is preparing a consultation towards the review of the DDA. All information regarding legislation, projects, submissions and consultations is distributed to the organisation's members for their approval prior to submitting the documents. In addition, the organisation has its own 'issues' group that is investigating concepts such as adaptable housing and the 'cost' of disability.

Val has been searching the internet since 1996 because, as she said: 'It just opens up a whole new world – in the sense that if you want to know something... you can get information. It's an atlas, it's a dictionary, it's a medical dictionary, and its contact through e-mail. At this point in time, I use it more than I do the phone.' When she needed a new environmental control unit[1] she did internet research as well as contacting the appropriate allied health professionals. On receipt of the new equipment, Val programmed in two television receivers, two videos and one stereo consisting of a CD player, many radio channels and a cassette player. She uses it by pressing the 'lolly' switch. She was thrilled by its versatility, and found she could manipulate it herself just by pressing a switch. She uses either a mouth-stick for typing or voice-recognition software and a microphone to access the computer.

What Bob loves about the internet (and he, like Val, has broadband) is being able to get information effortlessly. 'Any information! And to broadcast information!' He tends to be home often because of his acutely limited mobility. However, as he says, 'you can have all the communication in the world, but you can be locked at home and isolated. But the internet has the possibility of bringing the world to your doorstep. Information that you want is there at the doorstep... I use the internet to communicate and get information, to talk with people.' But as he points out:

> One could argue that that in many ways [it] is forcing me to stay home more, because if I wanted to find out information before the internet I'd have to go out. I'd have to go to the library and go somewhere to find information, so it pushed me out into the community. I'd have to use taxis and transport and accessible buildings and all that sort of stuff. So, the answer that I want to see out of the internet which is not happening yet [is]... connecting, connecting people with similar needs or with needs... bringing people together around issues.

Apart from information, he believes that the technology contributes to the 'relationship' category, and that there is a need to interconnect 'communities of place' for the exchange of information around happenings in that community not restricted to specific needs only. If this were the case and the cost barrier was removed, then according to him, 100 per cent of people could be online. He says: 'To me the internet is about people, it's about connecting people and it's how we connect those people that we really haven't solved as yet.'

Keith, like the other interviewees, uses the internet to gather information, primarily around social justice issues. Another reason is hobby-related – racehorses, which he regards as his social outlet.

> But all in all, as I think I said earlier, it's particularly good for getting information. Towards the end of my studies when the internet became a greater reality for me, it really saved well, I won't say time, but opened up equal opportunities to research. Like access the journals from libraries, access books from libraries, whereas I would've had to physically go there, try to find it by myself or feel that I was imposing upon a librarian, who was already overwhelmed because of under-resourcing etc. etc., to ask for help. So that aspect of it was a great equalising opportunity for me. Because of my physical disability, it was also about managing the paper. Using a computer, physically I could manage it quite

sufficiently and quickly and competently as opposed to dropping it on the floor and having to wait for somebody to come and pick it up, or losing paper, losing time and wasting time. So it is a vehicle that has created more opportunity and quality for me. Quality, I think, in the sense of efficiency and using your time and giving you some more, some greater capacity to have quality time with your family. But equally, I think it can take away from that as well.

The internet proved to be invaluable to Marcie for her information seeking. She used it for research for her recent master's degree and also to get information such as accessible holiday venues. In fact, regarding access, she finds the internet 'a fairly cheap way of finding out a lot of information without necessarily having to visit travel agents or ringing STD phone calls to different other hotels individually. But the only thing with that is, I don't always trust the information their websites give about wheelchair access.' Apart from the time and energy saving of being able to download academic articles from her home computer, Marcie also uses the internet for many recreational activities, for example checking movie times, etc. In fact, she says: 'I guess I'm very web based!'

As Sam uses computers all day at work, he only uses the internet at home when he is seeking 'disability' information relating to equipment and resources, accommodation, access and so forth. He uses this technology for booking accommodation and theatre tickets, banking, minimal general shopping and ordering disability equipment. Regarding the notion of a virtual community for people with disabilities, he believes that 'if I was part of the virtual community I'd be coming and going. I'd go in when I needed some information and then come out. I can see a definite need for a virtual community and for disability discussion groups, but I think it depends very much on the individual, how they like to get information.'

Interest category

A lot of the rationale behind people with disabilities using ICT takes on a level of 'moral purpose'. It allows them to explore disability rights issues, such as bioethics and stem-cell research, and also express their opinions about matters pertaining to these rights. In fact, many of the people with disabilities who have taken on a leadership role in this area have done so with a 'moral purpose' and been vocal about issues of disability rights.

Scope

For the category 'interest', the scope of the key concepts within it is defined by the properties (disability rights, leadership, moral purpose, social justice), the dimensions (access, equity, independence, mobility, participation, values-driven) and the subcategories (assistive technology, civil society, inclusion, self-determination, vision and voice). These are apparent in the discussion on the opportunities emanating from the interviews.

Opportunities

Joe, in his employment in a disability role within the local council since 1990, has used a social justice framework. This is based on the four principles of equity, access, participation and rights, where he basically has outlined goals, objectives and strategies with respect to the use of ICT by people with disabilities. In the last 15–20 years Tom, as the oldest interviewee, has witnessed dramatic changes in technology that have opened up wonderful new opportunities for people with disabilities.

> The technology available to us, particularly with information systems via computer technology, as well as the adaptive technology which assists in its use, can enable many more people with disabilities to be able to participate in society through paid employment or volunteering. And of course enjoying entertainment and, very importantly, environmental management systems. Absolutely enormous are the opportunities these have now offered all citizens who wish to participate.

Val well remembers her delight when she bought her first hands-free telephone. She could now make phone calls on demand and had the right to privacy. Her electric typewriter allowed her similar independence and freedom. She operates the typewriter, cassette recorder and hands-free phone with a mouth-stick. 'I thought I had it made! I left the spinal unit with nothing but a shower chair, a pushchair, a manual hoist and a pressure-relieving mattress. All necessities for my physical well-being, but no idea how to occupy my brain.' She did find ways to occupy her brain, however: she has spent her time grappling with ICT and other technology and ultimately set up the website Disability Forum, which has a definite 'moral purpose'.

As Tom sees the situation:

If you look particularly at spine injury, the highest risk group is the male age group 17–35, with 75 per cent of all spinal injury falling into this category, then you're looking at capturing significant lost potential. I think that if you have the vision, if you have the will and if we can then develop the resources to do it, I believe that there's a wonderful opportunity to start modelling this whole virtual community. We do have the technology available there for everybody that has the desire to use it. We could start at the spinal unit, part of the rehabilitation programme could be an introduction to the virtual community which says, you're not isolated, you are not devalued, but still have the potential to be a valuable contributor to the community. The start would be operating computers in the spinal unit, gaining the knowledge and becoming enthusiastic and confident about the opportunity on offer. Telemarketing positions offer significant opportunity for employment for people with disabilities working from home and would be a wonderful platform for the start of the virtual home community.

One of the major outcomes of the Advocacy Action 2001 Forum, according to its director Keith, was that it opened up 18 areas for discussion that had policy implications and convinced non-disabled participants that people with disabilities can provide great leadership and insight. For example, one area was bioethics, and an active e-mail discussion group on this topic has been operating, expressing a wide range of views. The government saw the forum as a positive undertaking with enormous potential for engaging people; however, it could only be a one-off activity of Keith's organisation, as it was not really its core business (Goggin and Newell, 2003: 137–40). Another outcome was a partnership with CONROD at the University of Queensland in working towards the Disability Lifestyles website that became available in mid-2004. Keith, in fact, argues that all the historical types of disability model are restrictive, except the rehabilitation or social model.[2] This model he describes as liberating, as well as potentially useful for the CONROD website, 'because I remember when I left the spinal unit, the doctor, who was a very good doctor, said you'll get it together in two or three years' time. He was right – it took me three years, but what a waste of three years. Something like this could've been very helpful.' With anecdotes like this by Keith, and Val's earlier one, it is easy to appreciate why some disabled people conduct themselves with overtones of moral purpose.

Technology, although the expense constitutes a barrier for people with disabilities, has a definitely positive role for the social disability model. Keith said: 'So I think if, from an academic point of view, if we think about it in terms of a social model, it's how we manage technology to be enhanced, empower, give greater autonomy and self-determination – then I think we can use technology in a strong and powerful way.' He links the notion of a virtual community with that of a global community or society. 'There is a community whether we want it or not and the good things for that community will be where technology is liberating and allows people greater self-determination and empowerment.' The barriers to a virtual community Keith sees as determined by whether one is socially and/or economically disadvantaged, and revolving around information and knowledge or lack thereof. He believes that 'people have got to contribute significantly towards creating a civil society in the virtual community'. This thought is based on the assumption that hopefully the leaders in the disability community have close enough experience and memory of their isolation, marginalisation, depression and being a burden and non-productive. If so, they can contribute significantly to making that virtual community a more fair and just society.

> So yes, there is a challenge I think, about how we provide, particularly for people who live in poverty. People who live isolated, whether it be in a city or a rural and remote community, particularly indigenous people who are socially and economically isolated, even within their own communities. I think these are some of the great struggles that we have about how we include people, irrespective of whether it's through technology or really how we value people and include people on a daily basis in our lives and in our communities. I think it's the greatest challenge and, to use jargon, a benchmark of a true civil society is how we treat our most vulnerable people – and the answer to that, I don't have.

Sally became involved in the disability sector in New Zealand in 1981 and in the International Year for Disabled Persons activities, and rose from secretarial positions to become director of the Disabled Persons Resource Centre in Christchurch, New Zealand. She moved to Australia in 1989 and has continued to work in the disability sector ever since – currently as an executive officer for the Physical Disability Council of Australia (www.pdca.org.au). Sally returned to university, upgraded her

New Zealand studies to a bachelor's in community work and is now completing her master's in disability leadership online. She is very happy to be employed as a teleworker representative of this national advocacy organisation, a virtual community instituted in 1995. The PDCA needed to find ways to assist the leadership and members to communicate easily and cost effectively. Government and ICT provided the answer. The PDCA also instituted an open discussion list (pdca@ozemail.com.au)[3] that has become very active over the years, as it is disseminated through other networks encouraging and empowering people with physical disabilities to tackle issues that directly affect their lives. Sally is the moderator of the discussion list and also produces a regular digest of relevant items from the list for recipients who do not want to be burdened by innumerable daily e-mails. The PDCA website has a downloadable information package about its leadership, role and activities. Since that innovation the direct membership has more than trebled. It has future plans for the website to be interactive so people can download and complete online the membership application forms, surveys, questionnaires, resource kits for federal and state government information, HREOC processes of complaint and so forth. Sally believes that if people with disabilities learn to use ICT in this way, it will function as 'a very big empowerment tool for the membership'.

ICT also had a positive role for disabled people in breaking down isolation, and Sally considers the notion of 'essential equipment' will have to be redefined. 'I just think that we need to look at the virtual world as more a right to have than anything else. It's like we all were taught how to write a letter once, so now we teach how to use computers to do the letter, send an e-mail so that we can talk to people. So I think the benefits far outweigh the cost, the initial cost.' Moreover, Sally argued that ICT was an imperative communication device for people with disabilities and necessary for equality of education and potential employment.

> I don't think it's an easy one, but I do think that the whole concept of what people use a computer for has to be looked at... as a communication device for people. It's really essential that we start to look at that because that can break down a lot of the isolation barriers – in that people can talk on the internet in much of the same way as School of the Air did for kids that lived in isolated areas in terms of their education.

She sees extra funding for people with disabilities for ICT as being essential – whether it is to get them off the disability support pension ultimately, or as part of income support.

> So, we were trying to impress upon governments that if you're really serious about wanting to get people off the disability support pension, then you're going to actually spend money in the first instance to do it. And I think that's the same anywhere, that if you're serious about getting people into the community and interactive, even if it's on a voluntary basis, then there has to be something put in first. It's not just going to happen on its own.

Relationship category

The majority of virtual community sites specific to disabled people are American-based. However, there are an increasing number of sites for people with disabilities becoming the concern of community and not-for-profit organisations. Opening Doors, for example, is a mentoring site set up by the University of Washington. The nature of a virtual community does not restrict its application to national borders, and many of the American sites have a variety of international visitors. Some of the larger sites have disability-specific chatrooms, and most sites also have discussion boards and e-mail broadcast lists.

Many of the websites can provide the opportunity for people with disabilities to develop friendships or share experiences with others, so they have an invaluable community role or peer support role (Seymour and Lupton, 2004). Chatrooms are generally for the relatively technology savvy, as well as physically able, because conversations often move in a rapid, disjointed fashion, and some disabilities may prevent people from interacting in this way. The webcasts and discussion boards seem to be an inclusive way to become more involved in virtual communities at a self-controlled pace. A unique site is Disability Friends Web Pals Around the World (www.geocities.com/dfriendswebpals/), where users may leave details about themselves and an e-mail address to facilitate one-on-one communication through e-mail. For those with at least a basic competence in ICT skills, sites such as these provide relatively simple ways to become involved in virtual communities.

Scope

For the category 'relationship', the scope of the key concepts within it is defined by the properties (community role, peer support,[4] systemic advocacy), the dimensions (collective experience, shared knowledge, self-esteem, valued role) and the subcategories (acceptance, identity, privacy and social networks), which are apparent in the discussion on opportunities arising from the interviews.

Opportunities

Val started the Disability Forum virtual community in June 2003. She enjoys sharing what she knows about technology with other people and likes to learn what other people have to offer. As a consequence, she 'wanted to set up an interactive website where people with disabilities who are confined to their houses can freely exchange information'. She realised that she had used a wheelchair for 23 years and had learnt a lot, not only about wheelchairs but about other issues related to living with a disability. While attending meetings, she met some remarkable people who had first-hand knowledge, ideas and strategies that could make life easier for someone else with a disability. She says that was what motivated her: 'People with disabilities have a wealth of knowledge to share, but nowhere to share it that I could identify. The best place that I could think of for people with disabilities to share their knowledge and experience with one another was over the internet.'

Disability Forum is a consumer-based website, launched on 26 June 2003 (Independent Living Centre Association of Queensland, 2003), where people with a disability can network, support each other and develop and maintain friendships in a supportive, interactive online community. It contains advice about everything 'from grooming tips to dislocated hips', as well as categories of information, government information and a discussion format. Val has found the experience an empowering one. She 'hopes this website will become a state-wide place for people with disabilities, parents of children with disabilities, parents with disabilities and interested parties to freely exchange information and learn from one another', and that it will be empowering for them too. She is 'constantly amazed how many people are not aware that they have a lot of knowledge to share just from experiencing life dealing with a disability'. The website has needed ongoing development support and subsequently has received funding towards its redevelopment to suit the needs of its users better. It is hoped to develop it so that it becomes a 'one-stop shop' in terms of information provided by users for users. Ultimately Val, as moderator, hopes the site will have an impact on a wider community.

Keith is the full-time director of an advocacy organisation. Its mission is to promote, protect and defend through advocacy the fundamental needs, rights and lives of the most vulnerable disabled people in its region. The organisation does this by engaging in systems advocacy work – through campaigns directed to attitudinal, legal and policy change, and by supporting the development of a range of advocacy initiatives. It provides independent, community-based systems and legal advocacy for people with disability.

Keith is justifiably very proud of the advocacy organisation's work in its three-month, three-phase process called Advocacy Action Forum 2001: Turning Rhetoric into Reality. This was a forum that deliberately used technology to engage people with disabilities to encourage them to begin to tell their stories. One of the criticisms of the forum was the fact that many disabled people do not have a computer, and thus were not able to participate. Nonetheless, Keith saw the forum process as about starting to create a civil society, not only in the real community but also in the virtual community (Goggin and Newell, 2003: 137–40). This collective experience of sharing and learning to talk about their lives and of assessing how they contributed to public policy debate was infinitely rewarding for all participants. The first phase was a moderated e-mail-based 'conversation' and resulted in some strong relationships being built. Some 220 people (mainly Australian) registered to join the group, and only about 20 per cent had previously experienced participating in this type of discussion. Keith believes that for many people with disabilities it required bravery on their part, in that it was the first time they were actually able to tell their stories and be honoured and respected for the experience. Many people realised that they were not alone and that many of their experiences were not unique. According to him, 'it also impassioned people and angered people to actually hear of some of the [neglectful] ways people live their lives'. There were two main reasons why the advocacy organisation in the first phase of the Advocacy Action Forum used e-mail postings: one related to its capacity to moderate allied discussions (there were some 780 postings over the 12 weeks), and the second was 'about trying to ensure that harmful discourse didn't get away too quickly'.

The next step in the process of the Advocacy Action 2001 Forum was a videoconference workshop between people from three different communities. They connected and participated in a facilitated discussion about what was happening for them in their communities.

> Each group presented something that they'd worked together to present about their lived experiences. It quite enlightened one of the paid workers from a large service provider just how sophisticated people could be, and was very empowering for the groups that had more sheltered and disempowering lifestyles. They saw and met people who may have had similar disabilities and experiences doing very different things with their lives. And also those people then participated in four days face to face. So I think that one of the things that technology can never replace is the face-to-face gathering. From that there was a vision developed about what a civil society would look like, and answering the question 'what is the place of people with a disability in a civil society?' So that is the long way round saying that technology has a very productive and constructive role to play in people with disabilities' lives, particularly people who are isolated because of their location or their physical capacity and I think intellectual capacity as well.

Simon sees himself as part of a virtual community, defined as: 'that's the way that I use my virtual community, or I call it a virtual community, because you're able to access the community from your own home. I don't know if that's the definition of it or not, but that's the way I feel that it is and it's like we're all linked together with wires.' He sells Art Union tickets for a charitable organisation by phone, and this role gave him the opportunity to speak to a lot of people in his community. It also allows him to work from home; if he were not able to work from home, he would not be employable because of the many problems associated with his disability. Apart from his telemarketing role, he is very active in three other organisations.

Bob requires 24-hour high-level support and has limited use of only his head and neck. Nonetheless, he was 'connected' even before the internet went public and is networked to his wife's computer in the next room. He is keenly aware of its potential as a 'two-edged sword' for persons with disabilities. He likes to define a virtual community as the peer support that people experience being connected. It could well be 'a group of people with spinal injuries, someone who's only been in a chair for six months and someone 20 years [in a chair], exchanging information... You come together and exchange holiday information. Exchange information about your disabilities, tips on how to manage aspects of your life – this could be a virtual community.' He sees the work and strength of a bulletin board being comparable with that of a chatroom or a virtual community.

> Generally being connected... but only a part of the community, means you can be sitting in the lounge room and never see a soul for weeks on end. So it begs the definition of what is a community, and so I think the definition of a community should come first, and then next you'll be telling me how to make it virtual after that. And I've often thought about communities, what sort of community I would live in. I live in a community, but it's not a very friendly community.

Joe, who is employed by the local council in a community disability role, became interested in the capacity of the web as a medium of contact for people who experience social isolation, are not able to access transport and are near or below the poverty line. He particularly finds the PDCA e-mail discussion list useful, as it is representative of people from all over the country and many of the participants are very well informed. Parking regulations and street crossings, for example, have been a recent area of investigation for him, and through the interstate dialogue and networking that has taken place during the developmental phase, standardised solutions that may be implemented nationwide become more viable and are adopted as part of other standards. He hopes there will be more such specific discussion lists available through Yahoo! for people with other disabilities in the future, so they too can discuss their shared concerns and problem-solving. As Joe said:

> Frequently people have already solved the problem in their own area and that information can be easily passed on, and it's invaluable. You're not reinventing the wheel and you're not coming up with 'local solutions' that are out of step with other 'local solutions' and that is extremely valuable. If, for example, a blind person or a physically disabled person changes city it's handy if the rules don't all change.

Joe sees electronic networks as useful and anticipates the positive effect for rural members being online. He also welcomes all the various 'donation' programmes promoted by voluntary organisations (for example, Green PCs, Info Exchange, Technical Aids for the Disabled and so on) and how government is keen for economic reasons to get people with disabilities and other low-income people online. Cheap personal computer (PC) units were difficult to acquire prior to the 'donation' programmes that are now available. Joe would like to see ISPs offer what he terms a 'social justice' package – indexed against the person's circumstances or 'filtered' to include only the sites most relevant to their needs. A partnership between Technical Aids for the Disabled (TAD) and the internet service provider ISPOne advised in June 2005 that it would provide internet access to people who receive the disability support pension.[5] Another of his 'affordable' suggestions for people with disabilities who wish to participate in the online benefits associated with our 'information economy' is 'micro-finance' to providers through the government's Centre Pay reimbursement process.

SMS (short message service) is a facility of Marcie's mobile telephone that she uses regularly[6] (Australian Mobile Telecommunications Association, 2006).

> It's a cheap way just to send a message… it's a good way to let someone know you're thinking about them without interrupting them or making a huge phone call… It is another tool that I use, which is what I mainly use the mobile for. I must say I'm not a huge chatter on the mobile because of the costs. I try to be as cost efficient as I can be. I use it for emergencies pretty much, yeah. I don't use my phone for internet, but I know it does have that feature. I think, because I have the internet at home I use it there – because it's so much easier to type rather than press tiny little buttons on a mobile phone.

In a preliminary study into the impact of the mobile phone in Australia, the researchers observed: 'We can see how the mobile telephone has provided us with new abilities to be more mobile, and sometimes not to have to be mobile' (Academy of the Social Sciences in Australia, 2004: 4). Marcie exemplifies this position exactly. She was the only person interviewed who described using digital telecommunication, mobile phone contacts and text messaging ('texting', as this practice is known) as merely another tool in the range of ICT technologies at her disposal. As Marcie would vouch, the mobile phone does not decrease her number of face-to-face contacts; on the contrary, the technology is a powerful social tool that increases and promotes her social and concrete control over situations.[7] As Rheingold (2002: 10) postulated: 'the real impact of mobile communications will come not from the technology itself, but from how people use it, resist it, adapt to it, and ultimately use it to transform themselves, their communities, and their institutions'. He welcomes the empowering and democratising potential of these transformative technologies.

Marcie likens ICT and specific websites to support groups and networks for people with disabilities – especially for those persons physically unable to attend support group meetings. In other words, they can function as a 'buddy' system through the social contact, but additionally as an information system for people with disabilities.

> So, I'm sure it could be aspects of people typing in their own writings or people saying: 'I've got this problem, does anyone have a solution to it?' I'm sure we all manage the same problem and we're all trying to solve them individually, but there is probably someone out there who has an answer for it, different problems, maybe there could also be some professional information provided on the website as well.

Tom believes that we are now living in exciting times with amazing opportunities developing that will enable us to set up virtual communities with a valued community role as well as offering peer support, not only for people with disabilities but for the general community. Furthermore, he argues that if we can develop a virtual community that has enormous potential for people from a wide range of disabilities to be able to achieve positive, productive, effective outcomes from it, then automatically it will be adapted and accepted by the rest of the community. However, he says the major hurdle is going to be finances.

> For a virtual community, it's not simply a matter of throwing heaps and heaps of money at a problem and believing it will be fixed... It's a problem of firstly, how do we build up the infrastructure in our community where people are valued and value themselves. Because I think one of the greatest tragedies we face in Australia is that we're one of the luckiest countries in the world, environmentally, economically, politically, and yet increasingly because of the ailments we've got in our society... the people are not building their self-esteem to the point where they recognise they're a valuable contributor to this community. Recognising that potential and then developing it... but, if we're looking at any sort of a successful virtual community, we have to recognise that there's some very significant inhibitors to being able to achieve the level of success that I believe the technology that's available can provide.

Transaction category

As discussed earlier, people with disabilities are overrepresented in low socio-economic groups compared to the population in general. This affects their ability to access ICT and further disadvantages them in a range of activities that are now conducted over the internet. Many commercial activities, for example bill paying and banking, offer discounts for business conducted over the internet (Buland and Thomas, 2000: 263). Thus lack of internet access further penalises people who are already under financial strain.[8] If people with disabilities are teleworking or have other financial means, however, they may access the stock market for share trading to provide finances (Mainelli, 2003).

Scope

For the category 'transaction', the scope of the key concepts within it is defined by the properties (e-commerce, employment), the dimensions (investments, shopping, ordering, bill paying) and the subcategories (teleworking and telemarketing), which are apparent in the discussion on the opportunities emanating from the interviews. It is interesting to note that online gambling was never mentioned within this category by any of the interviewees.

Opportunities

Simon pays bills by phone, and was glad of this opportunity because it afforded him a valued household role. He is also a regular contributor in the PDCA e-mail group. This group posts interesting information and discussions concerning people with a disability. He regularly uses the internet to purchase items, compare features of items he wants to buy, research information on any issue that interests him, e-mail friends swapping jokes and conversation and search for graphics for celebration cards. He would not be able to participate in many organisations and groups, and feel a valued member of his community, if it were not for today's ICT. After a number of idle years trying to come to terms with his spinal-cord injury, he became a telemarketer for a charitable organisation.

Keith also does all his banking and bill paying online after realising that it was secure enough, and he has found this to be very liberating – quick, easy, efficient and very cost-effective. Apart from using ICT for communication, security, information and in completing her tertiary education, Marcie too uses the technology for banking, but not shopping (preferring to see before she purchases), and is gratified by how much less paperwork is required.

From about 1998 onwards, as the World Wide Web grew exponentially, Joe's interest expanded to include an affordable ISP, affordable hardware, affordable adaptive software and affordable training. As a result, he informed people of the value of being connected and the many benefits it would bring. He is vehement that he will continue working in these areas – living in hope that people will use ICT, but fighting fiercely to prevent all information going online solely.

One of the significant aspects of a virtual community, according to Bob, is its potential for changing the paradigm of work (Baker and Fairchild, 2004). Certain categories of work might not need to be done at a particular office but are appropriate to the home virtual office, which is desirable for a person with a disability providing it does not 'normalise' their isolation.

> The hours are more flexible, taxi money/inconvenience is saved, and so on; however, the downside of it is, of course, that you end up with this isolation model which seems to be the trap for anyone with a disability, if you work from home. You don't have a job, you live at home, you can end up being trapped and with the internet it's even worse, because you can end up spending hours every day at home in front of your screen. You're not even communicating. The web can end up being a disaster, if we haven't really adequately thought through this isolation problem that we have. A bit like television...

As detailed earlier in this chapter, the two most obvious themes that emerged from Jack's interview were the need for a sense of control in and over his life and the need for independence and self-reliance where possible. ICT has met these needs to some extent for him. He has taken control of his own stock investments. Taking control over what he can in his life was very important to him given that so much of his life is out of his control, for example morning rising, bedtime and so on. However, he would like to be able to talk (easily) to his computer or even 'think' to it (known as 'mind control'), which would be more practical for him, but as he wirily observed, 'it won't help you get around'.[9] So, according to him, ICT was a poor substitute for lack of mobility.

This differed from Simon, a young indigenous man, who believed the opposite to Jack. Perhaps the different cultural and socio-economic backgrounds and expectations accounted for the difference. Sam (like Jack) did not favour teleworking. He preferred to be able to have ready access to his colleagues and their knowledge – but he factored in their companionship, as well as their knowledge. Jack's attitude was:

> I can't put my finger on what it is that makes it [going into the workplace] better or different, but for some reason being there and having that interaction I find more fulfilling and it's half the reason I work. So okay, everyone works to get paid, but for me I have to enjoy what I'm doing and if I'm just going to work by sitting at my desk at home [teleworking], then I'd probably rather not do it. I'd rather read a book in the sun.

Teleworking was a positive concept for people with disabilities, according to Sally, a teleworker herself for a national physical disability organisation. She acknowledged that it is not necessarily positive for everybody:

> I think that more people should have the opportunity to work from home, particularly people with a disability, because, in fact, you don't need to set it up. One of the biggest pitfalls for people in the workforce or studying is that they have to have special accommodations made – it might be access, it might transport, it might be all sorts of things. But doing it from home, you don't need those, because you're already in your own environment, which is established for you. I found that I have functioned more than adequately in the last six-and-a-half years working from home. It's a bonus for the employer, because although they compensate for the use of a room, it's not the same overhead costs, and there's no ongoing maintenance-type stuff. So you're not wasting [non-profit] funds in bricks and mortar.

Having retired, Tom still sought to be employed, but not in a full-time office job. He was of the opinion that the traditional workplace may have a negative impact on the quality of life for persons with high-level or debilitating disabilities, and the alternative of teleworking offered many positive possibilities (Roulstone, 1998; Midwest Institute for Telecommuting Education, 2003; Baker and Fairchild, 2004). He knew he needed technology if he was to work productively from home, and that working from home was a reality today. He was delighted with what he was now able to do from his home – everything that could be achieved in an office.

> So I agreed to work as a volunteer from home. I had my first desktop computer. It was very primitive compared to today's technology with very limited capability in the software. But it enabled me then to at least start to do letters and documents... I'm now at the stage where I have a completely self-contained office. I only go into the national office... whenever I need to pick up something. It's in Brisbane and I'm out at Robertson. I have a dedicated fax, the latest-level IBM laptop computer with XP Professional software and PowerPoint 2. I also have, obviously, connection to the internet, the e-mail, two telephone lines and all the bells and whistles that are available to anyone in the community that wants to work from home... A lot of my job is simply promoting memberships, which is obviously contacting people. A lot of it is a telemarketing-type work. I read something in the paper, or I'll hear something on the TV and I decide maybe there's an opportunity, because there's some synergy there. That organisation, or that person, may be interested in being part of what I call the community solution to spinal injury, through this funding solution. I'm very reliant on the telephone. I have a hands-free telephone headset, so I can just talk and still work away on my computer. I've got 200 memberships on my database where every detail about the member is recorded, with activity notes, follow-ups, revenue etc. So if I should depart tomorrow, somebody could pick that up and immediately see what's been happening and how to service them. We have a very comprehensive database of all 50,000 members.

As part of this exploratory process into employment or re-employment for people with disabilities, Tom elaborated a holistic approach. He outlined the need for an equipment and software assessment and provision plan, along with a training package, and then asked:

> What is the commercial potential of people within the quadriplegic community? And what are the personal and human benefits and most importantly what are the cost benefits to the community? When we talk about spinal injury, we estimate there's about 10,000 people in Australia at the moment with paraplegia or quadriplegia in a population of about 19 million/20 million. It increases at the

rate of about 300–500 a year and 250 of those will be quadriplegic. Therefore, we potentially have a very 'manageable problem' that is costing our society over $1 billion a year to fund. Therefore, the cost savings involved in us setting up a successful virtual community are very recognisable.

For him, there must be a cost-benefit statement to the community as an outcome of undertaking this process, as paraplegia and quadriplegia were the most expensive of all disabilities for society. Tom argued that it is a process that cannot be developed in isolation from people's other lifestyle needs. He acknowledged that it may not necessarily be cost justified in terms of achieving totally productive employment, but it could be recognised and reward those persons who showed less dependence on lifestyle support – even if they only managed voluntary work. Furthermore, he accepted that for some people with physical disabilities the notion of a virtual community or teleworking was not viable, because they were not interested in the technology challenge as a means of regaining active participation in their community. He said there was 'no point in trying to make people fit into typecast roles that they are not suited for'. However, Tom was very keen to put together a cost-benefit statement regarding the viability of virtual communities and telecommuting for the majority of persons with physical disabilities for presentation to government or funding bodies. He argued that without an understanding of the lived experience of marginalised people, many good ideas and potentially sound approaches and methodologies became perverted. For him, absolutely critical to the success of a test case for a virtual community and telecommuting, leading to its acceptance as a real model and subsequent wider implementation across the community, was to keep firmly in mind the long-term objectives.

- 'Clearly demonstrating that the model is a realistic representation of what a virtual community or telecommuting would look like if implemented more widely across the community.
- Ensuring the abilities and commitment of the participants involved (through ongoing nurturing and training).
- Making sure that the costs involved in the project are a realistic projection of the future costs of implementing similar projects as live working models within the community.
- Preparing an accurate cost-justification statement that includes both financial and human value benefits to the community.'

The EQUAL Telework Project (http://content.equaltelework.org/; info@telework.org.uk) is a site run by the UK Telework Association – a non-profit organisation set up in 1993 to encourage telework participation. The project provides background information and details of work for people who want to work from home. The information is mainly for people with disabilities and carers in the Leeds area as part of an EQUAL European Social Fund (ESF) supported project. In 1999, according to British Labour Force Survey figures, around 78,000 disabled people in Britain were teleworking, amounting to about 5 per cent of teleworkers (similar to the percentage of disabled people employed overall). A further 198,000 were unemployed. However, as of April 2003 the new UK Employment Act means that anyone with children aged under six years or a disabled child can request a variety of flexible working measures, including teleworking.

Merc@dis is another good example of the use of accessible web technology for the empowerment of people with a disability, helping them enter the Spanish labour market. It was launched by Foundation Telefonica at the end of 1999, and provides a virtual market of employment by internet. Most Spanish associations of people with disabilities are now involved in this project. Apart from offers and employment demands for people with disabilities, on the website (www.mercadis.com) it is possible to obtain information of interest for associations and employers. It is organised as a series of additional services: it allows access to and exchange of information on legal-fiscal aspects, grants, security in the workplace, risk prevention, workplace ergonomics, documents in a database and so on. An example of these services is the 'self-employment' section in which people with disabilities or groups of them give information about their professional activities, or the 'best practice' section containing case studies in employment and disability. After 18 months of operation the Merc@dis website had had more than 50,000 visits; 365 employment entities offered work; and it contained nearly 3,000 curricula vitae of people who were looking for employment. Up to 2001 more than 1,500 employee positions had been offered.[10] Finally, it is important to highlight that the Merc@dis website has received several prizes for its accessibility and design (Roe, 2001: 31–2).

While Australia does not yet have the equivalent of Merc@dis or the EQUAL Telework Project, early in 2005 the Australian Telework Advisory Committee (ATAC) was established to explore options and impediments to the development of telework for employees and businesses in Australia. This will have implications for people with disabilities, coupled with the Welfare to Work legislation that was passed on 6 December 2005. Furthermore, a national inquiry was launched in Australia on 4 March 2005 to address the low employment rate and earning potential for people with a disability. The inquiry's interim report, 'WORKability I: barriers' (Human Rights and Equal Opportunity Commission, 2005), found there were three sets of obstacles to higher employment rates: the lack of easily accessible and comprehensive information and advice; concern about the possible costs for employers and employees with disability; and the 'risk' factor or concern about the financial and personal impact on employers and employees if the job does not work out. People with disability represent a significant proportion of Australia's working-age population (16.6 per cent), yet they participate in the workforce at lower rates, are less likely to be employed when they do attempt to participate and will earn less if they do get a job. This has been the case for a long time, and indications are that the situation is getting worse.

A report,[11] 'WORKability II: solutions' (Human Rights and Equal Opportunity Commission, 2006), was tabled in the federal Parliament on 15 February 2006 in order to advance equal opportunity and more effective participation in the labour market for Australians with disabilities. The report recommends a national strategy to address various barriers as a matter of priority. Consequently, teleworking may become a more feasible opportunity for the employment of disabled people in Australia in the future, as it is elsewhere.

Barriers

There are both opportunities and barriers that emanate from all the categories discussed above. While the opportunities have been discussed individually for each category, the barriers (financial, physical, technological and social) are common to all categories, so for convenience they are aggregated below.

Sally, for example, was very cognisant of the use of ICT in online education, as well as the extra cost factors associated with training in and use of ICT and the associated necessary assistive technology for persons with disabilities. Sally said that it was the responsibility of people with disabilities to inform governments of their needs.

> The average person with a disability, who for instance might be on a low income, or may be on a disability support pension, has costs

that are over and above what their disability is – there aren't extra funds to allow for something like e-mail, or a modem, and so on. So a computer is seen to be quite a luxury when in actual fact a computer may be a necessary method of communication given that you live in a remote area or in a house that you can't get outside of.

Simon, in fact, saw ICT (and ultimately smart technology) as being the only viable way a person with a severe physical disability has of being employed, accessing the community and undertaking any valued role in the community. He, like Sally, did not see ICT as being a choice or a luxury for people with disabilities, but a necessity. They are both aware that the cost of this sort of technology was not factored into the additional living costs of people with a disability on a welfare benefit.

Online training was another contentious and difficult area for people with disabilities, according to Joe. Technical and further education (TAFE) courses were not necessarily available because of barriers like cost or inaccessibility. He urged people to utilise their local libraries for the free access to ICT, an e-mail address and internet searching. The major problems (apart from e-commerce) he had identified for those who were not technologically literate were being 'under-informed and missing out on social and other interactions'. Furthermore, he wanted to see people with disabilities mentor other such people wanting to gain online skills – he saw this as being very effective and empowering, and likened it to a 'ripple effect':

> They can go to all the government sites, all the legal sites. They can find out what their rights are. They can talk to people, they can workshop, they can discuss matters amongst themselves. They can actually get quite proactive. I've seen people organising national days of action on parking and whatever not, on the e-mail and it worked – it's a snapshot that governments can't ignore – [it] is quite a valid document which shows there's a problem.

Joe also has a very strong interest in any and all issues affecting people with disabilities – especially the digital divide, ICT, inclusion 'and our ability to actually run with the agenda for a change'. He, like so many, identifies the DD (which he sees as revolving around income and education) as a huge issue for people with disabilities – of whom some 58 per cent of working age are unemployed. As he says: 'They've not found the underlying causes of people being in those low income groups and low education groups, and it may well be that society has actually raised barriers up that prevent some people from moving forward, and there are other reasons of course. Not everyone in those groups has a disability by any means, but I think they'd be well and truly overrepresented.' Joe is cognisant of the barriers and extra costs associated with disability. Assistive software for a person with a disability is expensive and ISP costs can be prohibitive. If one cannot afford the broad bandwidth, PDF legislation files, for example, are very slow to download.

Assistive technology[12] (AT) is necessary for Bob to operate his computer. He uses a mouth-stick, as well as a track-ball and programmable keyboard. The term 'assistive technology' is used to refer to a broad range of devices, services, strategies and practices that are applied to ameliorate the problems faced by individuals who have disabilities (Cook and Hussey, 1995). Bob acknowledges voice-recognition software could be very useful instead of the AT that he uses, but the editing required makes it unattractive to him. What he really wants 'is to be connected to a headset or a radio that radios back to the computer, which would make me virtual (that is, independent) around the house'. He knows the wireless technology exists.

> It means you can take your computer and provided you're not too far from your base station you can pretty much work anywhere in your house and you're not locked into a little study. So that's got some great potential which takes us through to how virtual communities can work in real life. Wireless and extensions of that with technology can potentially connect communities. We just saw recently the Brisbane City Mall has gone wireless and so you can take your laptop, you can take it anywhere and sit it on your lap and be online whilst being part of the people environment.

Tom was introduced to technology very early in life, even though in those days it was very limited in delivering significant benefits for people with disabilities. He spent 28 years working for a large international information technology company – 17 years as an administration manager – and received many awards for excellence during that time. Before he left the company he tried (unsuccessfully) to convince it to fund a state-based adaptive technology centre for all of Australia, as it had done in the USA. Nonetheless, he may be credited with instigating the first adaptive technology in Australia for hearing-impaired children at a pre-school.

[The company] had introduced this software and the computer technology that would enable deaf kids to see how the spoken word looks when it's spoken correctly by the speech pathologist. The kids could then attempt to reproduce the sound patterns as they developed more legible speech. They could see the variation between their voice and the voice of the pathologist. The idea then being that it would encourage them to try to form words that they couldn't hear to achieve the most satisfactory response from the point of view of audible comprehensive sound.

Dan is acutely aware that more people with disabilities can now lead more independent lives and seek professional careers than ever before in history. However, as he puts it, it is about eliminating or minimising obstacles to living in the community and participating in the workforce. 'Technology is built into my life – so it's got to be simple to use.' The only assistive technology Marcie uses is a cordless keyboard and a cordless mouse.

The AT that Sam uses is a mouthpiece to access the computer and spreadsheet software, as he is unable to use his hands or arms. However, he does believe wireless and remote environmental control technology ultimately will be beneficial to him, if and when he could justify the costs. He has used mouse simulator and voice-recognition software in the past, but as he currently does not use word processing extensively, he believes it would not warrant the cost of his purchasing this software. Like many people with disabilities, he seemed to perceive voice-recognition software as an assistive device – despite the fact that he was particularly technologically aware and had published an article on the general effects of voice-recognition systems on writing styles and the implications for use in the education environment (Pell, 1998). Sam did not focus on internet connection costs as a barrier, but on the cost of specialised disability equipment as being quite prohibitive. From his past experience with voice-recognition software, he believes that to get maximum benefit out of it, you need to be using it consistently and over a long period of time. In order to use a mouse simulator, you need someone available in the office to attach it. Also, he commented, 'being in an office, people might think it's a little bit strange if you're talking to yourself'.

Innovations in AT are one key to successful community participation. Despite the assistance and promise of independence offered by many devices and the growth in AT options, the rate of AT non-use, abandonment and discontinuance remains high – on average about one-third of all devices provided to consumers. The single most important reason why devices are not used is lack of consumer involvement in their selection (Scherer, 2000). If the device meets the person's performance expectations and is easy and comfortable to use, then a good match of person and technology has been achieved. The perspective of the user must increasingly be the driving force in device selection, not the affordability of the equipment or the speed with which it is obtained. To reduce device discontinuance, non-use and abandonment, increasing attention needs to be paid to the disabled person as a unique user of a particular device. AT users differ as much personally as they do functionally. Functionality in use of technology is evident in all the interviews. Each potential user brings to the AT evaluation and selection process a unique set of needs and expectations, as well as readiness for use. To achieve better AT outcomes, these factors are ideally assessed so that the AT can be customised to the user, training and trial use of devices arranged and additional support identified.

Psychological readiness for technology use, or lack of readiness, is also a strong determinant of use. For many users of AT, their devices become an extension of self (certainly for Dan), not just for themselves but also as perceived by other people. The device is then incorporated into the individual's identity. This process can be difficult for some (for example, Jane), thus leading to underutilisation of AT. For an AT device to enhance a user's quality of life, it should be incorporated into the individual's accustomed routines and lifestyle and not introduce new, time-consuming and disruptive elements that are perceived as interfering with one's customary and desired activities. As outlined above, frequently little is understood of the needs of AT users and the quality of the outcomes achieved. Furthermore, while the Technology-Related Assistance for Individuals with Disabilities Act 1988 was introduced in the USA to create new funding systems for technology assistance (Galvin, 1997), there is no legislation relating specifically to the provision of AT in many Western countries. Consequently, AT resources/services are frequently fragmented and poorly funded, with uncertain futures (Smith, 1995).

Additional barriers Sam identified as detrimental for disabled people included lack of consideration of a person's individual needs, and whether training in groups in public libraries or at inaccessible TAFE colleges was desirable compared with the privacy of self-paced internet training and learning packages.

> Other than the physical disabilities, each person is individual and what works for me, what I've developed over the last ten years, isn't going to work for someone else. I think that's the big barrier for someone who is coming to use the technology: if you don't know what's possible then you don't know the right questions to ask, and you don't know the right sources to go and get the information.

He saw it as important that training in the use of computers and assistive devices was provided to people with physical disabilities at their point of rehabilitation, so they trialled the various devices before they faced society at large. 'The technology breaks down the problems that people with disability face. Technology being there, it's irrelevant whether someone is disabled or not. I think that a very large majority of people at work here wouldn't see me as disabled or even notice the chair any more. I'm sure they did initially.' Sam was aware of the lack of training in using the technology, and has written scholarly articles on the topic.

> Yes, definitely lack of training. A lot of people don't find the computer friendly, real user-friendly. You have to know how to use them and people have different learning styles. Some learn best by playing. The computer manuals are paper based, not computer based, and I guess in terms of training needed a lot of the training facilities just aren't set up for people in wheelchairs, because you do need higher desks and specialised software on the computer. They could be set up to be hospitable – the majority of places do their best to do it well, but if you need expensive desk renovations or assisted technology, it is difficult being able to open it to every person.

Marcie knows from her client experience that acceptance of the need to learn to use the technology can still be a barrier to be overcome initially. She suggests that TAFE courses may present yet another barrier if people have a physical impairment with which the tutors are unfamiliar. Furthermore, TAFE tutors would have no familiarity with assistive devices. She suggested that disability organisations might run small group courses for members who have not yet grasped using ICT. 'I think that's where I can see introducing it to people in a friendly environment could open up a lot of things for many people.' She also was concerned about costs and believes that 'it would be good if the government did have a discount for people with disabilities for internet use. Even if it's not a substantial discount, just some discount, because it can be a main means for us to communicate with other people, or get information.'

Keith, like Bob, saw technology for people with disabilities as a double-edged sword.

> I think the dangers of technology for people is that it can reinforce their isolation and that there can be some assumptions that people can only really have virtual relationships and that it can take the place of human contact and bonding and that intimacy isn't important. So I suppose, like everything, it has a solitary downside, I suspect. However, I certainly do think in the ways of overcoming some of the created man-made barriers, whether they be physical or attitudinal, technology certainly can be a vehicle to overcome some of those things.

A certain amount of space has been given recently in the literature to the risks of obsessive internet use or addiction. Only a small minority fall prey to this newest disorder. The literature tends to focus on the detrimental effect it can have on a person's life: research has revealed that people who spend too many hours at their computer increasingly withdraw from 'normal' social interaction with their family and peers (Young, 2004). Spending extended periods away from face-to-face interaction can affect people's ability to deal with real-life situations as opposed to cyberspace communication. The paradoxical effect of ICT in the lives of people with disabilities is a double-edged sword: on the one hand it 'overcomes' some mobility problems, but on the other hand too prolonged or too great a dependence on ICT leaves disabled people in danger of becoming addicted to the internet!

The two forms of communication are very different. Face-to-face communication involves many non-verbal forms of communication such as facial expressions, body language and learning how to respond to these non-verbal cues. These are not learnt while communicating using ICT. While accessing ICT is a positive activity (especially for people with disabilities), like everything in life a balance needs to be found so that the unhealthy possibility of becoming addicted does not occur.

Marcie thinks there are not enough websites available that are disability related, and would like them to specify their standards and criteria when they claim their venue is accessible. She believes that providing information of this nature to people with disabilities would relieve them of a great deal of stress. Marcie does not always find government websites especially easy to navigate for information, however, and frequently needs telephone confirmation.

> Probably one thing that I could find out more about is that when you do web searches I think that there are ways that you can learn to type in different words, that will let you search in ways that you can bring about better search results. I probably need to learn that because quite often I find I type something and it doesn't even come out basically what I'm looking for and that can be a little bit frustrating... So at those times I always try and find the information somewhere else, through phoning or some friends that I'd ring.

To Joe, the web is but one alternative of several media, and some people will choose not to go online and should not be disenfranchised for this choice. To give him the last word on this topic:

> My concern is that those who would go online, but are prevented from going online, get justice. But lots of people simply say 'I am not interested', and that's a valid choice. I don't need a television in my house but I would be an odd person if I didn't have one, but I don't need it. I don't have to have it. Now it's the same with the web; if they make that the only option for communication, banking etc., we are in trouble. Society is in trouble. We really need to make it an option. It's part of the solution, not *the* solution. It's a very useful tool, an extremely useful tool for so many people, but to rely on it wholly and solely disadvantages the many who will choose not to use it. When you only advertise for your positions online or when you only allow an internet banking service, you automatically lock out all of those people who have no idea of how to use it and no interest in using it. So that is a great inequity. The web cannot be overrated. It can't be underrated either, but it can't be overrated. It's not the answer. It's one more communication tool and it needs to be balanced against the existing communication tools that many people will, in some instances, much prefer.

Emerging theory or model

The primary research question that the present study sought to explore and analyse was 'how can virtual communities for persons with long-term physical disabilities best be facilitated?' The study also sought to develop a theoretical framework or model of 'best practice' for a virtual community for people with severe long-term physical disabilities. The population whose interviews are recounted in this chapter are a representative population. The procedures of theoretical sampling and constant comparison are allied with theoretical sensitivity, as has been described in the above processes (Strauss and Corbin, 1994: 280).

The well-being model for a virtual community for people with long-term, severe physical disabilities that emerged from the data collection and analysis based on the grounded theory methodology was a meld of six types of electronic communities: education-oriented, fantasy-oriented, information-oriented, interest-oriented, relationship-oriented and transaction-oriented, depending on the types of consumer demand. For the well-being model to be truly transformational, all six foci of virtual communities need to be built into portals developed for disabled persons. In fact, several of the above needs or orientations were met simultaneously. This possibility is presented diagrammatically in Figure 7.1. In the end it must be emphasised that if any one of these types of e-communities was ignored, the full virtual community experience would not be available to persons with disabilities. The findings also indicated that information and technological literacy enhanced access to the notion of a virtual community, while costs of connecting and various physical and technological aspects were barriers to a successful virtual community.

The proposed model differs from the Australian CONROD website Disability Lifestyles, launched in 2004, which provides a portal to seven key areas for those recently disabled: training, employment, recreation, transport, accommodation, personal support and relationships – of which only two overlap with the findings of this study. Each of the seven Disability Lifestyles key areas provides links to a variety of other relevant websites, and the primary aim of this website is to establish an online environment for people who are completing or have recently completed rehabilitation. Such people have vastly different and immediate needs from the needs of the long-term disabled relevant to the present study, who have already dealt with most of those basic lifestyle issues.

This work is unique in that a conceptual model can be developed that would provide the platform for building a virtual community that meets the specific needs of persons with severe long-term physical disabilities. The well-being model is innovative, sustainable and, if used to help guide the development and implementation of environments that support virtual communities, it would be likely to lead to reduced social isolation for people with physical disabilities and would be transferable across communities to some other disability types and timeframes. It is expected that this theoretical well-being model of 'best practice' would also contribute to the reduction of social isolation of other population groups, for example older people.

For the researcher and theorist, the experiences of opportunities and barriers obtained from the interviewee respondents, as well as the experience of the analysis itself, were affecting (Strauss and Corbin, 1994: 280). Each narrative was true, relevant and unique, and would be a rich source of motivation for other disabled users or potential users of ICT. The road to success is usually paved with setbacks, mistakes and enormous learning curves. In this study there are many inspiring examples of the ways people with physical disabilities have learnt to harness their personal strengths towards using ICT to gain 'a sense of control' in their lives again.

'Access' was a very important aspect of these findings. It was a component of functionality and technical specification, and contributed to both the dimensions and the subcategories. On the other hand, the interviewees identified four major types of 'barriers' to people with disabilities forming successful virtual communities: costs, and physical, technological and social barriers. Most of the interviewees were aware of barriers – including connection problems for rural and remote people, the 'isolation' double-edged sword controversy and the inaccessibility of chatrooms to people with physical disabilities. Other barriers included costs, because most people with disabilities have limited economic resources (Williamson et al., 1999: 9). Some cost barriers identified were the set-up costs for the hardware and software (for example, voice recognition), assistive technology, the ISP and the ongoing telecommunications or broadband cost. Some solutions to the cost barriers were suggested, however, such as cheap, recycled 'green' computers, or computers available from Brisbane City Council according to income/assets testing or from Technical Aids for the Disabled.

This analysis and findings provide the framework for the eventual well-being model. It is established to fulfil shortcomings and provide an appropriate model of a virtual community for people with severe long-term physical disabilities. The analysis and findings form the basis of the well-being model presented in Chapter 7.

Notes

1. The DEFIE (Disabled and Elderly People Flexible Integrated Environment) system is a UK multimedia integrated system that allows the elderly and motor- and/or sensory-impaired people to command and control domestic and working environments with a high degree of self-sufficiency and safety.

2. Due to the stigma, historically society has perceived disability in three main ways: moral, medical and minority. The first and oldest view is the moral model. In this view, disability is a defect caused by moral lapses or sins. It brings shame to the person with the disability and his or her family. They carry the blame for causing the disability. The medical model (or 'personal tragedy' model) began during the 1850s as medicine became more enlightened and humane. This perspective puts the person with the disability in the role of a patient who has a medical problem. The disability is a defect in, or failure of, a bodily system and as such is inherently abnormal, pathological and tragic. The goals of intervention are cure, treatment of the physical condition to the greatest extent possible and rehabilitation. The minority model gets its name from the view that persons with disabilities are a minority group. Like people in other minority groups, they have been denied their civil rights, equal access and protection. Key impediments for any minority group are prejudice and discrimination; these impediments are seen as major problems for those with disabilities. There is now a fourth way, according to Oliver (1990: 78–94), named the social model, which says that the problem of disability lies not within persons with disabilities, but as a social construct in the environment that fails to accommodate them and in the negative attitudes of people without disabilities. WWDA addresses disability within a social model that identifies the barriers and restrictions facing women with disabilities as the focus for reform. Shakespeare and Watson (2002) called for the social model to be overtaken by a more comprehensive approach.

3. The rules of the list are as follows.

   ■ The list is for items of interest to people with physical disabilities or associated individuals.

   ■ It is not to be used as a personal mechanism to communicate with individuals (reply off list in that case).

   ■ Delete previous messages that take up a lot of space in return e-mail, except the message replied to (e.g. sometimes people reply four or five times with four or five e-mails in the body).

   ■ No attachments are to be sent through the list to avoid viruses being passed on. If there are documents that people want, it is suggested they are sent individually or requested individually.

   ■ Respect one another's views and opinions.

   Messages are available in either traditional e-mail or by a daily digest that consists of only one e-mail.

4. Peer support is usually provided by someone who also has mobility impairment, is living successfully with it and has experience with handling the

same or similar situations. They are knowledgeable about living with severe mobility impairment and would like to pass this knowledge on. They provide information and practical advice gained from their personal knowledge and experiences. They are not healthcare professionals, professional counsellors or personal assistants/carers.

5. This access through TADAust Connect ISP is a 'dial-up' service now available for $5.50 a month – a service that usually costs $30–40 – with no set-up fee, no limit on downloads and no connect or disconnect fee, and is a local connect call on 1300 735 439 (toll-free across Australia).

6. The Australian Mobile Telecommunications Association (www.amta.org.au) includes links to AMTA's Disability Access webpage, as well as links to accessibility webpages maintained by industry members.

7. GSM mobile phone use may be 'out of a service area' for its provider and the 000 emergency number may not be reached. Dialling 112 from a GSM phone will enable the phone to access *any* service provider's network, and therefore vastly increases the possibility of getting through in an emergency. Further details can be reached from the Australian Communications Authority website (www.aca.org.au), following the links from 'Consumer issues' to 'Frequently asked questions', or direct via the URL www.aca.gov.au/consumer_info/frequently_asked_questions/emergency.htm#numbers. In areas where you are out of your service provider's coverage area but in another mobile carrier's coverage area, e.g. from anywhere overseas where there is GSM digital coverage, the call will be automatically transferred to that country's emergency number without having to key in a security protection personal identification number (PIN).

8. The Internet Society of Australia (ISOC-AU) (www.isoc-au.org.au) holds consumer consultation meetings. The aims of the consultation and discussion meetings are to foster consumer input into the development of the internet, fulfil the vision that 'the internet is for everyone!', ensure that maximum benefits flow to internet users as participants in society and the global information economy, and draw input from all relevant stakeholders and organisations.

9. Scientists led by Professor John Donoghue, a world expert in neuro-technology at Brown University in Rhode Island, used a computer to decipher the brain waves picked up by an implant. A severely paralysed man was the first person to be fitted with a brain implant (called BrainGate) that allows him to control everyday objects by thought alone. He uses a wheelchair and is unable to breathe without a respirator; doctors say he has no chance of regaining the use of his limbs. But he has become the first patient in a controversial trial of brain implants that could help disabled people to be more independent by tapping into their brain waves. Electrodes were attached to the surface of his brain, positioned just above the sensory motor cortex where the neural signals for controlling arm and hand movement are produced. Surgeons completed the operation by fitting a metal socket to his head so he could be hooked up to a computer. In early trials, the severely paralysed man learned to move a cursor around a computer screen simply by imagining moving his arm. By using software linked to devices around the room, he has since been able to think his TV on and off, change channels and

alter the volume. In the most recent tests, he was able to use thought to open and close an artificial prosthetic hand and move a robotic arm to grab sweets from one person's hand and drop them in another. Professor Donoghue hopes the implant will ultimately allow paraplegics to regain the use of their limbs. 'If we can find a way to hook this up to his own muscles, he could open and close his own hands and move his own arms,' he said (Sample, 2005). Research of this nature began in 1990 when Drs Philip Kennedy and Roy Bakay and a team of researchers created a basic but completely functional alternative interface using electrodes surgically implanted in the brain (Hockenberry, 2001).

10. By the end of April 2002 the Merc@dis website had had almost 75.000 visits; had 690 employment entities offer employment; contained 4,423 curricula vitae of people who were looking for employment; and had offered more than 1,500 work positions.

11. The report and other material from the inquiry are available at www.humanrights.gov.au/disabilityrights/employmentinquiry/index.htm.

12. The International Alliance of Assistive Technology Information Providers has used the term since 2003, when a memorandum of understanding was signed to increase knowledge sharing and networking internationally. Organisations from Italy, Denmark, Germany, Great Britain, Spain, the USA, Holland and France are part of the alliance (http://portale.siva.it/servizi/iaatip/default_eng.asp).

6

Findings from the narratives of the allied health/information/policy professionals: confirming the relevance of the emerging well-being model

The deconstruction, analysis and findings from the narratives of six allied health, information and policy professionals reinforced the in-depth interviews with the 12 people with physical disabilities discussed in the previous chapter. These further in-depth interviews revolved around the same one question: 'What can you tell me about your experience with persons with physical disabilities using virtual communities and how they use ICT both personally and professionally?' The professionals were also interviewed according to grounded theory principles: the interviews continued until 'theoretical saturation' of content occurred, as with the previous interviewees. This required six interviews before no new content emerged.

This chapter, phase 2 of the grounded theory analysis, has six components:

- the emergence and identification of themes and concepts;
- the central theme of 'a sense of control';
- the themes and concepts shared by the professional interviewees;
- the infrastructure barriers to participation for people with disabilities;
- the emerging theory, theoretical framework or well-being model;
- the methodological process employed in this study being evaluated and deemed trustworthy.

The six allied health, information and policy practitioners interviewed were professionals who had significant backgrounds in working with persons with disabilities in relation to using ICT. Again, pseudonyms have been used.

- A senior occupational therapist in a large teaching hospital (Jean: Interviewee 13).

- A manager in an assistive technology information centre (Clara: Interviewee 14).

- A university researcher (Barb: Interviewee 15).

- A project consultant for a telecommunications disability consumer representative group (Kerry: Interviewee 16).

- A manager in a specialist government post-rehabilitation health information service (Kate: Interviewee 17).

- A manager in a specialist government disability information service (Gerry: Interviewee 18).

Emergence and identification of themes and concepts

To reiterate Chapter 5, according to the grounded theory research methodology, 'phenomena' are the central ideas in the data, represented as concepts. Concepts are the building blocks of the theory. Categories are concepts that stand for phenomena; for example, in this study the major theme that emerged was 'a sense of control', which, as stated previously, initially surprised the researcher but on reflection made great sense. Properties are the characteristics of a category, the delineation of which defines it and gives it meaning. Dimensions are the ranges along which general properties of a category vary, giving specification to a category and variation to the theory. And subcategories are the concepts that pertain to a category, giving it further clarification, meaning and specification (Strauss and Corbin, 1998: 101).

Both Glaser (1978, 1992) and Strauss and Corbin (1990, 1998) described coding as an essential part of transforming the raw data into theoretical constructions of social processes (Kendall, 1999: 746). However, Glaser provided only two types of coding processes, substantive (or open) and theoretical; whereas Strauss and Corbin nominated three – open, axial and selective coding. Although they both used the two types of coding differently in their theoretical constructions and products, it was Strauss and Corbin's additional intermediary set of coding procedures (and possibly their paradigm model) that has proved to be so controversial. Although Glaser (1992) identified other differences such as the need for emergent conceptual analysis, the main controversy between the two approaches has focused primarily on the use of axial coding. This study has used open coding as the basis of the deconstruction and analysis process.

As indicated above, the central theme that emerged strongly when these 18 in-depth interviews were subjected to the open coding analytic process was that persons with long-term physical disabilities desired to regain 'a sense of control' over their lives. Increasingly, they have found that this concept of 'a sense of control' could be achieved by their use of ICT, and the professionals were as unanimous in their enthusiasm for the technology as the persons with disabilities. The other particularly significant themes to emerge from these interviews were the importance of education, the seeking of 'fantasy', the need for and use of information, 'interest', relationship and transactions. These six phenomena or concepts are the building blocks or cornerstones of the theoretical model or framework for a virtual community that would be useful to the users – people with long-term physical disabilities – and the facilitators of such communities. However, the degree to which these concepts were emphasised by the professionals varied from the emphasis given by the persons with disabilities.

As previously, another very important phenomenon or concept to emerge from the interview data was the notions of 'access' or 'accessibility' and 'barriers' to the success of a virtual community for people with long-term physical disabilities. The characteristics or properties of the 'barrier' category included costs or affordability, as well as availability and other physical and technological aspects of connectivity. The diversity and range of the barriers identified by interviewees that may limit successful use of ICT are termed 'dimensions' in grounded theory. They give specification to 'barriers' as a category in these findings, but add no significant variation to the theory or theoretical framework for a virtual community for people with long-term physical disabilities that emerged.

There are very crucial subcategories that also emerged from the analysis of these interview data. These include the necessity of a climate of 'access' by way of information literacy and technology literacy for users and facilitators of virtual communities for disabled people. Again, from this study it is such specific terms as awareness, mobility, social justice, inclusion, disability costs, empowerment, assistive equipment, technology literate, training, technology dependent, barriers (learning and technological), peer support, 'design for all', anti-discrimination and so on that give further meaningful clarification and specification to the phenomena, concepts and categories that emerged so readily from the professionals' interview data – as they did from the people with disabilities. All these aspects of the findings in terms of the grounded theory methodology will be developed more substantially in this chapter.

Central theme: 'a sense of control'

Again, the central theme that emerged from all the professional interviewees in this study into a virtual community for persons with physical disabilities, either overtly or implicitly, was that the use of ICT invariably provided 'a sense of control' for users. In assessing the value of the influences of technology, a virtual community and the choices offered to the clientele in a large teaching hospital, Jean (Interviewee 13) concluded that there were certain problems within the scope of the service. The staff in the specialist hospital unit found it really hard to make the time to achieve taking their clientele out into the real world for coffee or shopping – even though they encouraged this activity.

> It's kind of an informal observation, I think, I'd have to base my comments on – informal and very sort of individualised. There are some people that while they may be very effective with the computer and technology to enhance their virtual world and have a focus of control over activities like grocery shopping and do all their banking and the like – a lot of those individuals by their very nature are isolated from the world... Of course, that might not be an issue for them... I think that's where sometimes they still find there are barriers for some people to get a perception of how much they think is important for them to control or not.

Barb (Interviewee 15) tackled the issue of technology affording people with disabilities a greater sense of control from a slightly different perspective, and elaborated on her perception of the nature of that sense of control.

> I would think that would give people more control, because in the past people with disabilities have been dependent on service providers to give them information. They don't have to do that any more, because they can go and get a much broader range of information. They can actually access information from people who have similar life experiences, or a similar disability. So they get real-world information and then they're in a position to inform the service provider that what you're offering isn't what I need. Whereas before, they were only able to access or know of what was being offered and they weren't in a position to say, no thank you, actually what I need is something else.

She believes that it is when people have choices that they have the freedom to do more. If one does not have options, one does not have control – and technology can provide everybody, not just people with disabilities, with options. 'But if you can give people a range of options to choose from then at least they can direct the process in some way. So, communication devices I always felt was an area that really empowered people.' The professional notion of 'duty of care' she rated as possibly being very restrictive to the options that service providers may permit people with disabilities to have; she described this as a reflection of poor problem-solving.

> What became obvious to me as I talked to people is that people have the amazing capacity to take themselves where they need to go and some people need more control over that than others, but some of what's needed is not government and it's not service provision. What they need is the ability to make their own decisions about things and to use the personal capacity and their own social networks to achieve what they want to achieve. So sometimes service provision erodes that and we have to be really careful, us service providers, that we don't disconnect people from the supports that are going to be most useful to them and most powerful for them long term.

Barb's current research interests centre on the role of technology and environmental design in enabling people with disabilities to participate equitably in the community. She believes that technology in environmental design is now equally narrow and static as it was in reflecting the realities of mobility. For her, 'universal housing' and environmental design for people with disabilities was all about 'space', and space was about mobility and also about socialising. The current trends in universal housing and environmental design for people with disabilities have changed the nature of homes. When they were designed for people with disabilities they incorporated a very clinical-looking, open, cold environment. People with disabilities wanted exactly the same as anybody else in their homes.

> So what we're saying is, we want it to go back to being what a home should be. The first thing we need to find out is what people want out of a home. Do they want it to be cosy, warm and sort of encapsulating, or is it appropriate that they are simply given an open view and lots of large spaces? Let's get that right first and then look at what kind of compromises are necessary, because they are trade-offs. When you start designing for mobility and access, you do lose some of that feel that you get for a home. So let's find out what people want first and then these trade-offs become reasonable decisions that happen all the time.

Obviously this sequence of thinking about technology and environmental design in creating homes for people with disabilities was critical. People with disabilities particularly spend a lot of time at home and have many activities that are geared around the home. They do not want 'special facilities' or 'disabled facilities', but want to see features that are accessible because access has been mainstreamed by good design using universal design principles.

> Their social needs are no different to anybody else and in some ways they are even more important, because of the restricted options that people with disabilities have elsewhere. I don't know how you meet those in a virtual community or where a specialised virtual community is required, but I can imagine that they have a great need for creative expression. If that's channelled and exhausted in another way, it removes that need. But something that you have more control and more direction over could be quite useful. I'm just thinking that some of those webcam things, where you can go where you want to go, rather than doing what's on the schedule for that day, gives you a sense of control too.

Clara (Interviewee 14) said that technology such as voice output communication systems was designed to enable an individual to select a button or key or series of keys to create a message. The message was then spoken (and in some cases displayed on a screen or printed on paper). They include dedicated electronic communication devices (ECDs) or voice output communication devices (VOCDs) and specialised communication software for PCs and laptops. Computer access options refer to a range of strategies and equipment that are useful in assisting people with the difficulties encountered in using a computer, including alternative seating, positioning, keyboard, mouse and software options. Environmental control technology is equipment that enables people to control their environment when their ability to use standard methods of control has been lost or diminished. For example, specialised remote control devices are used in place of a number of standard remote controls and incorporate the on and off control of lighting and electrical appliances. Switch access provides a means of accessing a range of activities including communication, computers, leisure and environmental control. It is useful for people whose functional movement severely limits their ability to participate independently in such activities – an individualised switch set-up enables them to have some independence. Switch access is used in activities such as listening to music, working a computer or operating a communication device. A wide range of switches are available. For Clara, they were 'about enhancement, ability and to enable people to have as much control over their life, but I wouldn't rely on it in an emergency situation. Because you can't guarantee that it's going to be reliable and some of them may not be.'

The information professional Gerry began with a similar type of disclosure, or concept of empowerment, to the ideas mentioned above: 'I think really knowledge is a cliché, but it's also quite true, like knowledge is power. Like if you have good knowledge then the next step to greater power is to take life into your own hands really.' This is his philosophy for both his clients and himself. He argues that the specialist government disability information centre of which he is manager has witnessed a 'shift' in attitudes and values, in that its clientele are now seen more as having abilities as well as disabilities. He described it thus:

> Yeah, I think that's coming through more and more and I think the whole values sort of area is affected. But it finally comes down to somebody that they've got to change their values. And they're going to have to now because more and more people are going to have disabilities and the adage, if you want to have a good life sort of thing, is significant. The adage is in the community through the

technology stuff and through interaction with people and as other barriers are broken down and people interact, a lot of other barriers are being broken down towards people with disabilities.

Another of the interviewees, Kate, argued that people with disabilities find accessing a specialist government post-rehabilitation health information centre gives them a sense of control over their lives, and explained it in terms of the centre validating the information the disabled people have learned from their healthcare providers.

> Well, what I found working with people with spinal-cord injury is that they're in general a group of individuals who know a lot about their disability, but have a sense that in the wider community not a lot is known about it. So they often have to be the one to educate health professionals or the GP or the person in the street about what a spinal-cord injury is. So, for our purpose, I think we're really complementing the skills that a person is developing. Or, if they're at that stage where they're still evolving those skills, to be able to talk to service providers about what it is that they need, so that they can have a full, active participation in community life. That's really what our service is about. We're client directed and client focused in that sense, in that people tell us the information that they need or the assistance that they need and we try to facilitate, I guess, them linking in to whatever that is.

She also commented on how a client with a disability 'turned his life around with the use of technology, in that he has regained control over himself'.

These are a range of the comments extracted from the professionals' interviews to illustrate their awareness and concern for the 'sense of control' that the use of ICT afforded their clients with physical disabilities.

Themes and concepts shared by the professional interviewees

The additional themes or concepts of significance to emerge from these interviews, as in the previous interviews, were six major aspects: education, the virtual world or 'fantasy', the need for and use of information, the 'interest' that is derived from beliefs in equity and access for persons with disabilities, community awareness and relationship, and the transactions essential to living in the world of an e-economy in the information age.

Education

In assessing newly hospitalised spinal-cord-injured clientele, Jean looked at their abilities first, because she saw the basic environmental control unit as of foremost importance. It provided their initial independence in that institutional setting. In addition to this basic control unit, she looked to adding the personal computer. However, the first component that the occupational therapy (OT) staff sought to manage was the client's ability to operate the television or telephone. She says: 'You know, I believe in the philosophy of introducing people to technology. The earlier you can do it, is really important. The technology might influence someone's life, as simple as turning on the TV or whatever it is, So, to think about technology here within spinal injuries and rehabilitation, I'd probably look at it as different sorts of levels and in different ways.'

Jean's attitude towards the rehabilitation of persons with quadriplegia or paraplegia was that of starting a process of independence or empowerment in a way of thinking and a way of being for newly injured people: 'to plant a seed about what's possible for people whose independence is really important [because the staff] still face a lot of people who [are still adjusting to the injury and] have the attitude, if I've got to have a carer to cut my food up, why can't that carer turn the television on and off?' When the 40-bed hospital unit was originally planned and budgeted for, it was anticipated that every bed in the ward would have the appropriate technology so that the newly injured client would be able to adjust the bed and manipulate all the television controls. However, budget cuts prevented the installation of this technology. Subsequently, some commercially available independent technology for control of the unit's televisions was introduced, so the mobilising and rehabilitation process could start immediately after the spinal-cord injury.

The newly injured clientele were not offered the opportunity to use a computer until they had begun to mobilise, and then the technology was perceived as a rehabilitation or therapeutic tool in that it was used as a medium for arm-strengthening. As a result the computer was employed mainly for playing games; it was not perceived for its role in a return to work or as a communication aid at this stage. If the person had only head movement, they were taught firstly to operate low technology such as a switch for a page-turner before the computer was even considered. So, according to Jean, 'it's all about strengthening and control... so that they actually learn to be able to sit up in their wheelchair for more than ten minutes... I don't know that it's reasonable or realistic to expect at this stage of people's rehabilitation that they be trained in how to use a computer, or maybe being fully trained up in voice technology.'

Frequently, the hospital-based OT staff took their clients out to other disabled people's homes very early in the rehabilitation process so they actually saw how various technologies were used, 'just to see how people have their workplace and see how they use some low-technology solutions like workdesk design and more keyboards and simple sort of options like that, that actually can have a big impact on, you know, their workability. So you know, exposing people as much as possible to those individuals out there who are actually using technology, I think is really important.' The staff invited speakers, ran technology expositions and generally talked about the positive impact technology had in the lives of disabled people, as well as showing people with disabilities examples of what they did and expected to do with the technology. They wanted these projects 'to have an [ongoing] life' for the unit's clientele and not just validity for the one project:

> the push is so much to get people home. So the priority has to be given, what is it this person needs in order to get them home? To get them home and to get them home safely, they need to have a wheelchair. They need to have a hoist, they need to have a shower chair, they need to have a mattress. But they don't need to have a computer necessarily and they don't need to necessarily have environmental control and so, in that sense, we are in a way given our priorities.

If and when the client is ready to move to a higher level of quality of life, and where it can be demonstrated that it would impact positively on their personal sphere, the transitional rehabilitation programme (TRP) is the next step. Its role is to consolidate the opportunities and experiences begun in the hospital unit, 'because it's the seed that happens here. It's not the extensive skills.'

Clara is another OT who has worked in the area of assistive technology options to enhance ability for clients with disabilities for the past 16 years. During that time she has also been actively and regularly involved in a range of professional development activities to ensure currency of the information.

> Well, I think technology really is the door for people being able to demonstrate and use their abilities. The other side, I guess, that you know, so many people are limited in what they can do simply because they don't have the physical function to perform a lot of things that we do in our everyday life. To be able to sign a signature, to be able to go around to the bank, to be able to make a telephone call... It's just so great that people can come in when they've not been able to do very much and just go out and decide on the equipment or setting the equipment up... And it's very much a focus on ability, you know.

She worked extensively with Val (Interviewee 12), a person with severe disability and the developer of the Disability Forum website. She believed that this 'just opened up so much for her... and she's such a capable lady. Fortunately, she's persistent enough and she's assertive enough to try and find a solution herself. Well, I would hope that it would make her feel like a fully human being. More able to express herself, I would hope. And I would hope that it would give her more enjoyment in her life and a sense of control over her life.' While the assistive technology centre staff members were committed to the technology, they also realised the value of knowledge sharing between people with disabilities:

> we wanted to be part of that loop... It's much bigger than they initially expected... but really it's going to be shaped by the people who use the forum. It's an online community, so whether they want to share, it will grow and develop. But it's about sharing information and it's to make them, to empower them more and to value them. To value their knowledge, to value their input, I think is the word and that's the way we put it – the knowledge they want to share with others.

Clara also contrasted the abilities and motivation of Val, the web developer, with many of the assistive technology centre clients. As she observed, Val was self-reliant in her information seeking, used a diversity of information sources and was completely empowered to take charge of how she found information herself. 'I mean that's where people are really disadvantaged because they just don't have the means of finding out and even just about everything in their life is over to somebody else... You could, you know, communicate with friends and family yourself, without relying on somebody else to do it for you. I think that's, that really puts people at a very big dependent package.'

According to Gerry in his role as an information professional:

> probably about in the last 18 months, we've become increasingly aware of the advantages of information technology. So we've kept a close eye on the amount of things on our database and we do record the number of e-mail requests that come in, and even over 18 months, they've increased significantly. Yeah, and with that increase, we find that the source area of those calls has also increased. Yeah, well it used to be more phone calls generally, to be quite frank. You'd get the odd one from interstate and very rarely one from overseas. Now, we find we get a lot more e-mails from people who are living across Australia and even people living in England and in other countries who are wanting to find out information about how good the access is here in Queensland.

He wanted to see any and all relevant existing websites or virtual communities linking their pages and information into his specialist government disability information centre's database. It had plans costing some A$12 million for improving its database and making it more interactive so clients could provide feedback on the government disability information and referral service. In fact, a new sort of disability information system had been proposed, integrated across the whole of the government department, and the disability information centre's database was to become part of the new system. Gerry considered these changes appropriate, because the culture of doing business, such as online banking and online transport timetables, was changing rapidly. Nonetheless, he and his staff discussed whether these plans were 'a legitimate strategy or is it something that's bound to reinforce somebody to stay at home and not get out, you know', Ultimately, the government disability information centre was to be responsible for the information content and the actual website conforming to Web Content Accessibility Guidelines.

As Kate said in relation to her small post-rehabilitation health information service:

> We're really working with people who have a lot of experience of their disability, so they basically teach us a lot and we're able to

then pass that information on to health providers and services... back in '95 we undertook a needs assessment, and we contacted people with an injury, their families and service providers and asked them what they wanted in a service. And one of the biggest issues was that the spinal-injuries unit is located in Brisbane and people live basically all over the state, so they wanted access to information about using, changes, or problems that they were experiencing. Information they thought wasn't available in their local area, either because people didn't know how to access the resources that were in the local community, or they felt that once they had tried to access their local resources there wasn't the knowledge base and so they didn't have confidence. So we set up our model to say that we need to have a state-wide focus and we need to make that as accessible as possible to people wherever they are. But we also need to acknowledge that Queensland is a big state and we're only a team of seven-and-a-half people. So how were we going to do that? By setting up a system of having a webpage, having a free-call telephone number, having kind of e-mail and internet access was going to be vital for us, so really without that sort of communication infrastructure we would've just been viable. We do 12 regional trips a year and videoconferences are our other mechanism for sort of getting information, or using the regional Telehealth Network.

Most of the work was done on the telephone and by e-mail, providing consultancy and advice to those who wanted to access services in their local communities. The team still explore how to do that effectively without seeing somebody face to face, and regard it as very much an evolving process. All their work had been on an individual basis so far. They had set up a group to provide a rudimentary kind of virtual community, but it was informal; this area would interest them in the future. They had established an evaluation framework, and tried to incorporate some process measures into some of their outcome measures. They did satisfaction telephone surveys with clients on the post-discharge follow-up service.

The post-discharge follow-up service involves people who have been discharged from hospital admission at the spinal unit. We telephone clients at one month, three months, six months and 12 months. We go through a set pro forma of interview questions, so it's essentially qualitative and we ask them how they're going, and that's done by the social workers on the team. So they get a satisfaction survey basically when they've had at least three telephone calls about how they found that service. We also do a satisfaction survey with our general client group who are just accessing our consultancy and advice and we do one with people, those providers who contacted us for advice and for anybody who's participated in one of our education and training activities. We also use a goal attainment scaling. So for a percentage of our clients we look at what it was that their goal was when they contacted our service and whether we have achieved that goal and at what level. People are generally polite when they answer satisfaction surveys. So they're good in one sense, but you can't really rely on that as an indicator of how well your system is doing, so your goal attainment scaling is something that we've tried to use to be a more objective measure. It still has a subjective component to it because we're providing the goals with the person, so it's what they perceive is important to them at that time and it's their perception of whether or not that's been achieved at the end of it. And then we've got some other timeliness measures, you know, of what our response time is. Whether or not we're really meeting our goal of being a service that's accessible across the state.

The post-rehabilitation information service team, as part of their consultancy, are involved with education and training from an adult learning perspective for both their client group and the service providers. From their needs assessment exercise, they established that people do not necessarily know what information they are going to need, so they want to be able to access the post-rehabilitation health information service as issues arise for them. This specialist information service has a website that has been available for four years. It gets over 50,000 'hits' a year from around the state, on the government health intranet and via the public internet, and has a range of information on resources. The service has also prepared a kind of product guide. Over 1,000 people come through its online education sessions every year; most participants in these sessions are outside the 200-kilometre radius of the capital city and so are used to using the Telehealth Network. It is a really efficient way of providing information to a client group who are seeking independence and self-reliance. As Kate explained:

So, over time, we've developed a catalogue of in-service topics that we offered in the past. We asked people what they wanted and they were things like cushion prescription, how to access community resources, the adjustment that people might go through after spinal-cord injury, sexuality, pain, skincare. Skincare is a really big one for us, because that's a major, you know, complication after spinal-cord injury. It really has a huge cost to a person's life, because they really can't get up in the chair and have got to stay off an area and end up with lengthy hospitalisation and all sorts of things. So, we now have a library of things for when people ring us… We have a timetable of 12 regional trips every year and we publish that on the website and we do an annual newsletter in January of each year, so we advertise our timetable through that. So people know when we're coming and they can think about what issues are current. We also use the Telehealth Network to do our videoconference programme and we do like I think it's 16 topics, 16 conferences of eight topics every year, and this year the topics are things like sexuality, the spinal-cord injury, adjustment after spinal-cord injury. We're doing some stuff on pressure-releasing cushions, health, and wellness was a new topic that was introduced last year that was very successful. So, it's really an evolving roadmap.

Virtual activities or fantasy

Barb investigated the barriers and facilitators to people with disabilities when integrating assistive technology into the workplace as part of a research project. She was interested in 'who was using technology and how well they were using it, and what kind of process they went through to acquire their technology'. According to her:

What I liked about technology, it acknowledged that this is the given, so how can we enable people to be part of society and how to engage in the activities that they wanted to engage in through technology. It had a lot of potential. Whether it was environmental control that allowed them to have full control over how things happened in the home, or whether it was communication technology that allowed people who have indistinct voice or limited capacity to produce vocalisations a capacity to talk with other people. And increasingly then, what computer technology enabled people to do, initially in the first stages of being able to access education, and then employment, but then there's the birth of the internet technologies... Therefore, in terms of just being able to use the technologies to accommodate the impairment with assisted technologies that allowed them access to computer technology... so that they could get out in the community now – either in reality or virtually.

Furthermore, she argues that the workplace helps most of us by pushing the technological boundaries, so that we do not become isolated from the virtual world as it continues to grow. 'But that technology as it exists offers so much. And whilst they may not have a need for, or understanding of, how powerful that technology is, it's vital for people with disabilities to be informed of that fact. Often they're disadvantaged from that kind of information, because they might not have the financial resources to access that kind of technology.'

She, too, was cognisant of the fact that virtual activities and the virtual community have the potential to isolate people with disabilities further and keep them homebound. However, she chose to focus more on the opportunities it offered to the community.

[To] be able to plan your day, because you have information about how accessible and what's accessible... And the potential to have contact or encounters with people who aren't disabled through networks where your disability is invisible. So you can have conversations with people who you wouldn't necessarily encounter in the circles that you mix in. But also, if you want to talk to someone who is encountering similar frustration or similar issues, you can also do that through virtual communities as well. So you can share resources and share experiences, I guess. And I know that that's in some ways a virtual community and less physical contact, but to do that physically would cut down the number of encounters people have. And therefore, people have a broader range of options open to them.

Another aspect Barb felt was important was the way that comprehending mobility has expanded during her professional life. She had come to understand that a lot of assistive devices were really designed to accommodate a loss of function. In other words, the designer did not necessarily have an understanding or a vision of what a person with a disability aimed at doing. So, for example, a wheelchair was something that replaced walking. However, as she explained, that was not necessarily how we really mobilised. Invariably wheelchairs were designed to replace walking on a flat, smooth-glide surface, but in fact most surfaces are neither flat nor smooth.

> So really, if you give somebody a wheelchair that replaces walking, you've not increased their choices. You've actually restricted their choices, because you've just given them the capacity to move across small, flat surfaces, and mobility is about choices. I can go upstairs, I can go to the beach, I can go on a bush walk, and so if technology is well designed, it should offer people the ability to engage in a broad range of mobility activities.

If the technology could not be designed to cope with more than replacing basic loss of function in the most limited sense, it is easy to understand the attraction of the options that virtual reality offers people with disabilities.

> We have such a very narrow view of what technologies should offer and that's tied with this rehabilitation notion that we're replacing your lost function, but it's not a very real view of what it is people want to do. Therefore, what the technology needs to be able to do is to act for them in order to do those things. I don't know how long it's going to take before this experience will be possible.

It became easier to conclude that the virtual world and the physical world are becoming intermingled; in fact, frequently they are no longer the separate places they once were. This intermingling or lack of separation between the two worlds has certain obvious advantages for people with disabilities. The interviewees expressed this eloquently.

Information

Most of the research to date into people with long-duration spinal-cord injury has been from a physical and functional perspective rather than investigating how they can use the available technology to enhance the quality of their lives (Coutts, 1998). Jean believed it was likely that there were many people with long-duration spinal-cord injury who were not aware of the benefits of environmental controls or ICT. It was part of the roles of the specialist government post-rehabilitation health information service and the assistive technology information centre to make persons with disabilities aware of the new technologies. But some disabled people are not even aware of the post-rehabilitation health information service or the AT information centre. This deficit has to be solved before the new technologies can be promoted fully to people with disabilities – and then they have to be able to afford to purchase, maintain and upgrade them.

The AT information centre is a non-profit, non-government community organisation and the only specialised service of this type. It does not sell any equipment, nor is it aligned with only one equipment range or supplier – all suppliers are invited to display their relevant equipment. This service has a comprehensive range of state-of-the-art AT equipment, including alternative computer input devices, voice output devices, accessible hardware and software, electronic and wireless environmental control systems, switches, switch-operated equipment and positioning equipment. Both speech pathologists and occupational therapists staff the centre, specialising in the provision of professional, impartial advice, consultation and education about AT options. This consultation and information service enables people with disabilities, and those who support them, to trial a range of equipment options, customised to their individual needs and goals. Consequently, they are able to make an informed decision about the AT equipment options that best meet their individual needs, goals and physical limitations. In fact, this information centre has a referral process that is open to anyone wanting to explore AT options, including people with a disability, their family members, carers or their service providers. This is necessary, because as Clara said: 'They've got no chance of even knowing that there's something that could make their life easier or give them more choices, and their service providers don't know either.'

As defined in the previous chapter, the term 'assistive technology' is used to refer to a broad range of devices, services, strategies and practices that are applied to ameliorate the problems faced by individuals who have disabilities (Cook and Hussey, 1995). The AT information centre focuses on four areas: voice output communication devices, computer access hardware and software, environmental control systems, switches and switch-operated equipment, and positioning equipment necessary to support their effective use. The manager of this section finds they actually focus primarily on communication devices rather than environmental control systems, 'because for someone who can't communicate, they've lost all control there, haven't they?'

As this study is into a virtual community for people with severe long-term physical disabilities, and as ICT is the enabling vehicle, it is most appropriate to consider the AT information centre's computer access for people who are experiencing difficulty using standard computer equipment and are also seeking aids to independent living. People find operating a computer difficult for many different reasons (Seiler et al., 1997). According to the AT information centre, modifications to standard computer equipment and/or the use of modified techniques, including individualised set-up and positioning, help overcome some difficulties experienced by people with disabilities and are the first point of intervention. Sometimes there are simple strategies, and altering the position or height of the keyboard and/or the mouse is all that is required to enable a person to use a computer more efficiently.

> Yeah, trying to find a match from the range... I mean it's not always stuff that costs money, but it may be something that is standard software and the way they're positioned in relation to the equipment. Whatever, but we hope that we'll find a match within that person's available equipment, to a part of their life, every day. Quite a portion of their day may depend on what they're using equipment for. So therefore they push it to the limit and they find out a lot about it. So we try to match technology with people... and we try to expand it out, but you learn so much more from them, because I mean they're so good at finding out what suits them and they're always looking for more information on it.

Some people with disabilities require the use of specialised equipment as well. The best equipment for them to use is decided by the provision of information and advice on a range of options and, wherever possible, an individualised trial of the equipment. Of course, simple strategies of use are also teamed with non-standard or specialised equipment options for people with disabilities: 'They're things that don't cost anybody anything that can make a world of difference in the way someone uses something... We realise that it's not all about high end and high tech.'

Keyboard options include enlarged key areas, reduced-size keyboards, programmable keyboards, ergonomic keyboards and on-screen keyboards. Accessories are available for both standard and alternative keyboards, including a variety of stickers that are useful for enhancing the visual clarity of keyboard displays or key-guards. They are beneficial for some people who experience difficulty in targeting keys accurately. There are also various mouse options for people who have difficulty using a standard mouse, including trackballs, track-pads, joysticks and remote sensor units. Software is available to assist with specific mouse functions (for example, dwell – keep pointer still – for a set period of time and the software produces a mouse 'click', replacing the need to do this physically). There is also switch-operated scanning mouse software available.

If a person with disabilities is unable to use any keyboard options, speech-recognition software is a suitable option. This software is not specifically AT: it recognises the words spoken by a person and translates them into text or commands for the computer to carry out. As the software is quite complex, it is considered carefully for its suitability and back-up options (for example, an on-screen keyboard). The current versions have improved significantly with regards to both the training and operation of the software. Desktop USB microphones are also now available and are useful for people who are unable to position a standard headset microphone independently.

If a person with disabilities has difficulty in using standard computer software programs for any reason, there is a range of specialised software available that caters for a variety of needs and skills. Examples include word-processing software that speaks out what is typed or displays text and symbols. There is also access-enhancement software that enables text to be predicted or completed to reduce the number of keystrokes required. This increases typing efficiency and/or improves endurance. Specialised software for switch users or even those with literacy or numeracy difficulties is available for learning activities or just for fun. These are just some of the many ways in which computer use is assisted. Central to any computer access solution is also the positioning of both person and equipment. Each individual person with a disability requires a unique mix of techniques and/or equipment that enables her/him to be successful at using the computer.

Before Barb became a researcher she was involved with establishing the technology service at the AT information centre in 1989 (before Clara began there) and was an active member of the team for eight years.

> The centre wanted to set up a information system for people with disabilities around technology, because they had established systems for telling people about what kind of assisted devices existed in other areas, but not in technology. So I started there and helped to establish the information technology advice and assessment centre... I worked there as an occupational therapist to help people identify what their requirements were and to inform them about the range of technologies that existed, and to help them evaluate which technologies were going to be useful to them.

Barb realised very early in her career as an OT that if people with disabilities are to have 'successful' lives, they need to know specifically what they need and be able to use the 'system' to get it. Otherwise, the only way their needs are going to be met is by encountering a really well-informed service provider in that system who advocates directly on their behalf. So, to her, 'success' is a threefold activity of 'informing people with disabilities, or their service providers, about how to use the information, where to get information, and how to evaluate that information that is important'.

A different type of 'information' professional was Kerry, an information project consultant. She was asked by CONROD in Brisbane to investigate information usage by people with physical disabilities. This was ultimately to become the website Disability Lifestyles – the follow-up to the seminal *REHADAT Australia National Disability Database Linkage Project: Final Report* (Centre of National Research on Disability and Rehabilitation Medicine, 1998) originally mentioned in Chapter 1.

> What we did initially was an information-gathering exercise, I suppose. Using a variety of methodologies, we used some ethnographic studies, we used focus groups and we used telephone interviews and we contracted Patricia B., who is a well-respected social science researcher, to undertake this work. And the ethnographic studies were the most detailed piece of the work and there were approximately ten people who we studied, or she studied, and we had permission to go into their own homes and to see how they had their computer set up. Where it was in the home, how they used it, how they related to that computer and the programs they used. And so we asked them basically how they found particular information on the internet and they had particular tasks that we asked them to do.

In their 2003 investigation, Kerry indicated that the consultants' interest was in the process.

> We did ask them about particular websites they were interested in or found useful... but we were very interested in what type of search strategies they used, yeah, that sort of thing and how successful they were in using those. So we asked them first to search for something using a method they knew and then we asked them for other particular information. And so the idea was to see

first of all how they found information and also to observe them while they were doing this, where they had problems and so forth, and that was taped and there was also observations. And then we had focus groups. One in Adelaide and one in Brisbane and a very small one in Cairns looking at just discussing basically how people found information and also communicating online.

In 2004 CONROD launched the website Disability Lifestyles (see Chapter 4) based on the outcomes of the report and subsequent investigations. Its primary aim is to establish an attractive online environment for people who are usually young and coming out of rehabilitation.

They talk about their lives, how that's changed them. Frustration, satisfaction, where they saw their future going and so forth, and we tried to portray it in a way to be realistic. Not to be unrealistically positive, because everyone has frustration, but to say there is light at the end of the tunnel. And I think that is a really important message, that the Disability Lifestyles website is trying to get through, is that people who have been in a spinal-injuries unit for a long time are probably given a lot of information, but they are not ready to receive it. And so they might have gone out in the community and then they say, oh my goodness, what do I do now? And so the idea then is that they can log on to this website and just sit there and read at their own leisure, short snippets. It's not going to be totally in depth, there are links to other organisations where they can get better information if they like. This is a starting point, a stepping-stone for them, and the last important part of all this is a discussion forum and the discussion forum is an opportunity for anyone to have their own say. So something that they've read about on the website might trigger them to react and say, oh yes, that didn't work out for me like that, it happened like this instead. So they might want to provide some of their personal experience or they might have a question or whatever.

Gerry was regarded as a more traditional informational professional; his role is to provide central support and coordination to various government disability programmes that deliver information (2003–present). He also manages their specialist disability information service. Prior to then, between 2000 and 2003 he was an information officer for the specialist disability information service in a government department, providing information about services and support that assist people with a disability. He concluded: 'Yeah, I'm pretty comfortable with my knowledge and comfortable with trying to find out information, yes.'

Anyone who wants to know about support and services for people with a disability can call the information service using a range of contact numbers during standard business hours. The information officers are trained to provide up-to-date information to people with a disability, families, friends and carers, support workers, other professionals, community organisations, students, volunteers and anyone in the general community. This specialist service also is responsible for diverse publications covering news and events, information about the parent government department's support and services, key projects and community involvement. Gerry said:

> My involvement is from an information service point of view, particularly targeting people with disabilities, that's all types of disabilities. So predominantly a request for information comes in over the telephone and through e-mail [the commonest form of request] or sometimes for written information. We found a trend in the information service for increased usage of our website and e-mail facilities, purely out of convenience I'd imagine, because not everybody's got time between 9 and 5 to ring somebody up and talk on the telephone. So we've been receiving a lot more requests for information on e-mail and we also tend to be directing people who we do speak to on the telephone to go to our website and they can utilise the databases there. So if in future they want more information, they're aware of where it is and how to access it, rather than having to call us between 9 and 5.

The specialist disability service is a free information, resource and referral service available throughout the state. The type of information available includes details of services for people with a disability and information about different disabilities (physical, intellectual, sensory, psychiatric, neurological and learning difficulties).

> [The service] very generally is conscious of the disempowered status of people with disabilities... There is an underlying principle or value to things in [the information service] that the department's thought about. These are dealing with people with disabilities and the fact that they have the same rights and responsibilities as

anybody else. And it's having the right to lead your own life, yeah. I guess under that broad vision umbrella, we relay information to those who want it and the language that is used and encouraged is to help people make their own call in life.

Information is available through journals, newsletters and government publications. It is presented in the form of student factsheets, information kits and information on trends, philosophies and legislation. The specialist disability service has information about all services – government and community-based – including accommodation, employment, transport, respite care, recreation, independent living, education, advocacy, community access, family support, lifestyle support and post-school options. The staff have a mix of professional and life experience, communication ability, values and attitudes.

We have a person who had a spinal-cord injury about 15 years ago. He also conducts a lot of our disability information and training sessions for quite a lot of firms and a range of government and non-government organisations. So yeah, that one person has knowledge about wheelchairs for spinal injury and another person has cerebral palsy. She has worked in the families and disability area for probably about ten years. I guess she uses her own personal experience and understanding. There's another one who primarily has worked with people with intellectual disabilities and their families over the past couple of years and another person who works for people with psychiatric disability and mental health problems and she's also worked for the Commonwealth around the area of ageing. So we've got between us four staff a good mix of both professional and personal experience in working with groups and different people, yeah. A professional qualification as such, it might help, but it's not the priority.

The information people frequently seek that immediately springs to mind, according to Gerry, involves 'issues around access and accommodation. That could mean anything from people looking for permanent accommodation which is accessible – I cover real estate agents who might specialise in this area – and any particular services that assist people with disabilities to find accessible or purpose-built accommodation.' Other types of access-related information concern parking permits and holiday accommodation – especially sought by people who live interstate or overseas and use a wheelchair for mobility, and tourist companies or tourism providers which specialise in coordinating holidays for people with disabilities. Information about access and accommodation for people with disabilities covers a range of needs, such as train travel and sleeper accommodation and holiday support and carers. Sometimes broad advocacy information is required when an accessible toilet is non-existent, hidden away or not well planned. 'We'd direct them, in some cases, to perhaps even the Anti-Discrimination Commission or something like that. So yeah, the information service isn't about directly solving everybody's problems, unless it's about putting them in contact with the appropriate organisation.' Sometimes the access information request is from business. Gerry disclosed:

> Slightly off track, but I've been getting a call from a person who is setting up a, you know, one of those girl lap-dancing type of nightclubs and he wanted to make sure it was accessible. I was very impressed, yeah... So from my experience over the last few years I've seen a pleasant increase in awareness amongst the building industry to consider accessibility.

Access information takes many forms, for example:

> Like people wanting to get more involved in arts and choirs and singing and not knowing where to go. There's an increased sort of awareness in dramatic clubs that would be able to include people with disabilities. Yeah, we've had a number of people with a mindset that they should be in a choir for people with disabilities and so on. So it's good to explore different options for people in that way too.

Disabled people also seek employment, and this invariably has access implications. They are sometimes looking for permanent home assistance through community health, especially if they have been discharged from hospital recently. 'It's sort of like the calls where maybe the social worker in the hospital hasn't quite been thorough enough or had the opportunity to have enough contact with that person.' If, for example, what is required is information on where to obtain a wheelchair, Gerry perceives the role of the specialist information service is to provide a broad overview of the equipment. Then they assist the person in making contact with the AT information centre, where they receive individual advice and may trial the equipment. The range of information provided by the professionals to persons with disabilities is diverse, yet specific to both parties' abilities.

Interest

The 'interest' concept or theme examined in this section was derived from the range of research that many of the interviewees had undertaken or were pursuing into the needs or outcomes of persons with disabilities. The basis of the research invariably was derived from the respective researchers' beliefs in social justice, equity, access and participation for disabled people.

Following on from some of her earlier projects and as part of her ongoing commitment to working with and on behalf of persons with disabilities, Kerry began writing articles about web accessibility. She was then involved with some of the early work of the World Wide Web Consortium (W3C) and the web accessibility initiatives, 'because it was very clear that as the web moved from a text-oriented type of interface into the Windows interface, people who were blind or vision-impaired really had less opportunity to use the information... for them to lose it by having this particular graphical barrier placed in front of them was a real problem'.

Currently, Kerry is contracted to the organisation Blind Citizens' Australia (www.bca.org.au) as the policy adviser for TEDICORE, which has representatives from all the disability sectors. On behalf of TEDICORE she has ongoing input into government and industry reviews, inquiries and codes' and standards' development (Astbrink and Newell, 2002b). She initiates issues of concern relating to disability and communication technologies and seeks to raise awareness around these issues and provide information to people with disabilities and disability advocacy organisations, which then pass the information on to their members (Astbrink, 2004: 29). In 2004 she worked on an industry code on the provision of information from suppliers and manufacturers of telecommunication products and how they were to convey it to carriage service providers. There were also guidelines on accessible phone features to be determined in 2004–2005. The HREOC had a telecommunications forum at the end of November 2003, including key stakeholders from government, industry, regulatory bodies and people with disabilities, to discuss the key issues and concerns (Astbrink and Newell, 2002a). As she said:

It's a long and slow process, but we work to try and achieve a little bit each time and be it payphones, be it web accessibility, be it accessible phones, whatever it might be and just the way information is provided to the consumer. All of those things, they take time. But if we can encourage industry and government to consider accessibility and make them more aware of what people with disabilities really want, then we should have a community that will become more easily able to communicate with each other as time goes on.

Kerry has published many articles and given papers at Australian and international conferences on the internet, accessibility and disability. Early in 2004 she was invited by the Centre for Global Communications in Japan to speak at the Asia-Pacific Symposium on ICT Accessibility. She was elected in 2000 as a director on the board of the Internet Society of Australia and continued to serve into a second term. In a sense, her philosophy regarding the value of ICT for persons with disabilities is summed up by the following:

they are seen as equals. And that really makes such a difference, that people don't look at the physical person in front of them. They look at what's inside of that person and that to me I think has incredible value, and it means that people potentially can gain more confidence in expressing themselves, communicating better, broadening their interests. They might develop new hobbies, they can communicate with people not only where they live in their own town but anywhere in the world, and so this broadening of horizons and being able to communicate freely without prejudice I think is incredibly valuable. And that to me would be one of the chief aids, I suppose, of having virtual communities. Not specifically disability-oriented virtual communities, but any virtual community where a person who happens to have a disability could join in.

Kerry is also a particularly strong advocate of universal design, design for all or inclusive design. It is a very important concept for ensuring that mainstream manufacturers produce products into the future that are usable by all people in the community, and there are particular principles relating to that concept (Connell et al., 1997). There is always a need for particular assistive technologies. Some people have very severe disabilities, and it is unrealistic to expect a mainstream PC manufacturer to provide everything that assists such a person; for example puff and blow as an interface, a switch-in and so forth. COST 219 (European Commission Action on Telecommunications and Disability – www.cost219.org) suggests three levels to universal design. Make as many products as accessible as possible, recognising that there are some needs for AT and the mainstream equipment needs connected to the AT and vice versa. The third level is assisted technology (Roe, 2001). One of the issues is that in the IT area new products are readily available and part of a highly competitive market. For AT to be able to connect to and work with some of the new technology is always a challenge and national, regional and international standards are important. Considerable work is done in the major world regions to try to achieve standards that include accessibility. Kerry, the telecommunications policy adviser, is in a position to influence from the beginning the particular way a standard is compiled for accessibility.

The principle of social justice, according to Lyman's (1998: 5) experience, was a universal service, and this is particularly appropriate for persons with disabilities. In the USA universal service is based on telecommunications policy, and rural electrification before that. Although universal access may guarantee equal access, information itself is distributed by fee for service, thus creating a new kind of inequality that may be especially pernicious in an information society.

Kate has been involved in various interesting projects relevant to people with disabilities in recent years. She has received research funding over three years for a study entitled 'Outcomes in long-duration spinal-cord injury'. The research funding for the first three years is for telephone interviews. It is necessary to follow people for five years, beginning with those who are in a cohort of one-year post-injury through to, hopefully, 30 years post-injury. Six injury groups are asked a range of questions about their functional abilities.

> How people are going physically with their health complications that they might be having. How they perceive their quality of life and their satisfaction with life. So we're using a range of standard instruments to do that. We're using a World Health Organization quality-of-life questionnaire, a community integration scale, the functional independence measures, satisfaction with life scale, general health, pain questionnaire, because that's something that there's been a lot of literature about, pain and long-duration spinal-

cord injury. We're asking people to commit to an annual interview for five years, in the hope that we've got a cross-section of people of various levels of injury and that we'll be able to maybe start pinpointing information about where changes happen. What we know so far is that people start with a spinal-cord injury, their function improves for however many years post the spinal-cord injury and then at some point it drops off. In our earlier exploratory studies, when we were asking people to look at their last 20 years post-spinal-cord injury, it really was very much a curve. A typical bell curve, so people somewhere, when they reflected on the mid-point at ten years, started to talk about a decline. But we don't really know whether the decline was happening ten years post-injury, or it started two years post-injury, or five years post-injury or 25 years post-injury. So why is it that quality of life or people's satisfaction of life doesn't appear to be threatened by the functional changes that are certainly happening?

Additionally, Kate and her colleagues have received funding for research into physical and psychosocial changes in people with long-term spinal-cord injury. Although it is early in the stages of these research projects, Kate is speculating whether 'technology could play a role in this quality of life thing versus drop off in function and health and so on'. She sees the use of technology by people with disabilities as a positive aspect of the future:

because we're sort of shifting the focus for rehabilitation these days. I've only been in the area for eight years and I've seen a shift from, you know, more of this sort of 'if you don't use it, you'll lose it', to conserve it, to preserve it or whatever, some other little catchy thing. So that people will be now prescribed pressure-relieving cushions, when traditionally maybe they were thought to be in a group that could lift their own weight. But if you're going to be lifting your own weight every 20 minutes for the rest of your life, then your shoulders aren't really going to survive for that long haul. So, in that sense, technology provides a way for people being able to conserve their energy and, you know, they don't have to lift unnecessarily. If they can access an environmental control unit that can open and close doors and so forth then they can save that extra expenditure of energy.

Community awareness and relationship

The 'relationship' concept or theme examined here was derived from some of the range of research that some interviewees were undertaking into the needs of disabled people. The research was invariably based on the researchers' commitment to community awareness and support for persons with disabilities. For example, Kerry is associated with a research centre focused on internet technology and the user environments programme. Within this programme there is a user design project with three particular areas that are considered: small businesses, young people and people with disabilities. She believes in more collaboration between the user design project and the technology programmes, because then end users would be considered from the start of a research project rather than doing usability testing once a prototype has been completed.

> It's difficult because a user and the research and technology researcher speak different languages and have different approaches and methodologies. To try and bridge that takes time and that means that one has to have a number of different workshops in order to bridge the gap. It's a very interesting challenge and I think that we are starting to make some marks, but again it takes time.

She believes the involvement of government is very important to ensure there is funding and support to prop up good virtual communities. She argues:

> if people are able to communicate and share experiences, it means that they can hopefully develop more sense of identity and where they want to head in the future. It might help them to consider study, it might help them to consider employment and then become more and more part of the actual physical community, as well as being part of a virtual community. And so if government can assist that process, it should help people to become more and more contributing to society. Hopefully, the community generally will see that people with disabilities are not there just as someone they have to support by various funding programmes – and I'm not saying that those funding programmes should discontinue. But I'm saying that there is more of a possibility of people being out and about through maybe meeting socially on a discussion forum and then actually wanting to meet physically. So there are a lot of those sort

of opportunities, I think, and I strongly feel that government should support more research and development in this area.

There is very little research being done in Australia and very little funding available for research compared with internationally. 'It's one thing to take useful findings from other countries, but we have a unique society in Australia and we need to add that to international findings to suit our own environment. So I suppose that's a plea that there needs to be more funding available to achieve better outcomes generally.'

The notion of virtual communities for people with disabilities is not a specific priority of the specialist government post-rehabilitation health information centre manager or team members, or the organisations with which they have formed links. To date they are content to refer clients on to peer support networks or the member networks in the Spinal Injuries Association. Kate describes it thus:

> There's sort of networks that have cropped up, but they have really been kind of *ad hoc* and informal… I've got one or two clients that use technology a lot, who are chatting on forums and accessing sites wherever they might be. They e-mail me with, oh, I've just seen this bit of information. I find it's not something that we've looked at setting up here.

The post-rehabilitation health information service's main brief is to make its website accessible to everyone.

> So that might be something that we could then look at other people becoming involved in some kind of virtual community or a group, because clients typically don't access the Telehealth Network – it's really more the service providers. So, yeah, is there another way that we could get that information to people? Obviously, it's been valuable to have a lot of interest and the cost of accessing the internet for rural clients has been a problem and the quality of the access that they can get.

Kate describes people's adjustment post-spinal-cord injury and the changes to their self-esteem and their not wanting to be visible in the community as somebody in a wheelchair. She understands this urge for anonymity at the end of a chatline or forum, and feels that only with increasing community awareness and valued roles will this thinking change.

E-economy transactions

E-economy transactions occur in an economy that is characterised by extensive use of the internet and information technology. The second half of the past century introduced a host of brand-new terms into all languages of the world, such as computerisation, virtual reality, interactive communication, online payment and many others. A special role among them is assigned to the family of terms that start with the word 'electronic' – e-book, e-cash, e-document and so forth. Origination of the World Wide Web and its transformation into the internet global network, along with the globalisation of economic links, high levels of economic integration of countries and also the tendency of manufacturers to expand markets for sales and reduce the cost of production for the sake of higher profits, led to the internet becoming a source of revenue and generating a new concept – the e-economy. Thus the e-economy, in the broad sense, is an economy based upon the use of information, knowledge and ICT and grounded in the networking technologies and business-to-business/business-to-consumer models. As a rule, the term is applied in relation to distribution, marketing, sale or delivery of goods and services based on the wide use of ICT.

The electronic economy (EE) has a capacity to enable a country to expand its range of possibilities, become integrated in the process of creating the new, global market of goods and services and occupy its niche in the world economy. Besides expansion of the possibilities to access the new markets for goods and services, the EE ensures more cost-effectiveness and less complexity. Electronic transactions are essential for everybody living in the world of an e-economy in the information age, according to these interviewees, not just disabled people. However, for persons with disabilities the transactions of the e-economy are of more consequence than convenience. They are the very basis of their independence. 'If you can get on the internet you can do your banking yourself. No one needs to know what your account balances are or what you're taking money out for. You can do some of your own shopping yourself...'

Infrastructure barriers to participation for people with disabilities

Barriers to ICT use and the successful facilitation of a virtual community for people with long-term physical disabilities identified by the allied health, information and policy professionals were very similar to those specified by the persons with disabilities in the previous chapter. The characteristics or properties of the 'barrier' category using the grounded theory terminology included funding, costs and affordability, as well as inequities of availability and other physical and technological aspects of connectivity. It was the diversity and range of the barriers identified by interviewees that limited successful use of ICT.

The specialist hospital unit's clients and three OTs who facilitate their rehabilitation have access to the AT information centre when the initial assessment of their post-injury abilities is undertaken. One of the reasons for this is because none of the three specialist unit's occupational therapists has the level of ICT training that is required to be able to match the client's needs fully with the appropriate technology that is currently available. Jean sought funding for the specialist unit's OT staff to attend ICT training courses and to have the operating systems and games software upgraded on the computers their clients use as therapeutic tools in the resources room, but she feels that 'funding is always an issue on how much you can upgrade'. Another reason why the therapists and clients need regular access to the AT information centre is because the resources room at the hospital unit only has limited low technology, such as mouth-sticks, small environmental units and so on. Furthermore, there is no internet access for clients during their time in the unit, nor is ongoing training or technology support available for clients or staff. The hospital does not have a mandate to support the special technology required at the unit or for training their clientele.

Because intensive client ICT training is not available through either the specialist unit or the AT information centre, Jean constantly looks for alternatives according to the client's level of computer literacy. As she says:

> we can access the training manuals from the hospital staff, and tutorial programmes and things like that, but at the end of the day I don't think any of them are entirely effective because people want that direction. They want the facilitation, they want someone to be assisting them to drive that learning, because to do that on top of

just adjusting to the trauma of what happened to them is just a big ask, I think.

If the client is school-aged, she accesses the education department for some of their ICT training. She also tries to involve TAFE personnel, other external facilitators and even sometimes peer support people as trainers for recently injured people – all with varying degrees of success depending on the client's motivation. She proposes that an internet café be available to the specialist unit's clientele after hours and at weekends, because 'people really need to have these kinds of things outside therapy hours as well'.

Jean endeavours to work to clients' individual differences, especially in relation to the pace of adjustment to their newly acquired disability. She believes the OT staff need to be mindful that timing is an issue for some of the clients:

> probably just to be sure of adjustment, readiness to accept the technology could be seen as a barrier. I'm not sure it's so much a barrier. Do you know what I mean by that? I think I see that as a barrier, particularly with the environmental control technology where if someone is going to have a fair amount of care support it is not a barrier that can't be resolved, but a barrier that takes quite a lot of support before it's resolved. It's not just about control though. It's about accepting the disability. I think I've seen people who have taken three years to come to terms with the reality. They come in here and wouldn't even look at power chairs and that sort of thing, because they couldn't make that sort of quantum leap if you like, that that's how their life was going to be. And, I've worked with people in the Spinal Outreach Team, who two or three years down the track after leaving come to terms with their situation. They needed that time to really, yeah, get a sense of their situation and who now are probably some of the stauncher advocates of using technology within their home. But it's knowing how to tap into them and that includes knowing things like what is available, because this is a bit of a loop for people to get back into when they're ready.

Apart from the positive aspects of the technology, Clara also speaks about the barriers for people with disabilities – cost (without accident insurance), lack of support, lack of information:

It's hard for people to find out about things. But often, they're not empowered to find out themselves. They're so used to other people finding out for them... They can't pick up the telephone and make a phone call, they can't get on the internet and find out. So often perhaps the information they're getting is not always getting information directly.

Technology training and lack of control over one's life are also issues: 'if I put myself in that situation, and sometimes I do and I think if I couldn't use the phone or I couldn't use the TV or the radio. It's so isolating. I mean they're isolated by their mobility like a lot of people, but we must have contact with the outside world.' Clara identifies such barriers as, for example, if there is no support in the person's environment to set up the equipment 'it might mean that the person themselves doesn't have the dexterity to be able to programme in all the buttons. So that's when we rely on them having someone in their environment to do that for them.' She also believes that there are many funding inequities and unmet needs with respect to lifestyle support.

When you think about the things you do in your life every day, about turning the lights on, etc. How can anybody think that that's a luxury to be able to do that? It's not a luxury at all. You know, it's a core part of living, really. Absolutely fundamental... and if people don't have any means of calling for assistance at night, then that support system has got to be 100 per cent reliable... and that is very challenging for a lot of people with high-level injuries... Technology is not a magic wand either, and you can't get over some barriers like with people in the dead of night and... if they have a really bad experience at night and it becomes very dangerous. They might injure themselves, or even if it's not that, they need good switch access, so therefore it's not reliable for them any more. They're very vulnerable and so therefore it has to be reliable.

As an early senior OT in the AT information centre, Barb established thorough clinical assessment procedures that contributed to the development of AT service delivery. Nonetheless, she found some frustration and problems in this work. Although the need to help people function better is obvious, the technologies identified as meeting the needs are expensive and the follow-up evaluation training to ensure the person with the disability can actually use the technology effectively is not always available.

There's this mentality that there's one-off purchases and that what you see is what you get and that you don't need the word 'changes' in people's needs or what they want to do or their pain or whatever. We don't even acknowledge that people might experience pain as a result of wheelchair beds, prescriptions, yet that's coming through in the research now, that that's one of the major issues. And so customising things once people have them to make sure that it's working for them is just not on the agenda. There's no understanding of the complexities about this issue at all. There is no acknowledgement that the issue exists.

Other problems regarding AT also captured Barb's attention, for example the fact that there is no real 'system' in Australia to allow people to acquire the technology they need. Apparently, in Queensland there is a very traditional approach, where you are given a device to replace lost function and there is really no attention given to what your individual requirements are or what you aim to do. Furthermore, not only is the Queensland system not very discerning in determining different needs, but its focus is primarily on providing oxygen, incontinence and other basic medical aids, rather than assisted technology. In New South Wales, by comparison, medical aid support is drawn from the primary care hospital budget, so certain inequities exist from state to state that make it difficult for people with disabilities to acquire the various technologies they need. Another example of the kind of frustration professionals experience is the fact that high-level disability needs attract similar financial support to low-level needs. At this point, Barb gave vent to her frustration:

We have a service system that believes that a tilted wheelchair is a luxury. We have language-like needs and wants and it disturbs me enormously when service providers have the gall to be talking about someone's wants that aren't a need. And when you have, you know, artificial caps being put on equipment, because we have nothing more sophisticated to determine what people's requirements are. Part of my frustration when I was interviewing people in the research was that there's this cap of $5,000 to return them to work. So you have people with fairly minor disabilities using the $5,000 and you have people with quite significant disabilities whose needs aren't being met, because $5,000 isn't doing it! And you have service providers who think that $5,000 is about things and equipment. And other very astute service providers who work the system to get not just the equipment, but the training and customisation that's required to make that equipment work for the people with the disabilities.

Barb argues that these sorts of problems mean the 'disability dollar' is often dissipated. 'They set up this competitive model where services are competing with each other to get funding, so it becomes meted out to the loudest voice, yeah, rather than centres of excellence.' She concluded rather sadly:

> they weren't prepared to spend the money that had been allocated to them to buy in expertise, because they wanted to translate that money into things, and the things weren't useful. And so, yeah, you just get this really poor utilisation of services and fragmentation of services that results in really poor outcomes for consumers and a lot of amateurs running around doing things. You know, I call it the catalogue prescription method, yeah, open a catalogue, eenie meenie minie mo and choose something for somebody. Or consumers being told to go and investigate themselves – and I had some consumers who did that better than any service provider was ever going to be able to do it.

Barriers to people with disabilities having their technology needs met, according to Barb, again relate primarily to finances: 'they're frightened about the reality of the cost' of equipment. Their reduced earning capacity and the constant changes in technology exacerbate this problem. She estimates that technology changes approximately every two years, and the funding system is not geared to that short turn-around time. For example, it is expected that wheelchairs are replaced only every five years. She also identifies lack of training for people with disabilities in using the technology as another major barrier. She says that success is 'having a vision for what's possible and if you've lived normally, if one would like to say, well, you'll be engaged; but if you don't have an expectation, then you tend not to go after it'. For her, the most important thing is to give people with disabilities a vision of what is possible. 'If we don't, if our only vision is to meet the basic requirements, then it's not much of a vision. And that's really what we're doing, we're discharging people from hospital with the capacity to perform their self-care requirements that we'd expect of a seven-year-old.'

Gerry identifies three barriers that the specialist government disability information service clients have to deal with: awareness, time and cost.

'Not knowing what information is out there and where you can find it... Yeah, we get a number of calls from people who are at the end of their tether. They say, oh I've tried, I've been ringing up different places for weeks and weeks and I've been going around in circles.' He also considers that having the virtual technology option for people with disabilities really helps, but:

> Cost has probably been an issue for the majority of callers who ring up. It's very, very expensive to have an ISP and internet access for many people. From time to time people might have an idea, or they might've heard of some emerging technology and they'd really like to access it, but it isn't really commercially developed and some people find that frustrating.

As the manager of this specialist disability information service, he ensures that all incoming requests for information are tracked statistically. The key emerging themes or trends are reported monthly to senior departmental managers for policy formulation and input into a whole government approach to disability.

Emerging theory or well-being model

The theory and model that emerged from the interview data of the disabled persons, deconstructed and analysed in Chapter 5, were substantiated by the similarities in the deconstruction and analysis of the interview data from the allied health, information and policy professionals.

The well-being model for a virtual community for people with long-term, severe physical disabilities that emerged from the data collection and analysis, based on the grounded theory methodology and 18 interviews, was a meld of six types of electronic communities: empowerment-oriented, fantasy-oriented, information-oriented, interest-oriented, relationship-oriented and transaction-oriented, depending on the types of disability consumer needs they met. For the model to be truly transformational, it must reflect a number of different types of virtual communities. All six types that evolved from the interview data need to be built into portals and developed into virtual communities for persons with disabilities. It is also possible that the well-being model for a virtual community for people with long-term severe physical disabilities in fact met several of these needs or orientations simultaneously. The model had the expectation that it may meet several, if not all, of the purposes or orientations. However, if any one or more of these types of e-communities were to be ignored, then only fragments of the potential virtual community experience would be available to persons with disabilities. Furthermore, the findings from the interviews indicated that information and technological literacy enhanced access to the notion of a virtual community, while availability and affordability of connecting and various physical and technological aspects could cause barriers to a successful virtual community.

Methodological evaluation

Qualitative researchers work towards achieving what Lincoln and Guba defined as credibility, transferability, dependability and conformability: the 'trustworthiness of qualitative research' (cited in Bradley, 1993: 436). Strauss and Corbin (1998: 268–9) provided seven evaluative criteria against which the quality of the qualitative research that was designed to build the essential elements of theory for a virtual community for persons with severe long-term physical disabilities was judged. The criteria and brief attempts at addressing them are detailed below.

Criterion 1: how was the original sample selected? On what grounds?

In a sense, the participants chose themselves. Given that not everybody can afford access to the technology and the internet, and certainly people with disabilities are to be found usually at the lower end of the socio-economic spectrum, it was not expected that participants in the research would be plentiful or easy to find. Indicative of subjective research was the use of 'snowballing' or chain sampling – one of the 16 types of purposeful sampling identified by Patton (1990: 169–83) as the dominant strategy commonly used in qualitative research. Purposeful sampling seeks information-rich cases/participants who are studied in depth. This involves asking participants interviewed to help identify other future potential participants. There was no preconceived notion by the researcher of how many participants would make a reasonable 'sample'. Thus the participants helped to shape the actual research from the very beginning.

Although ideally participants should be selected according to the principle of theoretical sampling, the reality was that participants were selected from and by people with mobility impairments who were using ICT. However, the specific sampling decisions evolved during the research process itself (Strauss and Corbin, 1990: 192; 1998: 214). An exhaustive literature review was not done initially, so as to allow theory to emerge directly from the data and remain 'grounded in' the data. The literature was reviewed continuously, however, throughout data collection and analysis phases. Sampling included people who were experiencing the social process being investigated; and when the findings were being described, descriptive language was used to provide the reader with the steps in the process and the logic of the method.

Criterion 2: what major categories emerged?

The central or major category that emerged was that persons with long-term, severe physical disabilities desired to regain 'a sense of control' over their lives. Increasingly, they found that this concept of 'a sense of control' could be achieved by their use of ICT. The other major categories that emerged from the data were the importance of education, the seeking of virtual reality or 'fantasy', the need for and use of information, 'interest', relationship and transactions. These six phenomena or concepts were the building blocks or cornerstones of the theoretical model or framework of a virtual community that would be useful to the users – people with long-term, severe physical disabilities – and the facilitators of such a community. However, other very important phenomena that emerged from the interview data were the notions of 'access' and 'barriers' to the success of a virtual community for the demographic specified (see Chapter 5 and the earlier sections in this chapter).

Criterion 3: what were some of the events, incidents or actions (indicators) that pointed to some of these major categories?

The first incident that pointed to some of these major categories began with the interview with Interviewee 4. He took some three hours to complete the hour-long interview, because he was struggling with the pain of recalling and describing the loss and lack of control he now had over his life as a person with a severe physical disability. (Chapter 5 and earlier sections in this chapter give more detailed information about the six major categories.)

Criterion 4: on the basis of what categories did theoretical sampling proceed?

How did theoretical formulations guide some of the data collection? After the theoretical sampling was done, how representative of the data did the categories prove to be? While the selection of research participants may seem to have been somewhat serendipitous, it was based on intersecting suggestions of suitable participants by the people with physical disabilities. Therefore, they were likely to be a reasonable representation of the total possible set of suitable participants at the time of completing the interviews. Of course, in the IT field, which continues to develop so rapidly, any increase in timeframe undoubtedly sees more people with disabilities become involved with using ICT. There was a good cross-representation within the cohort: men and women of different ages, classes, educational backgrounds and different pre- and post-injury careers, as well as some members who had other physical disabilities as a result of other medical conditions. Their technology involvement varied between their private, public and commercial life spheres.

Criterion 5: what were some of the hypotheses pertaining to conceptual relations (among categories), and on what grounds were they formulated and validated?

Using grounded theory as the most appropriate methodology to undertake this qualitative study, the researcher was ever mindful of trying not to be precipitate or subjective in beginning to formulate hypotheses pertaining to conceptual relations (that is, among categories). Being a person with a physical disability, it was often difficult not to become a participant in the process itself. As described in Criterion 3, when the very protracted interview with Interviewee 4 was complete, considerable time was spent in reflection and reviewing the interview content and process. As a result of this reflection, it seemed for the first time that the major category was likely to be this issue of 'a sense of control'. Having become alert to the possibility of 'a sense of control' as being a or the major category, it became a possible hypothesis to be validated. However, mindful that grounded theory postulates that the methodology does not begin with a hypothesis to be proven or disproved, but rather an area to be fully explored by continuing to undertake in-depth interviews until it becomes apparent that 'saturation' of the topic has been completed, the process continued. Nonetheless, it was the formulation of 'a sense of control' as a possible major category that led to considering seeking validation of the perceived hypothesis.

What distinguished grounded theory was the method of 'constant comparison' to detect emerging categories and themes and direct the data collection process. The use of 'theoretical sampling' did not begin with a hypothesis that must be proven either true or false. This meant that the researcher had to cast a wide net for data. This method allowed the theory to emerge over the process of data collection and analysis – grounding the developing theory in the data themselves (obtained from the social research). Hence the theory formulation was allowed to evolve through an iterative process of data collection, reflection and analysis, rather than being the initial driving force behind the research.

Criterion 6: were there instances in which hypotheses did not explain what was happening in the data? How were these discrepancies accounted for? Were hypotheses modified?

Fortuitously, there were no instances in which the hypothesis, once formulated as described in Criterion 5, did not explain what was happening in the interview data. Grounded theory was reputed to be appropriate only for more sophisticated researchers. Initially, this statement was almost meaningless. However, as the iterative process of interviewing, reflecting, analysing and reviewing the interview data and published research literature progressed, it began to take on real meaning. Obviously, researchers who use grounded theory as their methodology would know the beginnings of their area of study. However, they would have no idea where it would end until it ended – this point being decided by the fact that 'saturation' of the data/analysis had occurred. So a grounded theory researcher would not have the initial security of having a readily formulated hypothesis to work towards proving or disproving; rather, the researcher has an area to explore and only knows completion has occurred with data saturation. It was from this mass of interview data and analysis that the categories and the theory emerged.

Criterion 7: how and why was the core category selected? Was this selection sudden or gradual, difficult or easy? On what grounds were the final analytic decisions made?

Criteria 5 and 6 above document how and why the core category of 'a sense of control' was initially selected and finally confirmed. The selection was quite gradual, becoming increasingly apparent over the iterative process of collecting the interview data and analysis against reading the research literature. The idea of the collection of the data towards the selection of the core category being either difficult or easy does not do justice to the processes involved in using grounded theory as a research methodology. The process of the categories emerging can best be likened to that of a flower unfolding – unknown, until it is revealed in its full beauty!

Conclusion

As concluded above, the theory and well-being model that emerged from the interview data of the persons with disabilities deconstructed and analysed in Chapter 5 were substantiated by the similarities to the deconstruction and analysis of the interview data from the allied health, information and policy professionals. Furthermore, these professionals were passionate in their commitment to and support of their clientele's independence and consequent well-being, and initiated their own perceptions regarding the importance to persons with physical disabilities of gaining 'a sense of control' over their lives.

This qualitative study using the grounded theory methodology satisfactorily addressed a number of questions. What are the strengths and weaknesses of various virtual communities? Are there features underpinning the general studies into virtual communities that are transferable to a specific virtual community with specific needs? What are the information practices of persons with long-term physical disabilities? What information is currently available to this community and how is it used? Exactly what information is required by this 'community of interest'? Has the legislative framework and government policy on information mitigated this information need, and is the information equitably accessible to persons with disabilities? Is information access used as a means of participating and thus feeling more included as a citizen? Or is it used to feel empowered to take control over one's life and well-being? And what of all the technology available – is it adaptable, flexible and accessible to people with disabilities, or are there barriers to its usefulness? These are some of the questions that had to be addressed in this study in order for the key components of a model to be identified. The characteristics of a useful and successful virtual community for persons with long-term, severe physical disabilities had to be ascertained for both the users of the technology and those who facilitate its use.

7

Model construction

> For the sake of persons of... different types, scientific truth should be presented in different forms, and should be regarded as equally scientific, whether it appears in the robust form and the vivid colouring of a physical illustration, or in the tenuity and paleness of a symbolic expression. (Maxwell, 1870)

This chapter, phase 3 of the grounded theory analysis, has a triple focus. Firstly, it considers briefly the potential implications of the study results in terms of the six identified categories, as well as access and barriers, in the consolidation of the emergent model. Then it discusses the opportunities and challenges of the six types of e-communities. Finally, it reconsiders the background theory to the study as derived from some of the literature reviewed in relation to the nature of the problem (how can virtual communities for persons with long-term disabilities best be facilitated?) being examined.

Potential implications of the results – the consolidation of the emergent well-being model

There were several considerations necessary prior to deciding to use a qualitative research methodology for this particular study. Strauss and Corbin (1990) claimed that qualitative methods were used to understand better any phenomenon about which little was yet known. They also could be used to gain new perspective on topics about which much was already known; or to gain more in-depth information that would be difficult to convey quantitatively. So, while information about many aspects of virtual communities has been available in the past decade, there is no recorded understanding about the needs of particular communities, such as persons with physical disabilities. The findings of the study establish that disabled people need virtual communities with specific characteristics.

Schuler (1996b) presented six core values and their attributes for community networks (as discussed in Chapter 2): democracy, education, health, equality, information exchange and communication. He wrote:

> They must rest on the solid foundations of principles and values and be flexible and adaptable, intelligent, and creative. They must be inclusive. Everyone must be allowed to participate. They will have to engage both governments and business because they both exist to provide services for people. These institutions must be accountable to the people, and not the reverse. (Ibid.: xi)

In this study into the needs or characteristics of virtual communities for people with mobility impairments, the six essential characteristics or concepts were identified as education and empowerment, fantasy or virtual activity, information, interest, relationship and transaction. These may be seen as presenting both opportunities and challenges. Thus the needs or characteristics of a virtual community for people with a physical disability overlapped strongly, although not completely, with the core values that Schuler identified for building community networks. However, there were further characteristics identified by this study that were unique to building a virtual community to meet the specific needs of people with a physical disability.

The central theme that emerged slowly but strongly from the open coding analysis to which all 18 in-depth interviews were subjected was that people with long-term physical disabilities desired to regain 'a sense of control' over their lives, and increasingly found that this was achieved by their use of ICT; the professionals were as unanimous in their enthusiasm for the technology for their clientele as were the clients themselves. The other particularly significant themes that emerged were the aforementioned six concepts that form the building blocks of the theoretical well-being model for this virtual community.

The desire to 'control' the world around us (that is, the desire for behaviour-event contingency or personal control) is a fundamental characteristic of human beings (Schultz et al., 1994; Haidt and Rodin,

1995; Burger, 1987; Rothbaum et al., 1982). 'Secondary control' reflects behaviour that, while not directly controlling events, promotes 'a sense of control' not by altering the environment but by altering oneself (for example, one's values, priorities or behaviour) so as to bring oneself in line with the environment. The central thesis of this formulation of perceived control is that 'persons perceive and are motivated to obtain secondary control in many situations previously assumed to be characterised by perceived uncontrollability and an absence of motivation for control' (Rothbaum et al., 1982: 27).

Another construct related to personal control is powerlessness (Seeman, 1975). Powerlessness is conceptualised in terms of an individual's general perceptions of lack of power (versus 'control'), encompassing elements of lack of autonomy, fatalism and inefficacy (Seeman and Seeman, 1983; Seeman, 1991). Personal control expectancies relate to judgements about whether actions can produce a given outcome (that is, the extent to which a given outcome is controllable) (Ferguson et al., 1994). There is considerable evidence linking 'a sense of control' to better psychological health (Haidt and Rodin, 1995), as well as evidence of links to better physical health outcomes (Marmot et al., 1997; Marmot and Wilkinson, 1999), better self-rated health and functional status (Seeman and Lewis, 1995), better maintenance of cognitive function (Seeman et al., 1993) and lower mortality risk (Seeman and Lewis, 1995).

Other very important phenomena or concepts that emerged from the interview data were the notions of 'access' or 'accessibility' and 'barriers' to the success of the proposed virtual community. The characteristics or properties of the barrier category included costs or affordability, availability and other physical and technological aspects of connectivity. The diverse range of identified barriers are termed 'dimensions' in grounded theory, and gave specification to 'barriers' as a category in the findings towards the theoretical framework for the virtual community. There were very crucial subcategories that also emerged from the analysis, including the necessity of a climate of 'access' by way of information literacy and technology literacy.

IL skills are fundamental to the success of a virtual community. Information literacy can contribute to participative citizenship; social inclusion; acquisition of skills; innovation and enterprise; the creation of new knowledge; personal, vocational, corporate and organisational empowerment; and learning for life (Australian Library and Information Association, 2003). While this definition of IL affords an insight into the notions encompassed by the term, there are several 'faces' of IL worth embracing (Bruce, 1997: 154). Library and information services professionals have chosen to undertake a responsibility to develop the IL of their clients. They support governments at all levels, and the corporate, community, professional, educational and trade union sectors, in promoting and facilitating the development of IL for all Australians as a high priority. The interviewees in this study were intuitively aware of their need for information, and to be information and technologically literate as deemed desirable by the 'thematic debate on information literacy' (UNESCO, 2005).

Strauss and Corbin (1998: 21–2) acknowledge that developing theory is a complex activity: 'we use the term "theorising" to denote this activity because developing theory is a process and often is a long one'. According to them, theorising is work that entails not only conceiving or intuiting ideas (concepts) but also formulating them into a logical, systematic and explanatory scheme. They argue that at the heart of theorising lies the interplay of making inductions (deriving concepts, their properties and dimensions from data) and deductions. Deductions are the hypothesising about the relationships between concepts; the relationships also are derived from data, but data that have been abstracted by the analyst from the raw data. For Strauss and Corbin (ibid.: 22), theory

> denotes a set of well-developed categories (that is, themes, concepts) that are systematically interrelated through statements of relationship to form a theoretical framework that explains some relevant social, psychological, educational, nursing, or other phenomenon. The statements of relationship explain who, what, when, where, why, how, and with what consequences an event occurs. Once concepts are related through statements of relationship into an explanatory theoretical framework, the research findings move beyond conceptual ordering to theory.

The e-communities or categories are systematically interrelated through statements of relationship to form the theoretical framework that explains the relevant social phenomenon, although they are presented here as separate units for the sake of graphical representation. The statements of relationship between these categories allow for objectification and explain who (relationship), what (information), when (interest), where (transaction), why (education), how (fantasy) and with what consequences (access and barriers) an event occurs – as discussed in the next section. For the model to be truly generalisable and

Figure 7.1 The framework of the virtual community well-being model

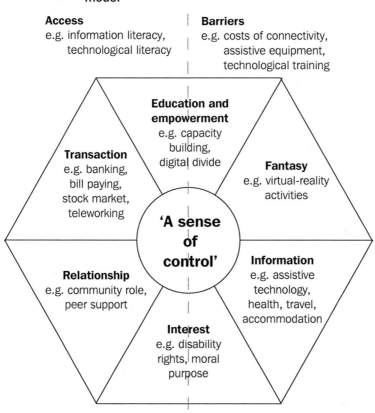

Access
e.g. information literacy,
technological literacy

Barriers
e.g. costs of connectivity,
assistive equipment,
technological training

Education and empowerment
e.g. capacity building, digital divide

Transaction
e.g. banking, bill paying, stock market, teleworking

Fantasy
e.g. virtual-reality activities

'A sense of control'

Relationship
e.g. community role, peer support

Information
e.g. assistive technology, health, travel, accommodation

Interest
e.g. disability rights, moral purpose

Note: 'Access' and 'Barriers' relate to all situations, not just those depicted left and right of the diagram – they are, in fact, 'two sides of one coin'.

transformational, all six types of virtual communities need to be built into portals developed for persons with disabilities (Jafari and Sheehan, 2003; Priebe, 2005). It is also possible that this well-being model for a virtual community meets several, if not all, of the above needs, purposes or orientations simultaneously. It is presented in greater detail diagrammatically in Figure 7.1.

If any one or more of these types of e-communities were ignored, only fragments of the potential virtual community experience would be available. The findings also indicate that information and technological literacy enhance access to a virtual community, while costs of connecting and various physical and technological aspects cause barriers. Barriers include, for example, connection problems for rural and remote people, the 'isolation' double-edged sword and the inaccessibility of chatrooms to people with physical disabilities.

Opportunities and challenges of the six types of e-communities

Category one: education

The first type of e-community is the community of education and empowerment that creates an environment for capacity building (or social capital), bridges information literacy and the digital divide and tackles inequities (discussed in Chapter 5). For this type of virtual community, being information literate means one has the prerequisites for 'participating effectively in the Information Society, and is part of the basic human right of life long learning' (International Meeting of Information Literacy Experts, 2003).

'Empowerment' means person-centred arrangements and relationships in social policy and service delivery, as distinct from institution- or agency-centred systems. Empowerment involves disabled people understanding their right to be citizens and being given the tools for equality and participation. It is achieved mainly by people with disabilities coming together to share their experiences, gain strength from one another and provide positive role models. It means breaking away from an identity of graceful passivity and finding the will and power to change one's own circumstances. This is not an easy process for people with disabilities or the wider community, but it is an essential component in their struggle for full participation and equality of opportunity (Friedmann, 1992).

Empowerment is a word used a lot by social activists and community developers. What does or can it mean for people with disabilities? Empowerment seems to mean taking hold of personal strengths, using them to develop personal power and directing that power to attain personal goals. For people with disabilities it also means sharing experience and outcomes with other disabled people so they can develop their own strengths and abilities. Taking hold of personal power is a huge challenge for someone with a disability, especially when the disability is so severe that it affects physical, economic and social independence.

Many communities devalue people with disabilities, a process compounded if the community also devalues females and people from different cultural backgrounds. The disadvantage can be multiplied if the disabled person stands out in other ways as well, such as being single when all the person's friends are married and so on. Accepting disadvantage is accepting the role of victim. Getting out of the role of victim means the person with the disability must establish their true goals, find out who shares them and determine what can be undertaken as a community to achieve social equity. Gaining power over the consequences of disability is hard and inevitably a lifetime battle. Those people with secondary disabilities caused by child-bearing, ageing or an unwise lifestyle know just how easy it is to slip into lethargy and give up.

Exercising the next power, the power of knowledge and experience, is difficult for people with disabilities. They are less confident about themselves. Disabled people have very few role models at the leadership level. Development of people with disabilities needs to be undertaken carefully so that they are empowered by many appropriate role models and significant shared knowledge to participate in decision-making at every level of society. Indeed, it is the potential of the new media and technology that offers these promises and affirms the abilities of disabled people and ways to change the wider community's perceptions of people with disabilities. Thus ownership and management of one's own life and control over resources and decision-making are seen as key components of empowered people. Access to information, ability to make choices, assertiveness and self-esteem have been identified as key elements of education and empowerment (Chamberlin, 1997).

Category two: fantasy

The second type of e-community is fantasy-oriented: users create new environments, personalities, stories and role-play and are drawn to virtual-reality 'activities' because of access and mobility issues. This has not emerged from the data as so relevant to the interviewees in this study as other issues, but nonetheless it was a concern under the guise of the 'double-edged sword' – that is, access versus isolation (Oliver, 1990).

On the business side of organisations (and many interviewees had employment as a priority), virtual reality enables a person to sample any purchase that traditionally had required examination in person – all without leaving home. Virtual reality enables people to do more than merely see and hear information (Levy, 1998). An employee with a disability puts his/her hand in a 'data-arm' connected to a computer to make a mechanical adjustment on a simulated piece of equipment illustrated on the computer screen. The employee is able to 'feel' and 'see' a rusty screw, see the 'hand' moving around coloured wires and see the results of the operation before it is performed on the actual equipment. Such types of processes enhance an organisation's business (and a disabled person's employability), cutting down on technical errors and down-time and improving performance and efficiency. Related to virtual reality, cyberspace as another technology goes one step further by incorporating the participant's thoughts into computer forms (as one interviewee suggested was useful for persons with physical disabilities). Furthermore, this is useful for brainstorming and new product generation and creation.

Category three: information

The third type of e-community that emerged from the data was information-oriented. The information-oriented community, for example, seeks a personal understanding of the availability and applicability of assistive technology, specific health information for persons with disabilities and information about accessible travel and accommodation, in addition to all the other general informational needs that any person might exhibit. In this study, sometimes this information-oriented type of e-community overlapped with the fourth type – the community of interest – but invariably it proved to be more 'personal'.

Burnett (2000: 4) contributed to the debate on virtual communities as information-oriented social spaces, developing a model of information exchange in virtual communities and a typology of the varieties of information behaviour to be found in them. He also drew attention to the fact that virtual communities can function as forums for both informational and social-emotional activities, and lamented the fact that little research had been undertaken to determine the relationship between these activities. He concluded that it may be possible that social activities, however trivial, were used in online environments to exchange information of various sorts, and that information sharing itself was a fundamentally social act. Effectively, the present study substantiated Burnett's thinking about virtual communities functioning as forums for both information and social-emotional activities – and as a means of accessing a wealth of information relatively easily, the internet may well excel.

An information-oriented virtual community implies that the community will be information literate and have an understanding and a set of abilities enabling individuals not only to recognise when information is needed but also to locate, evaluate and use effectively the needed information. Information pertaining to the availability and applicability of AT is a case in point (Tilley et al., 2007). Most of the large assistive equipment websites are based in the USA. The amount of equipment listed on each site varies greatly – from just a couple of devices to thousands. There is a great range of equipment available online, including items such as computer programs and specialised keyboards and mouse pads. Many sites also include general day-to-day assistive equipment for people with disabilities. The majority of sites have facilities to order online and almost all have contact details (phone or e-mail) for the company that produces the equipment. Much of the equipment listed online is fairly specific, but most sites do not provide enough background information for a user to rely on the website alone. These sites are best utilised for browsing and investigating the range of equipment that is available, and combining this with advice from specialists, friends and physiotherapists.

The past decade has seen people using computers to speak, write, read, study, manage finances, organise their own lives, express themselves creatively, develop skills and hobbies and gain employment. This has been an unequalled, historic opportunity for people with disabilities to become more independent and productive. And the future of virtual reality, robotics, videoconferencing, mind switches and so on continues to unfold. However, there are no coherent government policies on AT and there seems to be no bureaucratic understanding of the economic necessity for such technology. For example, it does not even feature in the Australian Commonwealth-State Disability Agreement, which allocates key policy responsibilities on disability matters between the Commonwealth and state governments.

President Bush signed the Assistive Technology Act 2004, as the previous Act was due to expire. This ensured that individuals with disabilities throughout the USA and its territories have access to the technology they need to help them be independent in school, home, the workplace and the community. This legislation represented an important commitment to people with disabilities from the president and Congress. Millions of disabled people rely on AT to help them gain and maintain independence. Every US state and territory has an Assistive Technology Act programme funded under the provisions of the Technology-Related Assistance Act 1988, but legislation supporting the state AT programmes was scheduled to sunset on 30 September 2004. The Assistive Technology Act 2004 supports the continuance of these programmes and eliminates the sunset provision; in this way the government sent a clear signal that it supports federal investment for people with disabilities, which paid off for communities, the economy, businesses and disabled people themselves.

The Association of Assistive Technology Act Programs (ATAP: www.ataporg.org) worked for several years to educate Congress about the significance of the Act in the lives of people with disabilities. ATAP was a national member-based organisation composed of state AT programmes funded under the Assistive Technology Act. Joined by other national disability organisations, technology companies and business representatives, ATAP shared with Congress the many successes of the programmes and the difference the law made for people with disabilities, and saluted the US Congress and the president for their important work in reauthorising this law and removing the sunset provision.

Smith, so commendable for his work in Australia, in 2003 pointed out the monumental policy failure in the area of assistive technology. There are at least four different Australian Commonwealth departments that cover AT issues (with responsibility for areas such as health, human services, employment, education and training), but none in fact did. Various state departments also covered AT, but only health departments flirted with the issue, through minimal and chaotic Program of Appliances for Disabled People schemes. Smith (ibid.) accused Australia of having nothing remotely comparable with the US Assistive Technology Act 1998, arguing that Australia needed creative government policies to fund AT research and testing, as well as widely available opportunities to trial and evaluate this technology. He suggested that tours were needed to take the technology to people who lived in rural and remote regions. In fact, Queensland's Independent Living Centre (ILC) had started doing regular regional tours just prior to his suggestion. He had a plethora of other ideas, such as technical support services for employers and job agencies, training for advisers and end users, publicised case studies of successes and funding for the equipment itself (perhaps in the form of a Higher Education Contribution Scheme (HECS) type of loan). He argued that these measures were all necessary adjuncts to such a policy, and asserted that, above all, channels of effective communication were needed to get usable information (in multimedia formats) out to therapists, teachers, job placement agencies, disability workers, employers and people with disabilities. Smith (ibid.: 20) declared that widespread use of AT by people with disabilities was an economic issue, in that the appropriate policies increased the employment and employability of such people, saved the government welfare money and enriched the lives of disabled people. It then became a win-win situation and made overwhelming good sense.

The main aim of Pell et al.'s 1999 study was to quantify the extent to which two types of technology, computers and assistive devices, were being used by people with physical disabilities. Additionally, the amount and types of computer education and training being undertaken by people with physical disabilities were examined (see Chapter 6, and the discussion on education above). The particular target group was chosen because the existing literature suggested that the technology helped its members overcome many of the mobility and access problems which were often the only barriers preventing them from obtaining greater levels of independence (ibid.: 56).

Furthermore, Pell et al. (ibid.) found that comparison between present computer ability and demographic variables indicated significant relationships between the level of computer ability and the age of the respondent, the age of disability onsct and the type of disability. Respondents with quadriplegia were more likely to have higher levels of present computer ability than persons with paraplegia. The findings also indicated that training was required in two main areas. The first was in the basic use of computers and standard productivity tools, followed by more advanced skills – such abilities would be highly sought in a society dominated by information production, transfer and analysis, and would improve employment prospects for people with disabilities. The second area for training was in the use of assistive devices (ibid.: 58–9).

In a 1997 study, Pell et al. examined the impact of computer and assistive device use on the employment status and vocational modes of people with physical disabilities in Australia. A survey was distributed to disabled people over 15 years old living in a capital city. Responses were received from 82 people, including those with spinal-cord injuries, cerebral palsy and muscular dystrophy. Of the respondents, 46 were employed, 22 were unemployed and 12 were either students or undertaking voluntary work. Three-quarters of respondents used a computer in their occupation, while 15 used assistive devices. Using logistic regression analysis, Pell et al. (ibid.: 332) found that gender, education, level of computer skill and computer training were significant predictors of employment outcomes. Neither the age of the respondent nor the use of assistive software was a significant predictor. From information obtained in this study, guidelines for a training programme designed to maximise the employability of people with physical disabilities were developed.

Category four: interest

The fourth type of community, the community of interest, was particularly relevant to the model developed for people with physical disabilities. This was where members had a significantly higher degree of interaction than in the community of information, and usually on topics of their interest that were especially relevant to the more general group interests of the interviewees in this study. These communities usually had chatrooms, message boards and discussion groups for extensive member interaction. Thus they were characterised by a significant amount of user-generated content around topics of moral purpose, disability rights, bioethics and such specific issues.

Category five: relationship

The fifth type of community, 'relationship', is as relevant to this study as it is to the Disability Lifestyles website. The community of relationship is built around certain life experiences that are usually very intense and lead to personal bonding between members. Again, when the same question was asked about a secret wish or fantasy, one person responded: 'free internet service provider access for all people with disabilities'. She clarified:

> This is not really a secret wish but a very practical one and one that has the potential to impact on people with disabilities in all areas of Australia. Today, people can use voice-activated programs to communicate, where once this was not possible. So let's hear it for a push to energise and empower the community for e-mail and internet provision for people with disabilities in Australia and provided free as a service to those who otherwise could not access the world.

SeniorNet was an early, important American organisation using digital network services to connect isolated elderly people into a vigorous online community. Studies of the use of SeniorNet suggest it was the interactive services that perpetuated its strong sense of community for that population, rather than its online information service (Furlong, 1989). Similarly, a decade later in a 2000 internet report, it was disclosed that another traditionally isolated, marginalised group had gone online for the first time in the past six months. More than 9 million American women were using the internet, and this surge had led to gender parity in the North American internet population. The researchers argued that this usage had reshaped America's social landscape, because women were using e-mail to enrich their important relationships and enlarge their networks. As with most of the disabled people interviewed in this study, the internet had the opposite of an isolating effect on these users. The women reported that e-mail helped them improve their connections to relatives and friends (Pew Internet & American Life Project, 2000: 7).

There is some research reporting on the internet's paradoxical or contradictory effect on social lives; given that the interviewees in this study identified four major types of barriers to people with disabilities forming successful virtual communities, this must be taken into account. Barriers included the 'isolation' double-edged sword issue (discussed in Chapter 5). So although the internet allows people to feel more connected to others by communicating and interacting, it may also result in perceptions of social isolation. Increased internet use may cause a decrease in interpersonal interaction. High use of the internet may very likely cause social isolation. If one is isolated to begin with, the internet may make one more isolated. If one is social to begin with, the internet may help one become more social (Carnegie-Mellon University, 2001). The results stemming from the longitudinal study were small and not generalisable, despite the methodology being good, and the study lends itself to future research (elaborated in Chapter 9).

Rheingold (1994b) explored how emerging digital networks were changing social groups in *The Virtual Community*. In his more recent book, *Smart Mobs*, Rheingold (2002) has again identified other transformative technologies that are converging to change the way we live – mobile communications, social networks, distributed processing and pervasive computing. He calls these new uses of mobile media 'smart mobs' and describes them as empowering media, because people can use them to summon their friends and keep their social network informed.

However, Rheingold (ibid.) says that he deliberately chose the word 'mob' to emphasise the double-edged nature of new technologies. They have emerged at a time when communication and computing technologies have developed such that they can enhance human talents for cooperation, and communication is facilitated by the new wireless, mobile, portable computing devices. Rheingold (ibid.) says that mobile telephones are a remote control for modern life. The people who constitute smart mobs are individuals who have the power to put themselves together in collectives of their own choosing, because through convergence they connect these real-time devices that possess communication and computing capabilities (for example, mobile phones, SMS and the emerging wireless internet). Their mobile devices connect them with other information devices in the environment, as well as with other people's telephones, and their wireless devices allow them to participate in a virtual social scene.

Category six: transaction

The sixth type, what may be described as transaction-oriented communities, primarily facilitate the buying and selling of products and services, and deliver information that is related to fulfilling those transactions. These communities do not address the members' social needs in any manner; instead there is little or no interaction between members, but the focus is purely to transact business or provide informational leads or consultations about other possible participants in financial-type transactions.

One of the major relevant aspects of computerisation to people with physical disabilities is in their working life, and they posed the question of whether computer and telecommunication systems improve the flexibility of work by enabling employed people to work from home part-time or full-time. Employers who hired disabled telecommuters gain a highly motivated – and often highly educated – workforce. Unfortunately, just as employers have been slow to accept telecommuting as an alternative for able-bodied employees, they have been equally reluctant to employ disabled persons.

If teleworking is not possible for people with disabilities, the UN Online Volunteering Service (www.onlinevolunteering.org) connects non-profit and non-governmental organisations with people willing to volunteer their skills over the internet. The organisations work to eradicate extreme poverty and hunger, empower women, educate children and stop the spread of killer diseases like AIDS. The online volunteers complement the work of these organisations by carrying out a multitude of tasks; for example, they develop fundraising strategies, build networks to generate support for projects, translate documents and create websites for publicity. At any given time there are between 150 and 300 opportunities available on the service's website.

Working life responsibilities were generally of two types: requirements that derived directly from personal needs, and professional and social activities that derived from the profession's obligation to the public in general and society at large. In order to conceptualise and measure working life and professional behaviour, Maslow's (1943) 'hierarchy of needs' of physiological, safety, belonging/social, esteem and autonomy/self-actualisation were again relevant and met through the six categories detailed above. The safety aspect included needs for job security and higher financial rewards (through education, information and transaction). The belonging/social aspect included the need for working-class affinity (through interest and relationship). The esteem aspect included the need for self-assurance associated with a position (again through interest and relationship). The autonomy aspect included the need for decisiveness, initiative and intelligence (through education and information), while self-actualisation included the need for personal growth and development in managerial ability and occupational achievement (through fantasy, interest and relationship).

Telework and broadband have provided mutual benefits for employees with disabilities and their employers alike – such as improved inclusion and collaboration in the workplace for distance e-workers, improved training and learning opportunities and internet equality. Because of the improved ability to deliver such technologies as videoconferences, document sharing and online collaboration, distance workers, both disabled and non-disabled, have worked together efficiently and effectively. These technologies allow all workers to participate more fully with colleagues in centralised locations and with other distance e-workers. Improvements in distance learning and computer-based training capabilities, as well as increased use of multimedia enhancements for students with varying learning styles and broadband technology, have made the delivery of this type of coursework over the internet a reality. This was especially appropriate for education and training for meaningful employment and careers for people with geographic difficulties and/or disabilities.

There are, of course, counter-arguments regarding teleworking. Telecommuting (as it is called in the USA) assists US employers with meeting the requirements of the Americans with Disabilities Act (ADA). While its benefits are not limited to people with disabilities, telecommuting provides organisations with the opportunity and flexibility to integrate successfully workers with disabilities for whom the traditional workplace presents obstacles. However, organisations must guard against using telecommuting to avoid face-to-face contact with people with disabilities. When it is possible for disabled employees to work in the office some or all of the time, that option is favoured. Forcing isolation through telecommuting is counterproductive for integrating disabled people into the organisation. It is considered a violation of the ADA if other reasonable accommodations could be made.

Light (2001) usefully explored how computer-mediated communications by people with physical disabilities had been promoted in the context of employment. She highlighted the fact that since the US Rehabilitation Act 1973, the legal concept of 'reasonable accommodation' had set the standard for bringing such people into the mainstream. At its origins, 'reasonable accommodation' was supposed to be synonymous with environmental barrier removal – even though implementation was highly uneven. Now, according to Light (ibid.), its definition has expanded to include telecommuting. As she pointed out, telecommuting offers superb opportunities for people with disabilities to earn a living. Yet its adoption may be described as a 'double-edged sword', in that it potentially reverses older policies of inclusion by substituting home-bound labour for changes in the workplace. To her, this new technology-centred definition of 'accommodation', which made the claim that cyberspace is space, threatened to undermine the original goal of integration.

The ADA 1990 mandated that reasonable accommodation decisions were to be made case by case, jointly by employer and employee. In fact, this individualised regulatory framework had the potential to lead to dramatic increases in telecommuting, yet simultaneously resulted in the collective consequence of reduced pressure for physical redesign; and as Light (ibid.) argued, physical redesign had implications for integration far beyond access to work. According to the law, the choice of telecommuting is independent of an accessible workplace. Light expressed the fear that without explicit efforts from policy-makers to articulate the benefits of telecommuting in the context of, not as an alternative to, physical barrier reduction, economic realities may easily lead to substitution effects. She argued that regulators had a role to play in reducing the likelihood that computer-mediated communications end up exacerbating the problem they were originally adopted to solve. She sensibly suggested that this might be accomplished by changing the enforcement of barrier removal legislation, keeping statistics on the relationship between telecommuting and physical redesign, or choosing some other strategy (ibid.: 243–4). In fact, employability is larger than the category 'transaction'. For people with disabilities, employability contributes not only to their self-esteem, but also to their 'sense of control'.

Many organisations want to keep employees with chronic disabilities employed and have incentives to do so:

- retain valued employees;
- reduce employee turnover and recruitment costs;
- control the rising cost of disability benefits;
- comply with the Americans with Disabilities Act (Midwest Institute for Telecommuting Education, 2003).

Nonetheless, it is worthwhile documenting how the internet has offered new ways for people with disabilities to participate in the world's activities as equals. Telework extends and broadens inclusiveness by offering advantages to those who cannot commute to the traditional office with ease, such as disabled people and seniors. Telework offers such persons much more than the ability to work from home – it is the conduit to a much richer life. One of the most important aspects of this richer, more inclusive life is the prospect of better economic conditions. Because knowledge work is less physically stressful, workers want to be productive until much later in life. Two types of people in the disability population who will be affected by telework are those who currently have disabilities and are underemployed or unemployed, and people who acquire disabilities in the future, as people live and work longer. Telework benefits both types as well as the employers, who have access to talent and intellectual capital that otherwise is inaccessible or retired. The employer and the economy in general benefit by having experienced, enthusiastic, productive workers (Burks, 2004).

Access

Goggin and Newell (2003) remind us that recent developments in ICT are commonly regarded as the panacea for persons with physical disabilities: the technology can give disabled people access to the total virtual world and many aspects of the real world previously inaccessible to them. Thus ICT has the capacity to be empowering for people with disabilities (Shearman, 1999: 3; Sheldon, 2003). However, we need to be ever mindful 'that in whatever we do we have the opportunity to disable or enable' (Goggin and Newell, 2003: 154). In fact, as they phrase it more fulsomely:

> In different accents and voices, we are ceaselessly promised that technology will deliver us from disability. Yet we would suggest not only that technology will never deliver society from the reality of disability, but that disability continues to be constructed through such technology… As a sociopolitical space, disability will continue to exist, and technology will remain an important site in which it is constructed. (Ibid.: 153)

Access to ICT and virtual communities for persons with disabilities is contingent on the likelihood of affordability and the adoption of universal design principles in equipment and information formats.

Barriers

Barriers, or inhibitors, to ICT usage for disabled people are the flip side of access.[1] Some of the more serious telecommunications issues for consumers with disabilities highlighted by the interviewees were the inaccessible, complex and confusing telecommunications product market, and the fact that ICT frequently created new and unforeseen barriers to equal participation and choice. This was particularly the case if developments took place without reference to the needs of all members of the disability community. Frequently there was a lack of knowledge on the part of staff about the telecommunications products they sold, and products designed to suit the needs of older people and people with disabilities were limited. Furthermore, there was usually a lack of disability equipment programme (DEP) knowledge by staff in telecoms shops, in conjunction with a lack of explanatory brochures or the DEP catalogue. There was a lack of access to a DEP when a consumer's primary carrier is not the major telecommunications company, thus often preventing a person with disabilities from taking advantage of competitive deals. As consumers, many interviewees suggested that there was a need for a comprehensive, independent, universally available DEP. There was a continuing need to address the manifold difficulties that prevent disabled people, especially those on low incomes, from bridging the digital divide. Being information literate, or technologically literate, usually meant that attitudinal or psychological barriers were also minimised.

Refining the theory

Strauss and Corbin (1998: 156) suggest that 'once the researcher has outlined the overarching theoretical scheme, it is time to refine the theory. Refining the theory consists of reviewing the scheme for internal consistency and for gaps in logic, filling in poorly developed categories and trimming excess ones, and validating the scheme.'

The main objective of using the grounded theory methodology was the discovery of theoretically comprehensive explanations about a particular social phenomenon, namely a virtual community for people with long-term, severe physical disabilities. The techniques and analytical procedures and process enabled the researcher to develop a substantive theory that is significant, theory-observation compatible, able to be generalised from (under specific situations), reproducible, rigorous and leads to new socially robust knowledge (Strauss, 1995). Grounded theory methodology is both deductive and inductive. Inductively, in this study the theory emerged from the interviews and the generated data (Kelle, 1997). This theory can then be empirically tested to develop forecasts or predictions from the general principles (Urquhart, 2001).

When the interviewees were asked 'What can you tell me about your experience with virtual communities and how you use ICT both personally and professionally?' the question elicited unanimously positive responses to the topic. However, the well-being model for a virtual community that emerged from the data collected for this study had some similarities to some models that already existed in fact and in the literature. The literature described essentially four major 'types' of e-communities in existence on the internet – depending on the types of consumer needs they met. Thus e-communities were likely to be primarily transaction-oriented, interest-oriented, fantasy-oriented or relationship-oriented, or a meld or hybrid of two or more of these orientations. It was interesting to note that the present theoretical model for a virtual community for people with severe long-term physical disabilities in fact expanded on the number of types of e-communities desirable to meet the needs of this particular sector (Armstrong and Hagel, 1995: 134–40; Chang et al., 1999: 2). This well-being model was innovative, sustainable and evidence-based, reduced social isolation for people with physical disabilities and was transferable across communities to some other disability types. It was expected that this theoretical well-being model of 'best practice' would also contribute to the reduction of social isolation in other population groups, for example older people.

There was concern as to how the investigator would know when an acceptable theory at the end of the 'grounded theory' process had emerged. Verification or 'truthfulness', according to Strauss and Corbin (1990: 108), involves 'looking for evidence in the data to verify our statements of relationship' while 'also looking for instances of when they might not hold up'. A crucial factor was that the verification process was not necessarily one of finding proof, but rather sought support for 'statements of relationships' between concepts and the developed theory, and was actually verified by the enquiry process (ibid.: 109). In this study the 'developed theory' was verified. Furthermore, Strauss and Corbin (1998: 269) provided seven evaluative criteria against which the quality of the qualitative research that was designed to build the theory may be judged (see Chapter 6).

The ACM-CHI Conference in 1997 identified five necessary multidisciplinary characteristics of a virtual community (see Chapter 2). Below are examples from the present study (summarised from Table 5.1 showing the grounded theory relationships derived from the study findings). The findings are compared with the ACM-CHI characteristics of a virtual community.

- *Members have a shared goal, interest, need or activity that provides the primary reason for belonging to the community.* In this study it became apparent that the shared goal, interest, need or activity for people with long-term, severe physical disabilities derived from the grounded theory 'phenomenon' that featured in all their interviews: to regain 'a sense of control' over their lives.

- *Members engage in repeated, active participation; often intense interactions, strong emotional ties and shared activities occur among participants.* In the case of people with physical disabilities, it is likely that members of the virtual community would engage in repeated, active participation accessing their online communities that support sociability through shared areas of need and interest (Burnett, 2000).

- *Members have access to shared resources, and policies determine the access to those resources.* In the case of disabled people, the members would have access to shared resources through portals, and would monitor the policies that governed access to those resources. According to grounded theory, policies would be described/ determined by the properties; for example the policy relating to 'capacity building' would in turn be determined by the 'education' policy.

■ *Reciprocity of information, support and services among members is important.* In the case of people with physical disabilities, as the study indicated, they would reciprocate information, support and services among the membership through discussion groups. The 'subcategories' of grounded theory would define the nature of the information exchanged.

■ *There is a shared context of social conventions, language and protocols.* For disabled people, the study confirmed that there would be a shared context based on shared experiences pertaining to technology, disability and so forth (Whittaker et al., 1997: 137). The 'dimensions' of grounded theory would outline their social conventions, language and protocols.

The well-being model (or theory) graphically represented in Figure 7.1 reflects the five necessary multidisciplinary characteristics of a virtual community as defined at the ACM-CHI Conference. These characteristics are implicit in the model developed in this study. Also, they overlap strongly with Schuler's (1996b) six core values and attributes for community networks: democracy, education, health, equality, information exchange and communication (as discussed in Chapter 2 and again at the beginning of this chapter). These characteristics highlight that access, equity, participation and self-empowerment are absolutely essential to any virtual community for persons with disabilities in the digital age. Furthermore, it meets Strauss's (1995: 10) dimensional location of a given theory in relation to abstraction, scope, range, specificity, conceptual complexity and applicability.

The online information and communication service proposed here would provide a portal to six key areas – a meld of six types of electronic communities – derived from the 'categories' established by the grounded theory method: education, fantasy, information, interest, relationship and transaction. Each area would provide links to a variety of relevant websites. The primary aim of this study is to establish an online environment for the provision and sharing of information about everyday life, in an informal and friendly manner, for people who have long-term, severe physical disabilities.

The literature has established that virtual communities traditionally are groups of strangers separated by geographical distance, but sharing common interests, expressed using ICT. Historically, many of the most successful sites run the gamut of providing scarce information about very specialised topics to providing a 'place' to talk about mutually relevant topics. Today, the tremendous growth of the internet is successfully making a variety of e-services a part of many citizens' everyday lives. E-services such as web-banking, web-shopping, e-learning, e-healthcare and e-government are available in most countries around the world.

The conceptualisation and development of a well-being model, based on grounded theory, attends to the experiences of a specific cohort. It may then be used by other researchers to explore the universality of the process of defining virtual communities for other groups of persons with mobility disabilities, for example the elderly.

Notes

1. The DCITA in Canberra has recently released a discussion paper on the role of ICT in building communities and social capital. Removing the barriers that exclude disabled and older people from ICT usage is critical in building social capital. Barriers may include lack of physical access; cost and quality of infrastructure, equipment and advice; geographical location; limited information literacy competence; disability; lack of skills and training or access to learning opportunities; attitudes such as a perceived lack of relevant content, fear and security concerns; and poor design – for example, some equipment, interactive voice response systems and websites (Department of Communication, Technology and the Arts, 2005).

8

Future directions for virtual communities for people with physical disabilities

Access to technology is the gateway into the twenty-first century to jobs, education and information. We have to make sure that people with disabilities can get through that gateway... in their communities, in their languages and on their terms. (Alliance for Technology Access, 1999)

This final chapter provides a synthesis of the study's findings and their relationship with the literature in order to highlight the unique outcomes of the study itself – that is, the set of six recommendations in the next section. These outcomes are derived from the key categories of relevance (see Chapter 7). This chapter achieves this purpose through a four-part approach:

- it considers how the study outcomes may be interpreted by key stakeholders and policy-makers;
- it determines what this study contributes to the understanding of the grounded theory methodology;
- it explores the study in relation to generalisability and other proposed further studies;
- it assesses what the study contributes to the understanding of virtual communities, specifically for people with long-term, severe physical disabilities.

In this way, the chapter demonstrates how access to ICT, information literacy, telecommunications and bridging the digital divide are all crucial components in a virtual community for people with physical disabilities and their regaining a 'sense of control'. Indeed, for many such people, all these components are equally vital to their social and economic lives.

In addition to all the general ICT applications, such as e-mail and other electronic communications, that enable successful virtual communities for people with disabilities, a variety of applications exist in which other members of the community with mobility restrictions, such as the elderly, have shown interest. These include alarms and other security services. The general ICT applications provide alternative modes of communication, information access and presentation. They give the opportunity for disabled people to undertake activities and transactions from home and permit remote access to care and other support services. Information services, teleshopping, telebanking and remote access-on-demand to entertainment, education and leisure offer new possibilities for people with disabilities.

Many people with disabilities need support from formal or informal care services if they are to live full, independent and secure lives in the community and participate in all aspects of social interaction. Technology plays an increasing role in this area. For example, it supports alarm and other security services based on voice or video connections. It enables remote social services to be provided through video telephony. It supports medical monitoring and consultation via data and video links. Furthermore, technology makes information accessible and communication possible in ways that best suit the abilities of each individual, while uncovering new opportunities for access, participation, inclusion and socio-economic integration. Although collectively making up some 19 per cent of the Australian population, disabled people have widely varying interests and needs. Their diverse requirements for ICT present both market opportunities for the telecommunications and computing industries and social challenges for policy-makers. In the time this study has been in progress, exciting new programmes have made joining the online community more affordable for people with disabilities.

For example, Green PC (www.greenpc.com.au) – a social enterprise initiative of the Info X-change – makes available low-cost, recycled personal computers to community organisations and individuals on low incomes. Major sponsorship of this effort was provided initially by the Department of Human Services and the Victorian state government's Community Jobs Program. The enterprise anticipates that future donations from corporate sponsors and other government departments will eventually lead to self-funding. Similarly, Brisbane City Council in Queensland has helped low-income earners with affordable access to computers and the internet since 2001.

How may the investigation outcomes be interpreted?

This section outlines the key insights gained from the study and establishes recommendations for the three main stakeholders and policy-makers – government, industry and consumer groups. The industry groupings involve the telecommunications services industry, the equipment providers and the information and online service providers. These stakeholders act to increase the availability of opportunities, increase the accessibility of products and services, enhance the affordability of products and services, and finally to increase public awareness (Cullen and Robinson, 1997: 203–12).

As part of the process of addressing the main research question – 'how can virtual communities best be facilitated for persons with long-term disabilities?' – the practical results from this study have answered the five research questions from Chapter 1 with varying degrees of satisfaction. The second question, in particular, was dealt with fulsomely and satisfactorily by the six allied health/information/policy adviser professionals whose interviews are deconstructed and analysed in Chapter 6. Answers to the five questions that define the research problem follow.

What are the information practices of people with disabilities?

People with disabilities, apart from their general information needs and uses, have information practices that focus on issues relating to their disability, mobility and access/barrier issues. They invariably use the internet, virtual forums and specific websites and virtual communities that are already in existence when they are looking for information about, for example, aspects of health and disability, travel, accessible accommodation and assistive technology (see Chapter 4). The implications are highlighted in Recommendation 1 below.

How does government policy on information provision influence the information needs of people with disabilities? How do consumers use this information?

In the past decade the DCITA in Canberra has taken responsibility for producing the government's information policy, which impacts on all Australians. Specifically, the National Office for the Information Economy (NOIE) initially provided a strategic framework for the information economy. During the drafting of the framework principles, several prevailing government policies, programmes and initiatives were referenced (Chapter 3). Disabled people access this government information not only through the NOIE website but also via other websites better targeted to their interests, such as that maintained by the federal government welfare office, Centrelink, the Physical Disability Council of Australia and so on (Chapters 3–6). They use the information to help establish and maintain their quality of life. The implications are highlighted in Recommendations 2, 4 and 5 below.

What other identifiable information needs – other than social, health and efficacy – would enhance the quality of life of people with disabilities?

The identifiable information needs of disabled people (apart from social, health and efficacy needs) are similar to those of any other information user, but include specific needs as well (see Chapters 4–6). For example, some of the identifiable information needs include pragmatic uses such as investments and online ordering, shopping and bill paying. More esoteric information needs might relate to life's moral purposes. The implications are highlighted in Recommendation 3 below.

What is the role of ICT in addressing the social, political, informational, health, efficacy and other needs of people with disabilities?

The primary role of ICT in addressing the range of needs specified above for persons with disabilities is in affording a 'sense of control' in their lives again (see Chapters 2, 3, 5 and 6). The implications are highlighted in Recommendation 6 below.

What are the perceived barriers for people with disabilities as the users of communication technology? How do the inherent technological limitations themselves impact on disabled people in their efforts to meet their information needs?

The interviewees identified four major types of barriers to people with disabilities forming successful virtual communities: costs, both economic and social, and physical and technological barriers, which included connection problems in rural and remote areas, the 'isolation' double-edged sword and the inaccessibility of chatrooms to people with physical disabilities (see Chapters 2–6). The implications are highlighted in Recommendations 1–6 below.

Recommendations

Consequently, there are certain recommendations and topics for future investigation that may be derived from the study outcomes. The recommendations come directly from the opportunities and challenges presented by the six categories (see Chapter 5). The recommendations are for assistive technology; accessibility or 'design for all'; availability and awareness of information and online services; industry standards, codes and practices regarding accessibility; affordability; and education and training. Tables 5.1 and 8.1 link the categories to these six recommendations.

Recommendation 1: assistive technology

Legislation similar to the US Assistive Technology Act 2004 should be introduced in other countries as required as soon as possible, and an independent disability equipment programme should be instituted. A possible future development would be to compile a webpage listing all the producers and distributors of assistive equipment to make the information specific and accessible for all users.

Rationale

The current situation for obtaining assistive telecommunications equipment is frequently inadequate. Customers with disabilities who need assistive equipment are not able to take advantage of competition in the marketplace. The situation is anti-competitive, discriminates against disabled people and limits their choice of carrier and type of service. Undoubtedly, this situation is not unique to Australia. Nguyen et al. (2004), in their research into telecommunications options for people with physical disabilities, also derived this conclusion. They present it as an ongoing challenge. Their research trialled and evaluated new configurable 'off-the-shelf' technological options that improve many lifestyle aspects for people with physical disabilities. They considered alternative solutions (such as car kits, voice-recognition software, hands-free technology and voice mail) to improve the awareness and telecommunications experiences of disabled people. Their research aimed to enable these members of the community to participate and experience telecommunications technology to the same extent as able-bodied people currently do. These researchers concluded that with the right policies, processes and support in place, current off-the-shelf solutions help to alleviate problems and improve the lifestyle, social interaction, security and independence of many people with physical disabilities.

The disability equipment programme, however, is only available to customers of Australia's major telecommunications company, Telstra, and customers of carriers that purchase wholesale landline infrastructure from Telstra. Thus not all telecommunications customers have access to the DEP. As the current universal service provider, Telstra has been obliged to develop and maintain its DEP. As a result, the Telstra DEP has by far the largest and most comprehensive range of any in Australia.[1]

Contact with the Telstra shopfront is the first step for the potential DEP customer. The next step is to contact the disability enquiry helpline (DEH). Many potential customers, however, make this their first action and bypass the visit to the shopfront. Those who have gone to a shopfront regard it as a fruitless and frustrating exercise due to the long and convoluted process required before suitable assistive technology can be obtained. In contrast, one telephone call to the DEH results in an immediate home visit to assess the best solution; the supply of the most suitable piece of equipment rapidly follows.

Telstra shopfronts have been the first point of contact for consumers with disabilities who want information or to inspect disability equipment for better access to phone services. Unfortunately, Telstra shopfronts do not have disability equipment on display. Theoretically, they have copies of the DEP catalogue and brochures about the DEP. Sales representatives also are expected to have some knowledge of the DEP and knowledge or training in how to interact with customers with disabilities.

In the competitive telecommunications marketplace, a radical rethink is needed to make sure that disabled consumers are not discriminated against in taking up competitive deals because of their lack of access to a DEP. Urgent action needs to be taken by the Commonwealth government and the Australian communications industry to investigate ways of operating a comprehensive, independent, centralised, consumer-involved and universally available DEP.[2] This model could be instituted in any country with similar deficits.

Recommendation 2: accessibility or 'design for all'

All services and equipment should be designed taking the needs of disabled and older users into account from the start of the design phase, in what is often referred to as 'design for all', 'universal design' or 'inclusive design'.

Rationale

Developers in all sectors of the telecommunications industry need to continue to increase the availability of opportunities and accessibility of products and services for disabled people (Human Rights and Equal Opportunity Commission, 2000). Needs and interests vary widely and many potential barriers remain (COST 219 bis Telecommunications Charter, 1999). As persons with disabilities do not have equitable access to the modern telecommunications medium, policy is required to address these aspects through anti-discrimination legislation and Universal Service Obligations. Telstra, the major Australian media-telecommunications company, expresses its USO as parity of service and parity of costs. Research and consultations undertaken by this study in relation to the general socio-economic position and ICT needs of people with disabilities indicate that they place an extremely high value on telephone services. Primarily, the telephone enables them to maintain contact with family and friends; in turn, this lessens their feelings of isolation brought about by reduced ability to access the wider community. Accessible phone services are also essential for making medical appointments necessary to regulate the effects of disabilities. Disabled people are more likely to need a reliable telephone service for medical and/or domestic violence emergency calls.

Recommendation 3: availability/awareness

The information and online service providers should take action to enhance public awareness of their interfaces and applications.

Rationale

Opportunities in this area not only depend on the availability and affordability of ICT products and services, but on policies, marketing and distribution.[3] Services like telebanking and teleshopping are essential for people with disabilities to live independently. More general access to online information services (for example, for weather, news, sports, lotto numbers, etc.) via the Wireless Application Protocol (WAP) is also invaluable.

Recommendation 4: industry standards, codes and practices regarding accessibility

The information technology and telecommunications services industries need to increase the accessibility of services to all consumers, because many potential barriers remain.

Rationale

Making services widely accessible increases the usage of the networks and value-added services, and improves the corporate image of the industry. Anti-discrimination legislation, USOs and customer service guarantees (CSGs) are increasingly required to ensure these services are available and accessible.

Bridging the digital divide for disabled people on low incomes, however, is an exercise fraught with difficulty, as the following problems illustrate. The purchase price of computers frequently presents a problem, even in a heavily subsidised computer refurbishment scheme. Similarly, the cost of accessing even the cheapest of ISPs is beyond the budget of many people on low incomes. Setting the system up in the home is also a problem. It is difficult to arrange and adds to the cost of the necessary hardware. Maintaining the set-up is problematic, both logistically and economically. Training is costly and logistically difficult to access. An in-home tutoring scheme carries the risk of having a 'stranger' in the home. Where a refurbished computer has shareware software that mimics commercial software, problems arise because the small differences in the programs are sufficient to confuse a learner.

Recommendation 5: affordability

Welfare income policies need to be coordinated with provisions under the USOs.

Rationale

The information technology and telecommunications industries need to enhance the affordability of products and services available to people with disabilities, because these people are more likely to fall within lower income groups. This may involve indirect financing of information and telecommunications equipment and packaging of service/tariff costs to meet the different needs of disabled people.

Furthermore, USOs and CSGs, as the relevant regulatory instruments, require review and upgrading at the legislative and administrative levels. Periodic review of these instruments will ensure that access to and functionality of telephone services for people with disabilities are improved, both in the short term and when new technologies are introduced.

Recommendation 6: education and training

In addition to ICT and AT education and training, people with disabilities need support to become information literate and committed to lifelong learning.

Rationale

In a paper on the use of technology by people with physical disabilities in Australia, Pell et al. (1999) strongly recommend that increased levels of training in the use of computers and assistive devices be provided to these people. As they point out, 'few studies have examined the extent to which technology is being used by persons with disabilities living in the community'. Basically, they found that in a 1999 survey of 295 disabled people in Brisbane, only some 60 per cent of respondents were computer users. The researchers concluded that 'increased levels of training in the use of computers and assistive devices needs to be provided to people with physical disabilities'. They state: 'It is suggested that such education, together with training in the use of computers, be carried out late in the rehabilitation program for people with spinal injuries' (ibid.: 57). The study concludes that while many people with disabilities use computers and assistive devices, many do not and are not taking full advantage of the opportunities presented by technology. The low rates of assistive device use, particularly by people with high-level quadriplegia, are of particular concern and suggest the need for better education about the capabilities and availability of these devices (ibid.: 60).

Implementing the recommendations

The stakeholder recommendations made during this study, summarised in Table 8.1, demonstrate that Pell et al.'s position remains relevant and needs to be addressed – undoubtedly not only in Australia, but also in other countries endeavouring to provide quality ICT standards for people with physical disabilities.

The recommendations are tabulated differently from the text describing them above in order to show more of the possible implications and relationships. 'General', 'availability' and 'accessibility' all include 'design for all'; 'accessibility' includes 'codes and standards'; 'affordability' incorporates 'assistive technology'; and 'awareness' incorporates 'education and training'.

These stakeholder recommendations are generalised and are applicable to groups other than people with disabilities. The adaptation of many of these approaches and findings on ICT in this specific area also indicates wider application to other groups, such as the elderly. Sectors within a global community need to be served specifically, and many of the concerns identified in this study establish guideposts for serving the future needs of all types of groups.

Some of the investigations undertaken in this study, however, highlight a number of serious telecommunications issues or barriers for people with disabilities, and these warrant addressing:

Table 8.1 Outline of recommendations for the various stakeholders

Stakeholders	General	Availability	Accessibility	Affordability	Awareness
Policy-makers	Coordinate policy Promote 'information society' Meet differentiated needs	Investment in infrastructure	Anti-discrimination USO Access to basic services (Telstra's Access for Everyone 2002 package) Access to advanced services 'Design for all' Obligatory standards	USO Social protection Assistive technology services	Public awareness Organisational innovation Service innovation Monitor social impacts Public debate Balance market and social needs within civil society
Information technology industry – general	Recognise potential Seek to understand market	Cooperation across sectors	Coordination of sectors 'Design for all' Implement standards Start with existing services More R&D Involve users	Flexible packages Cooperate with public sector	Marketing and distribution Information and awareness Support innovation
Telecoms services industry	Different needs	Broadband infrastructure Cooperate with public sector	Functional equivalence Implement standards Procurement policies	Flexible tariff structures	Marketing and distribution awareness Information and awareness Support innovation
Telecoms equipment industry	Mainstream 'design for all'	Mainstream 'design for all'	Equipment accessibility	Cheaper equipment	Marketing and distribution Information and awareness Support innovation
Information service providers	Recognise potential Understand market	Services of practical value	Service accessibility	Flexible packages Cooperate with public sector	Marketing and distribution Information and awareness Support innovation
Consumer groups	Awareness and expertise Identify common causes	Lobby policy-makers Lobby industry Provide services directly	Lobby policy-makers Lobby Telstra Lobby equipment industry Lobby information service providers Provide expert input Support user involvement	Lobby policy-makers Lobby industry Exercise consumer power	Awareness of members Wider awareness Technical support Monitor social impacts

Source: adapted from Cullen and Robinson (1997)

- the complex and confusing product market;
- lack of knowledge on the part of staff about the products they sell;
- lack of products designed to suit the needs of older and disabled people;
- the need to research the market potential for a mobile phone designed to meet the needs of older people and people with long-term or temporary disabilities;
- the lack of DEP[4] knowledge by staff in Telstra shopfronts, in conjunction with the lack of explanatory brochures or the DEP catalogue;
- lack of access to a DEP when a consumer's primary carrier is not Telstra;
- the need for a comprehensive, independent, universally available DEP;
- the continuing need to address the many difficulties that prevent disabled people, especially those on low incomes, from bridging the digital divide.

In Australia the Commonwealth government, individual carriers and carriage service providers, and the Australian Communications Industry Forum must continue to work closely with telecommunications disability advisory bodies to address and act to resolve these issues, especially when Telstra becomes fully privatised (see www.nowwearetalking. com.au for Telstra's dedicated telecommunications policy coverage). The risk that the Telstra DEP may eventually become a costly liability is palpable. This, of course, could have negative consequences for the range and availability of equipment held. It also means that development of new assistive equipment may be curtailed. The consequences for Australian people with disabilities would be inequitable and unsupportable under the Disability Discrimination Act 1992, the Telecommunications Act 1997 and the Telecommunications (Consumer Protection and Services Standards) Act 1999.

How does this investigation measure up against the criteria for assessing grounded theory?

Logical coherence and convincing grounding in the evidence are the key criteria for evaluating the validity of this type of study (Kvale, 1995). To evaluate how a study contributes to the understanding of grounded theory techniques, Strauss and Corbin (1998: 270–2) provide a series of questions that are equivalent to criteria for evaluating the empirical grounding of a study. These are addressed below (see also Table 5. 1 to support how these criteria are addressed).

- *The canon of reproducibility.* A researcher using the same methods ought to be able to come up with the same theoretical explanation.
- *The canon of generalisability.* A grounded theory study is generalisable to specific situations only (discussed later in this chapter).

> We are not suggesting that a substantive theory (one developed from the study of one small area of investigation and from one specific population) has the explanatory power of a larger, more general theory. It cannot, because it does not build in the variation or include the broad propositions of a more general theory. However, the real merit of a substantive theory lies in its ability to speak specifically for the populations from which it was derived and apply back to them. Naturally, the more systematic and widespread the theoretical sampling, the more conditions and variations will be discovered and built into the theory and, therefore, the greater its explanatory power (and precision). (Ibid.: 267)

Criterion 1: are concepts generated?

This criterion assesses whether the concepts are grounded in the data. Clearly, this study fits this criterion, as the concept 'a sense of control' is generated from the interview data (see Chapters 5 and 6).

Criterion 2: are the concepts systematically related?

This criterion asks if conceptual linkages have been made, and whether they are grounded in the data. The study explores the data of linkages between the concept of 'a sense of control' and the categories, properties, dimensions and subcategories, and so fits this criterion (see Chapters 5 and 6).

Criterion 3: are there many conceptual linkages and are the categories well developed? Do categories have conceptual density?

This criterion questions whether the categories (education, fantasy, information, interest, relationship and transaction) and subcategories (for example, access and choice are the subcategories for the category 'information') are tightly linked; and also if the categories are theoretically dense with respect to their properties (for example, e-searching, equality and virtual communities for the category 'information'). The coding processes used in this study did result in categories of dense properties with innumerable dimensions. Therefore, the study fits this criterion (see Chapters 5 and 6).

Criterion 4: is variation built into the theory?

This criterion states that variation is important, because it signifies that a concept has been examined under a series of different conditions and developed across its range of dimensions. While the study reports only a single phenomenon or concept ('a sense of control'), it does establish many conditions under which it appears, so it fits this criterion (see Chapters 5 and 6).

Criterion 5: are the conditions under which variation can be found built into the study and explained?

This criterion, according to Urquhart (1997: 172), specifies that the analysis should not be so 'microscopic' as to disregard 'macroscopic' sources such as economic conditions, social movements, trends, cultural values and so forth. The variation or dimensions for the category 'interest', for example, include access and equity. Again, this study fits within the criterion (see Chapters 5 and 6).

Criterion 6: has process been taken into account?

This criterion questions whether processes/stages in the research have been identified and marks this as important, because it enables theory users to explain action under changing conditions. Nonetheless, Strauss and Corbin (1998: 272) observe that 'the conceptual scheme used to explain process is less important than attempts to bring it into the analysis'. The findings from this study are presented in such a manner as to satisfy this criterion.

Criterion 7: do the theoretical findings seem significant, and to what extent?

This criterion states that a grounded theory study can fail to produce findings of any significance if the theory 'canons' or procedures are applied without creativity or insight. 'By this, we mean that the research fails to deliver new information or to produce guidelines for action' (ibid.). Strauss and Corbin believe significant findings depend on three characteristics in the researcher (in addition to the quality of the data collected): analytical ability, theoretical sensitivity and sufficient writing ability to convey the findings. The study's analysis and findings do seem to fit within Strauss and Corbin's characteristics and this criterion for evaluating the empirical grounding of a study (see Chapters 5–8).

Criterion 8: does the theory stand the test of time and become part of the discussions and ideas exchanged among relevant social and professional groups?

Certainly, the process of undertaking this study has contributed profoundly to the understanding of a virtual community for people with disabilities – and produced rich data and robust theory. The real impact of the concept of 'a sense of control' on persons with long-term, severe physical disabilities through ICT use in a virtual community will only become apparent when the theory developed from the study's findings is published in a scholarly, international, refereed journal, and also as a monograph by an international scholarly publisher, and is then implemented fully for its stakeholders. Hopefully, implementation of the model will be undertaken by CONROD Australia.

Generalisability

This study acknowledges that small qualitative studies are not generalisable in the traditional sense, yet have redeeming qualities which effectively set them above that requirement (Myers, 2000). People who lack familiarity with qualitative methodology processes may be surprised by the sheer volume of data and the detailed level of analysis that results, even when the study is limited to a small number of subjects. Furthermore, a complete analysis can provide evidence of the relationships among variables and may stimulate additional research questions in the particular area of study. There is agreement that the most rewarding results do not come from the ability to do extensive generalisations, but rather from the ability to seek answers to how people make sense of their experiences.

Virtual communities, disability and qualitative research share the mutual characteristics of dealing with subjectivity, describing the complexity of lived experience and appreciating realities where holism and intuition are valued. Qualitative methodology, therefore, lends itself to research that attempts to understand such human experiences as disability, lack of control, barriers to accessibility of technological services and the human impact of the digital divide.

How does this investigation contribute to understanding virtual communities for people with disabilities?

The CONROD Australia project established an online environment for the provision and sharing of information about everyday life for people who were completing or had recently completed rehabilitation after a traumatic spinal injury. This Disability Lifestyles website was an online stepping-stone between rehabilitation services and full adjustment back into the community. However, it was the two analyses of findings in Chapters 5 and 6 that presented the framework or theoretical well-being model, including the socio-political components, for a virtual community for people with mobility impairments – a need that had not been previously investigated.

The primary research question that the present study explored and analysed was: how can virtual communities for persons with long-term, physical disabilities best be facilitated? The study also developed a theoretical framework or model of 'best practice' for a virtual community for such people. They were the population interviewed in this study (as well as allied health workers, policy and information personnel involved with service provision to persons with disabilities), and were regarded as a representative population.

The key findings, well-being model and theory for the this study specific to a virtual community for people with long-term, severe physical disabilities did parallel and extend the general findings elaborated by Beamish (1995). The key findings, model and theory of this study also upheld the five necessary multidisciplinary characteristics that Whittaker et al. (1997: 137) found essential to a virtual community. Beamish (1995) described community networks as sharing three characteristics, also found to be integral to the theoretical framework for a virtual community for people with long-term physical disabilities.

- *A focus on local issues.* In addition to information services, community networks provide forums for discussion of local issues. For example, in this study the participants focused on their shared 'interests' – that is, on disability rights.

- *Access.* The network is concerned to reflect and include all members of the community. For example, in this study the participants accessed information using assistive technology.

- *Social change and community development.* There is a belief that the system with its communication and information can strengthen and vitalise the community. For example, in this study the participants were empowered to pursue aspects of capacity building as part of strengthening and vitalising their community.

Preece's (2000) idea of 'designing usability and supporting sociability' with 'lifelong learning as their central focus' (such as Britain has created in its 'learning cities') offers a powerful model for virtual communities for people with long-term, severe physical disabilities to emulate (Longworth, 2002: 14–15).

> Yet from our own experiences at the local level we know that community networking is not so much about the technologies as the people. The technologies are a means to an end – not a goal in themselves. Access is about the ability to use the technologies in ways that seem relevant to people's everyday lives and interests. Access is not about having a PC or TV... The potential that technology offers people to improve their lives is less about accessing information and electronic commerce and much more about building up self-confidence, learning... (Shearman, 1999: 3)

Virtual communities in the developed world form, grow and change rapidly in ways that must be considered for their applicability to the Australian case as well as other situations.

Proposed further studies

While this work provides an overall view of a virtual community for people with long-term, severe physical disabilities, much research still needs to be done, and a number of further studies invite consideration. These proposed studies would supplement the current investigation and CONROD Australia's work in providing the portal for Disability Lifestyles as it now stands.

The current findings reported that disabled people experienced 'a sense of control' from the use of ICT and the notion of a virtual community. Further studies undertaken in this area would contribute to the generalisability of the work. They would also provide useful information to the public and the disability sector for planning, policy development and national coordination, as well as help to identify community training and education needs. Some further possibilities might include:

- the development of projects, tools and resources to monitor progress and track and document the impact of ICT use in the establishment of virtual communities for all the various disability types;
- the development of a generic disability virtual community model for a national group of people with mobility disabilities, and then an international group of such people;
- the development and ongoing maintenance of a generic disability virtual community 'toolkit' and resource guide;
- a study into the role of a generic disability virtual community model in the development of social capital and community building;
- the development of accountability and evaluation methodologies for ICT and virtual community projects that have a disability community impact;
- the implementation of longitudinal studies into the social, economic, environmental and technological implications of telecommunications developments with respect to people with impairments;

- an investigation into whether high internet use actually causes isolation, and whether this has any different effect with respect to people with disabilities;
- an investigation to determine the level of internet use that is socially isolating.

A major step, in addition to any quantitative studies into virtual communities for people with long-term, severe physical disabilities, would be to undertake a series of qualitative studies into virtual communities for various other disability types. This would provide more specific evidence of the benefits of ICT to the various disability sectors, and refine understanding of the contribution of ICT to specific disability communities. It would also illuminate the economic impacts and employment options (beneficial or otherwise) that influence the day-to-day activities of people with various types of disability.

In the process of completing this work, the notion that people with severe long-term physical disabilities can achieve 'a sense of control' irrespective of the extent of their disabilities has become a reality. Extensive IT development and society's capacity to embrace technological change mean that people with disabilities can anticipate, and participate in, a 'virtual community' where factors over which they themselves have control are the main limits to their connectivity.

The most recent major change has been the advent of the new wireless technology. This WiFi[5] technology affords unbridled power to connect and the freedom to move. As wireless technologies continue to evolve, the future will be definitely wireless, and the potential of this technology for the physically disabled presents opportunities for freedom to be 'sensed' and physical limitations to be continuously challenged and shifted.

This work has significance in that it contributes to the development of virtual communities for people with physical disabilities. Its extends the knowledge and understanding of the allied health and information professionals who provide services to them. It provides a serious stimulus to the IT community and the telecommunications industry to respond to more than the general needs of the markets they serve. It achieves these three things through its outcomes, which have made possible the addition of a valuable well-being model to the developing research agenda in this area of virtual communities for people with disabilities.

In addition to liaising with these stakeholders, the policy-makers must undertake other actions to remove identified barriers. These include targeting those initiatives that necessarily intersect with a number of policy areas, especially in ICT, telecommunications and social policy. The information technology and telecommunications policy areas of relevance include the regulation of services and prices, legislation on and regulation of accessibility and investment in infrastructure development. The relevant social policy has to include income support, cost subsidies and legislation governing aspects of accessibility. The current 'information age' initiatives encourage a climate that permits a range of ICT applications to meet the different needs of persons with disabilities in an optimal way. The difficult challenge for the policy-makers is to balance the needs of all their clientele equitably, but nevertheless this must be achieved (see Table 8.1).

The grounded theory approach has successfully identified key categories of relevance to the groups interviewed. Virtual community, disability and qualitative research share the mutual characteristic of dealing with subjectivity. They help successfully describe the complexity of lived experience and lead to an appreciation of realities where holism and intuition are valued. Qualitative methodology, upon which this research has relied, yields outcomes that create greater understanding of the many human experiences that disability so often engenders.

Great opportunities and immense challenges lie ahead. The stakeholders need to be challenged to develop strategies and initiatives that meet not only the informational but also the socio-political needs of people with disabilities as determined by this 'well-being model' of 'best practice'. Additionally, they must foster a collaborative approach to resolving the problems that will be of value, and impact, to that specific group of people with disabilities in our wide, global world.

Notes

1. In a letter from Matthew Stafford, adviser to Senator the Hon. Helen Coonan, Minister for Communications, Information Technology and the Arts, Australia, received on 29 August 2005, he wrote:

   The Government is aware of the importance of ensuring that people with disabilities have equitable access to telecommunications services in the competitive telecommunications environment. In relation to your concerns about the full privatisation of Telstra, the legislated safeguards which will ensure access to telecommunications for people with disabilities will continue regardless of the ownership structure of Telstra, including the requirements under the 'Telecommunications (Consumer Protection and Service Standards) Act 1999' and the 'Disability Discrimination Act 1992' (DDA).

The Government does not support an expansion of the existing legal and financial requirements which are placed on the telecommunications industry in this regard. Placing additional imposts on service providers that do not supply telecommunications equipment as part of their business activities would go beyond the requirements of the DDA and would treat telecommunications companies differently from other industry sectors. Given the large number of service providers that are small and medium sized businesses, placing additional financial and regulatory burdens on the sector is likely to adversely affect competition and industry development.

The supply of telecommunication equipment for people with disabilities was considered as part of the Telecommunications Service Inquiry (TSI). The TSI Report found that further obligations need not be set through telecommunications legislation because the DDA already provides appropriate avenues for people with disabilities to pursue their concerns in relation to equipment provision. The Inquiry noted that if a consumer feels that they are not receiving adequate service from their telecommunications provider, then there are processes for redress available through advocacy groups and the Telecommunication Industry Ombudsman.

With respect to your proposal for further discussion to be held between consumers, regulators, industry and government agencies, I note that the Australian Communications Industry Forum agreed in 2004 to organise such a seminar but considered it prudent to wait until after the work of its Customer Equipment and Cable Reference Panel Working Committee 19 has been completed. The Government will continue to monitor the Disability Equipment Program provided by the Universal Service Provider and consider any views presented on these issues.

2. The Australian DCITA commissioned the Allen Consulting Group (www.allenconculting.com.au) to undertake a review of the DEP and present their findings by 12 June 2006. Part of the brief was to conduct small focus groups of consumers who use the DEP. It also consulted with advocacy groups, regulators and equipment providers throughout March/April 2006.
3. The Wireless Association has an accessibility website (www. accesswireless.org/product/comsumer_access_guides.htm).
4. Telstra and Optus operate DEPs that provide specialist terminal equipment for disabled people at rental rates equivalent to those paid by people without disabilities for the same equipment functionality.
5. WiFi is wireless fidelity – the popular term for a high-frequency wireless LAN. WiFi uses the Ethernet protocol and gives access speeds up to 11 Mbit/s.

Appendix I: Synopses of participants

Interviewee 1: Jane (50s, lives in a large regional town) has been involved in the social welfare field since 1978, after an accident some years earlier that resulted in quadriplegia. She completed university studies in community development and social welfare as well as a social work degree between 1981 and 1984. She has held a variety of positions in the disability sector for the past two decades, including working in individual and systems advocacy development. She has several years' experience in community development projects, service delivery and management issues for disability services, and wide experience of consultation processes with local, state and federal governments. Jane has been a member of several disability reference groups and advisory councils for many years.

Interviewee 2: Dan (50s, lives in a large regional town) became a quadriplegic at the age of 14, but it was not until many years later that his involvement in the disability sector began. He joined a committee to build a regional respite centre, and has continued to undertake a leadership role in the disabled community since that time. He completed an advanced diploma in information technology and began a consultancy business in database development using Visual Basic for Applications and Microsoft Access. He organised a successful workshop on adaptive technology, was an advocate for an adaptive technology aids and services exposition, and helped coordinate a number of subsequent successful expositions. He also has a leadership role in disability organisations.

Interviewee 3: Bob (50s, lives in a capital city), prior to receiving a spinal-cord injury, pursued a career as a chartered chemist and state analyst, specialising in water chemistry and environmental science. Since then he has worked in consulting, training and teaching. Although now semi-retired, he retains registration as a chartered chemist. His interest in disability issues led him to join the management committees of several disability organisations, and he is also a member of the Transport Lobby Group. He is attracted to people and organisations that are values-driven, and is focused on positive outcomes for people with disability ('particularly those that harness our knowledge, experience and wisdom to tackle the issues that affect our lives'). He said: 'Our voice on issues that affect us!'

Interviewee 4: Jack (30s, lives in a capital city) was born in a different capital city and had started university law/commerce degrees when he incurred a spinal-cord injury as a passenger in a motor-vehicle accident. This was during his first year at university and he was hospitalised for 12 months. He subsequently recommenced studies after his health issues had stabilised and completed a bachelor of law degree with honours. He was admitted to practise as a barrister and solicitor and was employed as a commercial litigator. He then moved north in 1997 (a lifestyle decision) and was admitted as a solicitor. He completed a master of business administration (MBA) as an external university student substantially by means of technology (internet, teleconferencing and CD-ROM), and then worked for the federal government in business education on tax reform. He is a director and company secretary of a southern, national disability organisation and has been a member of the management committee of a peak disability organisation since his relocation.

Interviewee 5: Joe (40s, lives in a capital city) received his spinal-cord injury in 1978. He was appointed to a disability role in the city council in 1990. He sat on the working group for the development of the Disability Services Queensland publication *People with Sensory Disability: Communication and Information Guidelines* in 1996. He then became interested in the capacity of the web as a medium of contact for people who are socially isolated, not able to access transport and near or below the poverty line. From about 1998, as the web grew exponentially, he expanded his interests to include affordable internet service providers, affordable hardware, affordable adaptive software, affordable training and informing people of the value and many benefits of being connected. He continues working in these areas, living in hope that people go online, but fighting fiercely to prevent all information going online solely (the web is only one alternative of several media), as some people choose not to go online and are not to be disenfranchised for this choice.

Interviewee 6: Sally (50s, lives in a capital city) is married with three adult children and one grandchild. She contracted polio at the age of 20 months in New South Wales, Australia, and spent over three years in various hospitals. She attended a special school for children with physical disabilities, then later went to a state school. In 1981, while living in New Zealand, she was involved in an accident which resulted in multiple fractures, leaving her no longer able to walk and having to use a wheelchair. At the time she had three small children and a failing marriage. She became involved in the disability sector in New Zealand and in the International Year of the Disabled Programme (1981), and rose from secretarial positions to become director of the Disabled Persons Resource Centre in Christchurch. Since her return to Australia in 1989 she has continued to work in the disability sector. Sally returned to university in Australia and upgraded her New Zealand studies into a bachelor's degree in community work. She is now studying for her master's in disability leadership from a southern university.

Interviewee 7: Simon (30s, lives in far north Queensland) was very sports-oriented as a youth. In 1986 he suffered a spinal-cord injury in a motorcycle accident, smashing the fifth vertebra in his neck, which left him a complete quadriplegic and resulted in ten months in hospital. After a number of idle years trying to come to terms with his injury, he became a telemarketer. This gave him the opportunity to speak to a lot of people in his community, and also allowed him to work from home. If he were not able to work from home, he would not be able to hold down a paid position, because of the many problems associated with his disability. Then, with his wife's support, he began to become more involved in his community and with issues affecting people who had a disability. He became a facilitator for a north Queensland member network for a disability organisation. Facilitators are the communication link between members and the organisation. He edits the local network's newsletter and e-mails it to network managers and local members. Facilitators also participate in teleconferences every three months. He is in contact with other facilitators, members and staff of the disability organisation by e-mail and phone on a regular basis. Now he is on the management committee of the organisation and, as the head office is in the capital city, management documentation is regularly e-mailed to him and he participates in many board meetings by teleconference. Simon also helped form a local advisory group (Burdekin Disability Advisory Group), whose aim is to be an effective community forum for disability issues. They work hard to raise awareness of the needs of people with a disability in their community, as well as on local, state and federal government levels. Much of Simon's work for this group is information sharing and is carried out using ICT. He also became a north Queensland presenter in spinal awareness education for a Queensland disability organisation. Furthermore, Simon is the disability representative on a number of different local disability organisations, with which he remains in regular contact by ICT. He is also a regular contributor to the Physical Disability Council of Australia's e-mail group, which posts interesting information and discussions concerning people with a disability. He uses the internet for personal use to purchase items, compare features of items he wants to buy, research information on any issue that interests him and e-mail friends. He would not be able to participate in these many organisations and groups if it were not for ICT.

Interviewee 8: Keith (40s, lives in a capital city) is the director of an independent community-based systems and legal advocacy organisation for people with disability in Queensland, Australia. Its mission is to promote, protect and defend, through advocacy, the fundamental needs, rights and lives of the most vulnerable people with disability in Queensland. The organisation achieves its mission by engaging in systems advocacy work through campaigns directed to attitudinal, law and policy change, and by supporting the development of a range of advocacy initiatives in the state. Keith undertook all his tertiary studies after a football accident in the 1980s that resulted in a spinal injury. He completed a master's degree in social welfare and administration. Prior to his position in advocacy, Keith was employed as a policy officer in the Queensland government.

Interviewee 9: Marcie (28, lives in a capital city) has been studying for eight years. First she completed a BA with a double major in psychology, then she gained honours in psychology part-time and has recently finished her master's in clinical psychology. She has been unable to walk since she was eight years old due to an auto-immune muscle-wasting condition known as dermatomyocitis (essentially the immune system becomes overactive and eats away at the muscle tissue). She uses a manual wheelchair at home and when out driving or working, but uses an electric wheelchair for mobility around the university campus. She is fully independent at home with cooking, showering, dressing and all activities involved in daily living.

Interviewee 10: Tom (60s, lives in a capital city) became paraplegic at the age of nine as a result of a gunshot wound. He has been married some 40 years and has four adopted adult children. He was the first person in a wheelchair in New South Wales to adopt children. He gained his leaving certificate and was the first person to attend a New South

Wales high school in a wheelchair. He was introduced to technology very early in his life, even though in those days it was very limited in delivering significant benefits. He has a radio operator's licence and a business management diploma, and spent 28 years working for a large, well-known, international technology company, including 17 years as administration manager, receiving seven Excellence in Management awards during that time. In fact, before he retired he tried – unsuccessfully – to convince this international technology company to fund an adaptive technology centre for all of Australia, as it had done in the USA. Nonetheless, he is credited with instigating the first adaptive technology in Australia – for hearing-impaired pre-school children in the capital city in which he lives. He has held management positions in various voluntary organisations; currently he is a membership promoter for a charitable organisation. He was a high achiever in many areas, and received the Order of Australia Award for service to the community. He is available as a motivational presenter. He recalled that 50 years ago people with disabilities did not aspire to high achievement, because society did not embrace such people and did not believe they had a future. He has a vision that science will prevent, or cure, paraplegia and quadriplegia in the future. He also looks forward to the quality-of-living needs of people with paraplegia or quadriplegia being adequately funded. His current perception of the future for persons with severe physical disabilities is for them to gain, or regain, a sense of control over their lives and independence through access to environmental controls and employment through telecommuting.

Interviewee 11: Sam (35, lives in a capital city) moved to Australia from England with his family when he was aged six. He began his tertiary education at Adelaide University and completed a PhD at the Australian National University in Canberra in 1994. While undertaking fieldwork for the doctorate he was involved in a vehicle roll, resulting in cervical (C4/5) quadriplegia. He moved to Brisbane to undertake a graduate diploma in education (with majors in computer science and chemistry). He was married in 1997, and in 2002 he became the proud father of a daughter. He is employed in the petrochemical industry.

Interviewee 12: Val (40s, lives in a capital city) grew up in a small country town in central Queensland. She went to school there until grade 10; then did various jobs before attending senior school as a mature student and going to university to study journalism. In 1981 she broke her neck in a car accident while still at university: this changed her lifestyle and her career. She has travelled all over the eastern seaboard of Australia and to Europe and Hong Kong. She has learnt so much from other people with a disability. She is a 'technology junkie' and uses a lot of gadgets to make life more comfortable. She enjoys sharing what she knows about technology with other people, and likes to learn what other people have to offer. Currently, she is active on a disability council. She has countless friends and relatives who have given her solid support over the years. Val has used a wheelchair for 21 years and learnt a lot not only about wheelchairs but also about other issues related to living with a disability. She has met some remarkable people who have first-hand knowledge about making life easier for someone with a disability. She said: 'People with disabilities have a wealth of knowledge to share, but nowhere to share it that I could identify. The best place that I could think of for people with disabilities to share their knowledge and experience with one another was over the internet.' This led to her establishing the website Disability Forum in September 2002, with help from a Brisbane-based assistive technology information centre. Disability Forum is a consumer-based website, officially launched on 26 June 2003, where people with a disability network, support each other and develop and maintain friendships in a supportive, interactive online community. Val hopes this site will become a place for people with disabilities, parents of children with disabilities, parents with disabilities and interested parties to exchange information freely and learn from one another. She is constantly amazed how many people are not aware that they have a lot of knowledge to share just from experiencing life dealing with a disability. The Brisbane-based AT information centre continues to support her in the ongoing development of the website. In 2005 it was further developed in conjunction with the state government department Disability Services Queensland, so that it is a 'one-stop shop' in terms of information provided by users for users.

Interviewee 13: Jean is a senior occupational therapist (OT) at a large teaching hospital in a capital city. She has specialised in spinal-cord injury (SCI) rehabilitation since 1985 when the specialist hospital unit first opened. In 1990 she was awarded a Churchill Fellowship to study advances in SCI rehabilitation overseas. In 1992 she was a senior OT at the SCI unit in Toronto, Canada. When she returned to Australia, she lobbied to establish the Spinal Outreach Team (SPOT), a community-based post-rehabilitation health information service in Brisbane, and the transitional rehabilitation programme (TRP). She undertook to work part-time with SPOT initially, and then resumed work as a senior OT in the specialist unit of the teaching hospital.

Interviewee 14: Clara is one of the managers in the assistive technology information centre in a capital city. She graduated with a university bachelor's degree in occupational therapy. Since graduating she has worked with a broad range of people of all ages. Her particular interest in assistive technology began during her work at a special school, where she became the key staff member for investigating, initiating and integrating AT programmes for a range of students. The use of assistive technology enabled students at the special school to become active participants in their environment rather than passive observers excluded by the nature of their disability. Hence her interest in, and commitment to, the value of AT for people with disabilities grew from an awareness of how it empowered individuals simply by allowing them to use what abilities they had rather than being constantly restricted by their 'disabilities'. She has worked in the area of AT options to enhance abilities for the past 16 years, and during that time she has been actively and regularly involved in a range of professional development activities that ensure currency of information. She has worked at the AT information centre since 1995, as a consultant OT for the first five years and then in a managerial role. Initially she specialised in providing information, advice, consultation and education in relation to voice output communication devices, computer access, switch access and environmental control. Currently, she is responsible for service development and management.

Interviewee 15: Barb is an OT with 20 years' experience. In 1989 she was involved with establishing the technology service at an AT information centre based in a capital city, and was an active member of the team for eight years. As a senior OT she established thorough clinical assessment procedures that contributed to the development of AT service delivery. She was the project officer for a joint research initiative that addressed the experience of people with disabilities using AT in the workplace. Barb has a long association with a university and has been instrumental in introducing technology as a key component in the occupational therapy curriculum. She completed her research master's degree investigating the barriers and facilitators for people with disabilities when integrating AT into the workplace. Her current research interests centre on the role of technology and environmental design in enabling people with disabilities to participate equitably in the community.

Interviewee 16: Kerry has over 15 years' experience in disability and technology issues both in Australia and internationally. She has extensive experience of research and policy in disability, the internet and ICT. She manages her own information consultancy business, as well as being employed as a senior research fellow at a university working with smart technology. Currently she is contracted as a policy adviser with TEDICORE (Telecommunications and Disability Consumer Representation) and has ongoing input into government and industry reviews, inquiries and codes' and standards' development. TEDICORE is supported by the Australian Commonwealth through the DCITA Grants to Fund Telecommunications Consumer Representations programme. Kerry is also involved in an advisory capacity with many Australian telecommunications groups. She has initiated and led the disability component of a project with a university that aimed to incorporate user-centred design and accessibility in technology research programmes. This led to the funding of a project on the use of natural language in mobile devices for sight-impaired people. Previously, Kerry worked with the Telematics and Disability Centre of Swedish Telecom (now Telia) and was secretary of the Nordic Forum on Telecommunications and Disability and chair of the Information Transfer Working Group of COST 219, a European Commission Action on telecommunications and disability. She is currently the Australian member of COST 219 ter. She is listed as an expert evaluator of research proposals with the European Commission. She has written many articles and given papers at Australian and international conferences on the internet, accessibility and disability. Early in 2004 she was invited by the Center for Global Communications in Japan to speak at the Asia-Pacific Symposium on ICT Accessibility. She was elected in 2000 as a director on the board of the Internet Society of Australia, and continued to serve into a second term.

Interviewee 17: Kate has been a programme manager at the specialist government post-rehabilitation health information service since 2002. She was a social worker with this service from 1997, and prior to that appointment she was a project officer/social worker with the Spinal Injuries Ambulatory Care Project (SIACP) in a large public teaching hospital. In her capacity as a programme manager for the post-rehabilitation health information service, Kate is expected to show leadership in research on the impact of long-duration spinal-cord injury, have a high level of social work clinical expertise in the management of SCI, be a professional consultant to services state-wide on issues relating to SCI and have a high level of skills in developing, delivering and evaluating education and training on SCI. She has been involved in various funded research projects in recent years, such as 'An Ambulatory Outreach Service and Description of an "Episode of Care"'.

Interviewee 18: Gerry is a senior programme officer at a state government department in a capital city – the first disability-focused government department in this city. Before the department's formation in 1999, the disability programme was part of Family, Youth and Community Care. His role is to provide central support and coordination to various departmental programmes that are delivered across the state. Prior to this appointment, he was an information officer for the specialist disability information and referral service in that government department. He provided information about services and support to assist people with a disability. Other posts he has held in the same government department were regional coordinator of the Volunteer Friends Program, in which he assisted adults with an intellectual disability to connect to their communities through meeting other people and forming friendships; and acting state coordinator of the Volunteer Friends Program/Friendship Program (part-time), working closely with people with a disability and their families to plan and provide high-quality services to enhance the inclusion of disabled people in the community. Before his various roles with the state government, Gerry was a registered nurse/unit manager, specialising in intellectual and psychiatric disability. During this time he worked primarily with people who presented violent and aggressive behaviours. Prior to that he was a youth worker, and created and implemented a range of recreational and skills development programmes for young offenders on remand.

Appendix II: Data analysis sample

Grounded theory

This appendix provides details of the data analysis. As noted in Chapter 5, this analysis is based on the grounded theory method. Grounded theory is defined as 'a qualitative research method that uses a systematic set of procedures to develop an inductively derived grounded theory about a phenomenon' (Strauss and Corbin, 1990: 24). Barney Glaser and Anselm Strauss originally developed this method. Their view was that 'Not everyone can be equally skilled at discovering theory' (Glaser and Strauss, 1967: viii). They suggest that creative and intuitive arrivals at insight are the province of genius, but contend that 'it does not take a "genius" to generate a useful grounded theory' (ibid.: 11).

The grounded theory approach advocates the use of a 'constant comparative method' in which conceptual categories and their properties that emerge from data gathered in one context are tested for relevance in other contexts of the same phenomena (ibid.: 21). The conceptual categories referred to here are preferably developed from the data, but can be borrowed from existing theory. Using categories from existing theory has the danger of selecting data to fit the categories rather than developing categories out of the data. Data are collected to illuminate categories to the point of 'theoretical saturation', which is when 'no additional data are being found whereby the sociologist can develop properties of the category' (ibid.: 61).

The process of analysis

Strauss and Corbin (1998: 12–13) say: 'In this method, data collection, analysis, and eventual theory stand in close relationship to one another.'

They also remind us that 'Analysis is the interplay between researchers and data' and that 'There are procedures to help provide some standardisation and rigour to the process. However, these procedures were designed not to be followed dogmatically, but rather to be used creatively and flexibly by researchers as they deem appropriate.'

After the interview with Bob (Interviewee 3), and without hearing the tape again, the investigator wrote in her fieldnotes her perceptions of the main concepts, questions and issues. Later, after receiving and reading the transcript of the interview, the investigator had further occasion to form a 'feeling' for these concepts, questions and issues. Then an 'open coding' procedure was carried out, as described by Strauss and Corbin (ibid.: 223–9). This is the part of analysis where 'by making comparisons and asking theoretically relevant questions, the theory begins to emerge' (ibid.: 224). As recommended by Strauss and Corbin, a line-by-line analysis was made from which conceptual labels were generated. As the conceptual label was generated, the relevant line numbers were written beside it. Where a comment fitted into more than one conceptual label, the line number was entered beside each relevant label. In later coding an attempt to be more prescriptive was made, and only code for the more significant concepts was written. Some conceptual labels were immediately apparent, and some evolved during the analysis and had to be coded by revisiting the transcript. At the end of coding, the conceptual labels were grouped to establish the categories, as described by Strauss and Corbin. At this stage it became obvious that some conceptual labels contained undifferentiated ideas and were actually categories. This material was then selectively recoded, searching for greater differentiation. Strauss and Corbin (ibid.) maintain that 'Early notes include categories, the concepts that point to categories, and some properties and dimensions.' Table A.1 shows the coding details of Bob's interview.

After generating the conceptual categories as outlined above, a process of cross-checking the material began. A narrative of Bob's interview as an ICT user was drafted from concepts determined as above, in order to test the adequacy of the data obtained from the interview. This was a second analytical step, as well as the beginnings of a reporting procedure that formed the basis of the findings reported in Chapter 6. In drafting the narrative of Bob's interview, the material was organised in a conceptual way and illustrative quotes were selected. Sometimes the material coded under one conceptual label fitted more naturally into another label, and this became more apparent when the narrative was being constructed. This second analytical procedure was invaluable in refining the coding, identifying key issues and testing methodological decisions regarding reporting.

The concept labels and the transcript were entered into the computer using QSR N4Classic (for Microsoft Windows or Macintosh) qualitative data management software. In N4Classic the concept labels are called 'nodes' and the transcript becomes a 'raw file'. The raw file was then re-examined line by line and recoded without reference to the original coding. The original and the recoded versions were then compared and adjustments made where necessary. This extra process provided a useful check on concept labelling and coding. The framework thus developed confirmed the basis of the interview structure for later interviews and ultimately the basis for the hypothesis. Richards and Richards (1991: 53) suggest the potential of computer programs is that the goals of grounded theory become accessible without the risk of jettisoning evidence for emerging themes and with new abilities to interrogate them. That evidence can be examined in simultaneous analysis or subsequent re-analysis of data using different techniques.

Interviewing and coding proceeded in tandem, and modifications of the N4Classic structure were made throughout the timeframe of the study. Some further modifications were made at the reporting stage, but these were minimal. At the reporting stage N4Classic proved invaluable, as it allowed all data in a particular category to be made available with relative ease. This enabled a more complete analysis of data than would have been possible without this electronic assistance.

Table A.1   Coding details of interview from which conceptual categories/properties/dimensions were generated

Concept	Code	Line number
ICT in education/learning for persons with disabilities (EL-)		
Technologically literate	EL-LIT	24–5, 163–9, 280–4, 285–93
Empowerment	EL-EMP	1–3, 126–7, 205–8
Capacity building	EL-CAP	1–3, 116–27
Digital divide	EL-DIG	29–30
Challenging	EL-CHAL	111–12
Shared vision	EL-SHAR	1, 155–6, 272
Stimulating	EL-STIM	205–8
Well-being	EL-WELL	1–3, 199
Information exchange	EL-INFO	116–27, 146–50, 197
Morale	EL-MOR	207, 216–17
Motivation	EL-MOT	1, 204
Skills	EL-SKIL	1–3
Values-driven	EL-VAL	2
Leadership	EL-LEAD	3, 155–6, 225, 272–5
Engagement	EL-ENG	116–27, 207–8, 212–13
Voice	EL-VOI	3
Confidence	EL-CON	126–7
Fantasy or virtual reality for persons with disabilities (FA-)		
Virtual activities	FA-VIR	23, 176, 208–11
Access	FA-ACC	102, 195, 196, 222, 243
Communication	FA-COM	126–7, 165, 212, 250, 284
Interaction	FA-INT	116–27
Barrier-free	FA-BAR	84–90, 176–81
Virtual community	FA-VIRT	20–2, 24–5, 62–75, 85–97, 111–27, 128–39, 261–2
Entertainment	FA-ENT	265
Recreation	FA-REC	123, 125
Participation	FA-PART	126–7, 149–52
Technology-dependent	FA-DEP	32–42
ICT provides information 'at your doorstep' (INFO-)		
Health	INFO-HEA	197–9
Search engines	INFO-SEA	103–6, 288
Disability	INFO-DISA	114–27, 222, 244–7
Assistive technology	INFO-ASS	173–5
Information searching	INFO-INFO	103–6, 191–5, 208, 212, 214, 219, 220–1, 225, 258–9
Information literate	INFO-LIT	48–101
Lifelong learning	INFO-LIFE	191–2, 280–4, 285–93
Discussion groups	INFO-DIS	128–39, 217–18, 220
Freedom	INFO-FREE	98, 101

Interests that ICT makes possible for persons with disabilities (INT-)		
Social conscience	INT-SOC	270–2
Moral purpose	INT-MOR	1–3
Disability rights	INT-DISR	1–3, 199, 272–6
Equity	INT-EQUI	1–3, 155–6
Vision	INT-VIS	1, 180
Autonomy	INT-AUTO	1–3, 180
Self-determination	INT-SELF	3
Civil society	INT-CIV	1–2
Attitudinal change	INT-ATT	2, 155–6, 250–2
ICT-enabled relationships for persons with disabilities (RE-)		
Self-esteem	RE-EST	3, 118
Peer support	RE-PEER	119–27, 133–4
Social networks	RE-SOC	128, 133–4, 165, 212–14, 265–9
Systemic advocacy	RE-SYS	3
Being connected	RE-CONN	23–5, 64, 87, 112, 166, 196, 199, 207, 213, 215, 225, 262, 277
Valued community role	RE-VAL	119–27
Privacy	RE-PRIV	114, 125
Collective experience	RE-COLL	3, 121–7
Transactions (TR-)		
Book tickets/travel	TR-BOOK	123–6
Teleworking	TR-WORK	229–45
Intellectual	TR-INT	256–7, 290–2
Liberating	TR-LIB	191–2, 230–6
Perceived barriers in ICT use (PB-)		
Technological – lack of training	PB-TECH	28, 48–55, 62, 281, 285–9
Physical – assistive equipment	PB-PHY	29–30, 170–2
Costs of connectivity	PB-COST	28, 31–5, 46–7, 56–60, 156–61
Psychological/social costs	PB-PSY	36
Frustrations/irritations	PB-FRUS	172, 253, 199
Inaccessibility	PB-INACC	35–40, 195, 196
Isolation	PB-ISO	36, 65–6, 84–5, 207, 246–55

Appendix III: Glossary

Accessibility means making computers accessible to a wider range of users than would otherwise be the case.

Alienation is the process whereby people become foreign to the world they are living in.

ARATA is the Australian Rehabilitation and Assistive Technology Association, formed in 1995 to serve as a national forum on relevant rehabilitation technology issues.

Assistive technology refers to a broad range of devices, services, strategies and practices that are applied to ameliorate the problems faced by individuals who have disabilities (Cook and Hussey, 1995).

Axial coding is an intermediate coding procedure in which data are put back in new ways after open coding.

Broadband is high-speed internet access technology and is delivered via asymmetrical digital subscriber lines (ADSL), optical fibre cables or microwave and satellite networks.

CONROD (Centre of National Research on Disability and Rehabilitation Medicine, Australia) is a joint initiative of the Motor Accident Insurance Commission (MAIC), the Queensland Institute of Medical Research (QIMR) and the University of Queensland.

COST has the main purpose of coordinating national telecommunications research on a European level. The COST cooperation consists of the European Commission, the 27 EU member states and ten non-member states.

'Design for all', 'universal design' or 'inclusive design' refers to all services and equipment that should be designed taking account of the needs of disabled and older users right from the design phase.

Disablement or disability as defined by the World Health Organization is a restriction or lack of ability (resulting from an impairment) to perform an activity in the manner or within the range considered normal for a human being.

Empowerment refers to each individual's ability to have control over and participate in the decisions that affect his/her life.

Environmental control units (ECUs) or devices provide an alternative means of operating various appliances within the home. Over the past few years there has been a significant growth in the range of equipment available, and this has greatly enhanced the possibilities for people who are unable to use the standard methods of environmental control.

Impairment as defined by the World Health Organization is any loss of function directly resulting from injury or disease

Locus of control refers to an individual's perception of what are the main causes of events in life.

Maslow's 'hierarchy of needs' theory proposes that lower needs must be satisfied before higher needs can be met. The basic need to be satisfied is physiological or survival; only when this need is satisfied will the next highest (safety or security) become important. The hierarchy shows self-actualisation to be the highest and last need, and that can only be reached when all other needs are met.

Mobility (or physical) impairment occurs when disability affects movement, ranging from gross motor skills such as walking to fine motor movements involving manipulation of objects by hand.

Paraplegia is the permanent and total paralysis of both legs.

Quadriplegia is the permanent and total paralysis of both arms and both legs.

Reference group theory is based on the principle that people take the standards of significant others as a basis for making self-appraisals, comparisons and choices regarding need for and use of information.

Social justice is everyone's fundamental right to equal well-being regardless of race, culture, gender, age, income, sexual orientation or geographic location.

Universal Service Obligation (USO) is the obligation under s. 9 of the Telecommunications (Consumer Protection and Service Standards) Act 1999 to ensure that standard telephone service, payphones and prescribed carriage services are reasonably accessible to all Australians on an equitable basis.

Virtual (community) has been used in computing for some time and usually refers to a quality of apparency; that is, something appears to be something it is not. For some people the preferred term is 'online community'.

References, legislation and websites

References

Abramson, L.Y., Garber, J. and Seligman, M.E.P. (1980) 'Learned helplessness in humans: an attributional analysis', in J. Garber and M.E.P. Seligman (eds) *Human Helplessness*. New York: Academic Press, pp. 3–35.

Academy of the Social Sciences in Australia (2004) 'The impact of the mobile telephone in Australia: social science research opportunities', discussion paper prepared by J. Beaton and J. Wajcman, with contributions. Canberra: AMTA.

Alliance for Technology Access (1999) 'Assistive technology connections: meeting the needs of Californians with disabilities', report to California Endowment, March; available at: *www.apt.org/policy/study/art2.html* (accessed: 20 February 2004).

Alm, N., Arnott, J.L., Murray, I.R. and Buchanan, I. (1998) 'Virtual reality for putting people with disabilities in control', in *Systems, Man, and Cybernetics, Proceedings of 1998 IEEE International Conference, San Diego, 11–14 October*, Vol. 2. New York: IEEE, pp. 1174–9.

American Library Association (1989) 'Final report of the Presidential Committee on Information Literacy'; available at: *www.ala.org.au* (accessed: 11 August 2002).

Appleton, K., Tu, A., van de Hoef, K. and Humphries, V. (2004) 'The highs and lows of living with technology: Vicki's day-to-day experience of taking control', paper presented at Australian Rehabilitation and Assistive Technology Association Conference, Melbourne, 2–4 June;

available at: *www.e-bility.com/arataconf/abstracts/appleton.html* (accessed: 16 July 2004).

Armstrong, A. and Hagel, J. (1995) 'The real value of on-line communities', *Harvard Business Review*, 73(3): 134–40.

Astbrink, G. (2002) *Best Practice in Telecommunications for People with a Disability in Australia*. Melbourne: Blind Citizens Australia for Telecommunications and Disability Consumer Representation; available at: *www.bca.org.au/ebmain.htm#contents* (accessed: 11 July 2004).

Astbrink, G. (2004) 'TEDICORE – improving access to telecommunications for people with disabilities', *Accord: Journal of Spinal Cord Injuries Australia*, 6: 29; available at: *www. spinalcordinjuries.com.au* (accessed: 24 September 2004).

Astbrink, G. and Newell, C. (2002a) 'Anomalies in the provision of disability equipment in Australian telecommunications', *Telecommunications Journal of Australia*, 52(4): 39–44.

Astbrink, G. and Newell, C. (2002b) 'Fostering access to telecommunications for Australians with disabilities: the TEDICORE approach', *Telecommunications Journal of Australia*, 52(1): 10–14.

Astbrink, G. and Newell, C. (2002c) 'Towards enabling competition: anomalies in the provision of disability equipment in Australian telecommunications', *Telecommunications Journal of Australia*, 52(4): 27–31.

Australian Bureau of Statistics (2000) *Disability and Long-term Health Conditions*. Canberra: AGPS.

Australian Bureau of Statistics (2004) 'Preliminary findings of the 2003 survey of disability, aging and carers', September. Canberra: AGPS; available at: *www.abs.gov.au/Ausstats* (accessed: 22 October 2004).

Australian Bureau of Statistics (2005) '8153.0 – internet activity, Australia, March 2005'; available at: *www.abs.gov.au/ausstats/abs @.nsf* (accessed: 20 April 2006).

Australian Communications Authority (2000) 'Implementation of Universal Service Obligation contestability pilot projects'; available at: *www.aca.gov.au/consumer/uso/usoimplement_dp.htm* (accessed: 23 October 2000).

Australian Communications Authority (2001) 'Monitoring and reporting on quality of service: possible enhancements in light of the government's action plan in response to the Telecommunications Service Inquiry', discussion paper. Melbourne: ACA.

Australian Communications Industry Forum (2001) 'Industry guidelines: access to telecommunications for people with disabilities', ACIF G586. Sydney: ACIF.

Australian Institute of Health and Welfare (2000) 'Disability – national picture'; available at: *www.aihw.gov.au* (accessed: 22 October 2004).

Australian Library and Information Association (1996a) 'Statement on National Information Policy 1996'; available at: *www.alia.org.au/alia/policies/national.information.html* (accessed: 19 April 2001).

Australian Library and Information Association (1996b) 'Policy statement on information as a commodity and its importance to economic development'; available at: *www.alia.org.au/policies/information.commodity.html* (accessed: 17 February 2005).

Australian Library and Information Association (2002) 'Library and information services for people with a disability'; available at: *www.alia.org.au/policies/disabilities.html* (accessed: 22 October 2007).

Australian Library and Information Association (2003) 'Statement on information literacy for all Australians'; available at: *www.alia.org.au/policies/information.literacy.html* (accessed: 17 February 2005).

Australian Mobile Telecommunications Association (2006) *Mobile Phone Industry Good Practice Guide: Accessibility for People with Disabilities*. Manuka: AMTA.

Australian National Training Authority (2004) 'Shaping our future: Australia's national strategy for vocational education and training (VET) 2004–2010', March; available at: *www.dest.gov.au/sectors/training_skills/policy_issues_reviews/key_issues/nts* (accessed: 20 March 2006).

Australian Regional Telecommunications Infrastructure Fund Secretariat (1998) 'Improving regional telecommunications: the Regional Telecommunications Infrastructure Fund', *Media International Australia: Incorporating Culture & Policy*, 88: 11–24.

Badley, E.M. (1993) 'An introduction to the concepts and classifications of the international classification of impairments, disabilities, and handicaps', *Disability and Rehabilitation*, 15(4): 161–78.

Baker, P.M.A. and Fairchild, A. (2004) 'The virtual workspace: telework, disabilities and public policy'; available at: *http://scholar.google.com/scholar?q=virtual+communities+for+people+with+disabilities&hl=en&lr=&ie=UTF-8&start=170&sa=N* (accessed: 17 May 2006).

Bandura, A. (1997) *Self-efficacy: The Exercise of Control*. New York: W.H. Freeman.

Bar-tal, Y. (1994) 'Uncertainty and the perception of sufficiency of social support, control, and information', *Psychological Record*, 44: 13–24.

Bartle, R.A. (2004) *Designing Virtual Worlds*. Indianapolis, IN: New Riders.

Baumeister, R.F. and Leary, M.R. (1995) 'The need to belong: desire for interpersonal attachments as a fundamental human motivation', *Psychological Bulletin*, 117: 497–529.

Beamish, A. (1995) 'Communities on-line: community-based computer networks', master's thesis, Massachusetts Institute of Technology; available at: *http://hdl.handle.net/1721.1/11860* (accessed: 14 December 2005).

Beattie, K. (1989) 'Alternative community information', *Australian Library Journal*, 38(4): 326–32.

Benton Foundation (1998) 'What's going on – losing ground bit by bit: low-income communities in the information age'; available at: *www.benton.org/Library/Low-Income/* (accessed: 20 May 2002).

Berkman, L.F. and Breslow, L. (1983) *Health and Ways of Living: The Alameda County Study*. New York: Oxford University Press.

Besley, M.A., Bennett, J. and Braithwaite, R. (2000) *Connecting Australia: Report of the Telecommunications Service Inquiry*. Canberra: DCITA; available at: *www.telinquiry.gov.au/final_report. html* (accessed: 17 July 2001).

Bourdieu, P. (1992) 'Think about limits', *Theory, Culture & Society*, 9: 37–49.

Bourk, M.J. (2000) 'Universal service? Telecommunications policy in Australia and people with disabilities'; available at: *www.tomw.net.au/ uso* (accessed: 18 May 2001).

Bradley, J. (1993) 'Methodological issues and practices in qualitative research', *Library Quarterly*, 63: 431–49.

Brenders, D.A. (1987) 'Perceived control: foundations and directions for communications research', in *Communication Yearbook 10*. Beverley Hills, CA: Sage Publications.

Britz, J.J. and Blignaut, J.N. (2001) 'Information poverty and social justice', *South African Journal of Libraries and Information Science*, 67(2): 63–9.

Browne, M. and Edwards, S. (1992) 'How users assess the quality of an information service', in *Priorities for the Future*, Proceedings of First National Reference and Information Service Section Conference and University, College and Research Libraries Section Workshop on Research 1991. Canberra: Australian Library and Information Association, Reference and Information Section, pp. 87–91.

Brownsell, S. and Bradley, D. (2003) 'Assistive technology and telecare: forging solutions for independent living', *Journal of Telemedicine and Telecare*, 9(4): 247–8.

Bruce, C.S. (1997) *The Seven Faces of Information Literacy*. Adelaide: Auslib Press.

Bruce, C.S. (1999) 'Information literacy: an international review of programs and research'; available at: *www.auckland.ac.nz/lbr/conf99/bruce.htm* (accessed: 31 July 2000).

Bruce, C.S. (2000) 'Information literacy research: dimensions of the emerging collective consciousness', *Australian Academic & Research Libraries*, 31(2): 91–109.

Buland, T. and Thomas, D. (2000) 'Technological visions for social change – information technology, tele-work, and the integration of disabled persons', in *Proceedings of ISTAS 2000, IEEE International Symposium on Technology and Society*. Rome: IEEE, pp. 263–8.

Burger, J.M. (1987) 'Desire for control and conformity to a perceived norm', *Journal of Personality and Social Psychology*, 53(2): 355–60.

Burgstahler, S. (1997) 'Peer support: what role can the internet play?', *Information Technology & Disabilities*, 4(4); available at: *www.rit.edu/~easi/itd/itdv04n4/article2.htm* (accessed: 14 July 2000).

Burks, M. (2004) 'Telework and the inclusive workforce'; available at: *www.att.com/telework/article_library/workforce.html* (accessed: 20 February 2004).

Burnett, G. (2000) 'Information exchange in virtual communities: a typology', *Information Research*, 5(4); available at: *http://informationr.net/ir/5-4/paper82.html* (accessed: 25 January 2005).

Burnett, G. and Buerkle, H. (2004) 'Information exchange in virtual communities: a comparative study', *Journal of Computer-Mediated Communication*, 9(2); available at: *http://jcmc.indiana.edu/vol9/issue2/burnett.html* (accessed: 17 May 2006).

Butler, C., Douglas, R.M. and McMichael, A.J. (2001) 'Globalisation and environmental change: implications for health and health inequalities', in R. Eckersley, J. Dixon and R.M. Douglas (eds) *The Social Origins of Health and Well-Being*. Cambridge: Cambridge University Press, pp. 34–50.

Calhoun, C. (2004) 'Information technology and the international public sphere', in D. Schuler and P. Day (eds) *Shaping the Network Society: The New Role of Civil Society in Cyberspace*. Cambridge, MA: MIT Press, pp. 229–51.

Carnegie-Mellon University (2001) 'HomeNet study'; available at: *www-cse.stanford.edu/classes/cs201/projects-00-01/personal-lives/cmu.html* (accessed: 26 May 2003).

Carroll, J.M. (2001) *Human-Computer Interaction in the New Millennium*. Reading, MA: Addison-Wesley.

Casalegno, F. and Kavanaugh, A. (1998) 'Concerning communities and telecommunications networks', *Societies*, 59: 63–77.

Centre of National Research on Disability and Rehabilitation Medicine (1998) *REHADAT Australia National Disability Database Linkage Project: Final Report*. Brisbane: CONROD.

Chamberlin, J.A. (1997) 'A working definition of empowerment', *Psychiatric Rehabilitation Journal*, 20(4): 43–6.

Chang, A., Kannan, P.K. and Whinston, A.B. (1999) 'Electronic communities as intermediaries: the issues and economics', in R.H. Sprague (ed.) *Proceedings of Thirty-second Hawaii International Conference on System Sciences*. Los Alamitos, CA: IEEE Computer Society Press, pp. 1–10.

Chatman, E.A. (1988) 'Opinion, leadership, poverty and information sharing', *Reference Quarterly*, 26(3): 341–53.

Chatman, E.A. (1991) 'Life in a small world: applicability of gratification theory to information-seeking behavior', *Journal of American Society for Information Science*, 42(6): 438–49.

Chatman, E.A. (1996) 'The impoverished life-world of outsiders', *Journal of American Society for Information Science*, 47(3): 193–206.

Chatman, E.A. (1999) 'A theory of life in the round', *Journal of American Society for Information Science*, 50(3): 207–17.

Chatman, E.A. (2000) 'Framing social life in theory and research', in L. Hoglund (ed.) *The New Review of Information Behaviour Research: Studies of Information Seeking in Context*. London: Graham Taylor.

Chatman, E.A. and Pendleton, V.E.M. (1995) 'Knowledge gap, information-seeking and the poor', in J.B. Whitlatch (ed.) *Library Users and Reference Services*. New York: Hawthorn Press, pp. 135–45.

Cheuk, B. (1998) 'An information seeking and using process model in the workplace: a constructivist approach', *Asian Libraries*, 7(12): 375–90.

Childers, T. (1975) *The Information Poor in America*. Metuchen, NJ: Scarecrow Press.

Civille, R. (1995) 'The internet and the poor', in B. Kahan and J. Keller (eds) *Public Access to the Internet*. Cambridge, MA: MIT Press, pp. 175–207.

Cohen, S. and Syme, S.L. (1984) *Social Support and Health*. Orlando, FL: Academic Press.

Cohill, A. and Kavanaugh, A. (1997) *Community Networks: Lessons from Blacksburg, Virginia*. Norwood, MA: Artech House Publishers.

Cole, C. (1997) 'Calculating the information content of an information process for a domain expert using Shannon's mathematical theory of communication: a preliminary analysis', *Information Processing and Management*, 33(6): 715–26.

Commonwealth Procurement Guidelines and Best Practice Guidance (2001) *Communicating with Customers Who Are Disabled: A Guide for Telecom Companies*, Oftel; available at: *www.ofcom.org.uk/publications/consumer/gpm0901.htm* (accessed: 23 February 1999).

Community Network Movement (undated) 'Seattle Community Network principles'; available at: *www.scn.org/ip/commnet/principles.html* (accessed: 11 July 2000).

Compaine, B.M. (2001) *The Digital Divide: Facing a Crisis or Creating a Myth?* Cambridge, MA: MIT Press.

Connell, B., Jones, M., Mace, R., Mueller, J., Mullick, A., Ostroff, E., Sanford, J., Steinfeld, E., Story, M. and Vanderheiden, G. (1997) *Principles of Universal Design*. Raleigh, NC: North Carolina State University, Center for Universal Design; available at: *www.design.ncsu.edu:8120/cud/univ_design/principles/udprinciples.htm* (accessed: 23 February 1999).

Cook, A.M. and Hussey, S.M. (1995) *Assistive Technologies: Principles and Practice*. St Louis, MO: Mosby.

Coopers & Lybrand (1988) *The Information Needs of Disabled People, Their Carers and Service Providers*. London: Department of Health and Social Services.

Council of Australian University Librarians (2001) *Information Literacy Standards*. Canberra: CAUL; available at: *www.caul.org.au/policy/p_infol.htm* (accessed: 17 February 2005).

Coutts, P. (1998) 'A user needs methodology – identifying the telecommunications needs of services supporting people with a disability', paper presented at ARATA SA Conference, Adelaide, November; available at: *http://regencyrehab.cca.org.au/arata/userneed.htm* (accessed: 22 March 1999).

Cox, E. (1995) 'Raising social capital', Lecture 2 in 'The Boyer Lectures: a truly civil society', 14 November. Sydney: Australian Broadcasting Corporation – Radio National.

Crawley, H.D. (2002) 'The best of both worlds', in *Electronic Networking 2002 – Building Community*, Proceedings of Fifth

Community Networking Conference, Monash University, Melbourne, 3–5 July; available at: *www.ccnr.net/2002/* (accessed: 29 July 2004).

Cullen, K. and Robinson, S. (1997) *Telecommunications for Older People and Disabled People in Europe: Preparing for the Information Society*. Amsterdam: IOS Press.

Dawson, E.M. and Chatman, E.A. (2001) 'Reference group theory with implications for information studies: a theoretical essay', *Information Research*, 6(3): 1–32; available at: *http://informationr.net/ir/6-3/paper105.html* (accessed: 25 January 2005).

De Cindio, F. (2004) 'The role of community networks in shaping the network society: enabling people to develop their own projects', in D. Schuler and P. Day (eds) *Shaping the Network Society: The New Role of Civil Society in Cyberspace*. Cambridge, MA: MIT Press, pp. 199–225.

Department of Communications, Information Technology and the Arts (2000) 'Second progress report'. Canberra: DCITA.

Department of Communications, Information Technology and the Arts (2002) 'Advancing Australia – the information economy progress report 2002'. Canberra: DCITA.

Department of Communications, Information Technology and the Arts (2003) 'Enabling our future: a framework for the information and communications technology industry', report of the Framework for the Future Steering Committee, April. Canberra: DCITA.

Department of Communications, Information Technology and the Arts (2004) 'Strategic framework for the information economy 2004–2006: opportunities and challenges for the information age'. Canberra: DCITA.

Department of Communications, Information Technology and the Arts (2005) 'The role of ICT in building communities and social capital: a discussion paper'; available at: *www.dcita.gov.au/ie/community_connectivity/community_ict_transformationdiscussion_papers_and_case_studies* (accessed: 16 March 2005).

Dervin, B. (1992) 'From the mind's eye of the user: the sense-making qualitative/quantitative methodology', in J.D. Glaser and R.R. Powell (eds) *Qualitative Research in Information Management*. Englewood, CO: Libraries Unlimited, pp. 61–84; available at: *www.mcc.ufc. br/etagi/projetobb/zendervinpowell92.html* (accessed: 18 March 2005).

Diaper, D. and Stanton, N. (2004) *The Handbook of Task Analysis for Human-Computer Interaction*. Mahwah, NJ: Lawrence Erlbaum.

Dixon, J., Douglas, R.M. and Eckersley, R. (2000) 'Making a difference to socio-economic determinants of health in Australia: a research and development strategy', *Medical Journal of Australia*, 172: 541–4.

Doyle, C. (1992) 'Outcome measures for information literacy within the national education goals of 1990: final report to the National Forum on Information Literacy – summary of findings', ERIC ED 351033; available at: *http://eric.ed.gov:80/ERICWebPortal/custom/portlets/ recordDetailsdetailmini.jsp_nfpb=true&_&ERICExtSearch_Search Value_0=ED351033&ERICExtSearch_SearchType_0=no&accno= ED351033* (accessed: 22 June 2004).

Dube, T., Hurst, R., Light, R. and Malinga, J. (2005) *Promoting Inclusion? Disabled People, Legislation and Public Policy.* London: DAA.

Eckersley, R., Dixon, J. and Douglas, R.M. (2001) *The Social Origins of Health and Well-being.* Cambridge: Cambridge University Press.

Edwards, S., Bruce, C. and McAllister, L. (2004) 'Information literacy research: the consolidation of a theme', paper presented at Research Applications in Information and Library Studies, QUT Brisbane, 20 September; available at: *www.csu.edu.au/* (accessed: 17 May 2006).

Emiliani, P.L. (1997) 'Information technology, telecommunications and disability: an approach towards integration', *ERCIM News*, 28, January; available at: *www.ercim.org/publication/Ercim_News/ en w28/emiliani.html* (accessed: 20 February 2004).

Epstein, J. (1980) *The Information Needs of the Elderly.* London: Department of Health and Social Services.

Estens, D., Bennett, J. and Braithwaite, R. (2002) *Connecting Regional Australia: Report of the Telecommunications Regional Service Inquiry.* Canberra: DCITA; available at: *www.telinquiry.gov.au/rti-report.html* (accessed: 2 May 2003).

Feeney, M. and Grieves, M. (eds) (1994) *The Value and Impact of Information.* London: Bowker Saur.

Ferguson, E., Dodds, A., Ng, L. and Flannigan, H. (1994) 'Perceived control: distinct but related levels of analysis?', *Personal Individual Differences*, 16(3): 425–32.

Figello, C. (1998) *Hosting Web Communities.* New York: John Wiley & Sons.

Foley, M.W. and Edwards, B. (1998) 'Beyond Tocqueville: civil society and social capital in comparative perspective', *American Behavioral Scientist*, 42(1): 5–20.

Folkman, S. (1984) 'Personal control and stress and coping processes: a theoretical analysis', *Journal of Personality and Social Psychology*, 46(4): 839–52.

Friedmann, J. (1992) *Empowerment: The Politics of Alternative Development*. Cambridge, MA: Blackwell.

Furlong, M.S. (1989) 'An electronic community for older adults: the SeniorNet network', *Journal of Communication,* 39: 145–53.

Galvin, J.C. (1997) 'Assistive technology: federal policy and practice since 1982', *Technology and Disability*, 6: 3–15.

Gaziano, C. (1997) 'Forecast 2000: widening knowledge gaps', *Journalism and Mass Communications Quarterly*, 74(2): 237–64.

Glaser, B.G. (1978) *Theoretical Sensitivity: Advances in the Methodology of Grounded Theory*. Mill Valley, CA: Sociology Press.

Glaser, B.G. (1992) *Basics of Grounded Theory Analysis: Emergence vs Forcing*. Mill Valley, CA: Sociology Press.

Glaser, B.G. and Strauss, A.L. (1967) *Discovery of Grounded Theory: Strategies for Qualitative Research*. New York: Aldine.

Glasgow, R.E. and Eakin, E.G. (2000) 'Medical office-based interventions', in F.J. Snoek and T.C. Skinner (eds) *Psychology in Diabetes Care*. Chichester: John Wiley & Sons, pp. 141–68.

Goggin, G. and Newell, C. (2000a) 'An end to disabling policies? Towards enlightened universal service', *Information Society*, 16: 127–33.

Goggin, G. and Newell, C. (2000b) 'Twenty-five years of disabling technologies: the case of telecommunications', in M. Clear (ed.) *Promises Promises: Disability and Terms of Inclusion*. Leichhardt, NSW: Federation Press, pp. 148–58.

Goggin, G. and Newell, C. (2003) *Digital Disability: The Social Construction of Disability in New Media*. Lanham, MD: Rowman & Littlefield Publishers.

Goggin, G. and Newell, C. (2004) 'Disabled e-nation: telecommunications, disability, and national policy', *Prometheus*, 22(4): 411–22.

Guo, B., Bricout, J.C. and Huang, J. (2005) 'A common open space or a digital divide? A social model perspective on the on-line disability community in China', *Disability & Society*, 20(1): 49–66; available at: *http://taylorandfrancis.metapress.com/* (accessed: 15 May 2006).

Gygi, K. (1995) 'Developing an evaluation framework for community computer networks', unpublished report, Community and Regional Planning Program, University of New Mexico.

Habermas, J. (1991) *Communication and the Evolution of Society*. Cambridge: Polity Press.

Haidt, J. and Rodin, J. (1995) 'Control and efficacy: an integrative review', report to MacArthur Foundation Program on Mental Health and Human Development, John D. and Catherine T. MacArthur Research Network on Socioeconomic Status and Health; available at: *www.macses.ucsf.edu/Publications/pubchron.html* (accessed: 6 August 2005).

Hakkinen, M.T. and Velasco, C.A. (2004) *Including Accessibility as a Component of Web-related Research: Ensuring that the Fruits of Your Work Will Be Usable by All*. New York: ACM Press; available at: *http://doi.acm.org/10.1145/985921.986163* (accessed: 16 May 2006).

Hargittai, E. (2002) 'Second level digital divide: differences in people's online skills', *First Monday*; available at: *www.firstmonday. dk/issues/issue7_4/hargittai/index.html* (accessed: 15 January 2004).

Harper, V.B. (2000) 'Digital divide (DD): redirecting the efforts of the scholarly community'; available at: *http://users.cnu.edu/~vharper/ documents/Digital%20Divide%20position%20paper1(hypertext%20 version)* (accessed: 10 July 2002).

Haythornthwaite, C. and Wellman, B. (1998) 'Work, friendship, and media use for information exchange in a networked organisation', *Journal of American Society for Information Science*, 49(12): 1101–14.

Hirose, M. (ed.) (2001) *Human-Computer Interaction*, Proceedings of INTERACT 2001, Tokyo, July. Amsterdam: IOS Press.

Hockenberry, J. (2001) 'This is the story of the most fearless entrepreneur ever: the human brain', *Wired*, August: 4–15.

Hoffman, D.L. and Novak, T.P. (1998) 'Bridging the digital divide: the impact of race on computer access and internet use', *Science*, 280: 390–401.

Hughes, H., Middleton, M., Edwards, S., Bruce, C. and McAllister, L. (2005) 'Information literacy research in Australia 2000–2005', pre-print in English, translated by Oristelle Bonis and published as 'La recherche australienne en maitrise de l'information 2000–2005', *Bulletin des Bibliotheques de France*, 50(6): 45–55; available at: *http://bbf.enssib.fr/* (accessed: 17 May 2006).

Human Rights and Equal Opportunity Commission (2000) 'Accessibility of electronic commerce and new service and information technologies for older Australians and people with a disability: a HREOC report on a reference from the Attorney-General', 31 March; available at:

www.hreoc.gov.au/disability_rights/inquiries/ecom/ecomrep.htm (accessed: 19 April 2001).

Human Rights and Equal Opportunity Commission (2005) 'WORKability I: barriers – people with disability in the open workplace', HREOC, Sydney; available at: *www.hreoc.gov.au/ disability_rights/employment_inquiry/final/ch3.htm* (accessed: 17 February 2007).

Human Rights and Equal Opportunity Commission (2006) 'WORKability II: solutions – a report'; available at: *www. humanrights.gov.au/disabilityrights/employmentinquiry/index.htm* (accessed: 17 February 2007).

Ife, J.W. (2001) *Community Development: Community-based Alternatives in an Age of Globalisation*, 2nd edn. Frenchs Forest, NSW: Pearson Education.

Independent Living Centre Association of Queensland (2003) 'Sharing wheel knowledge', *From Ocean to Outback*, 2(3): 1.

International Meeting of Information Literacy Experts (2003) *The Prague Declaration: Towards an Information Literate Society*; available at: *www.infolit.org/International_Conference/Prague Declaration.doc* (accessed: 14 March 2005).

Jafari, A. and Sheehan, M. (eds) (2003) *Designing Portals: Opportunities and Challenges*. Purdue University IN and Montana State University: Information Science Publishing.

Jolley, W. (2003) 'When the tide comes in: towards accessible telecommunications for people with disabilities in Australia', discussion paper commissioned by Human Rights and Equal Opportunity Commission. Sydney: William Jolley & Associates for HREOC.

Jones, Q. (1997) 'Virtual-communities, virtual-settlements and cyber-archeology: a theoretical outline', *Journal of Computer-Mediated Communication*, 3(3); available at: *www.ascusc.org/jcmc/vol3/ issue3/jones.html* (accessed: 10 July 2005).

Jones, Q. and Rafaeli, S. (2000) 'Time to split, virtually: discourse architecture and community building as a means to creating vibrant virtual public and electronic markets', *International Journal of Electronic Commerce and Business Media*, 10(4): 214–23.

Julien, H.E. (1999) 'Barriers to adolescents' information seeking for career decision making', *Journal of the American Society for Information Science*, 50(1): 38–48.

Kelle, U. (1997) 'Theory building in qualitative research and computer programs for the management of textual data', *Sociological Research*

Online, 2(2); available at: *www.socresonline.org.uk/socresonline/2/2/1.html* (accessed: 5 March 2001).

Kempson, E. (1987) *Informing Health Consumers: A Review of Consumer Health Information Needs and Services*. London: College of Health.

Kendall, J. (1999) 'Axial coding and the grounded theory controversy', *Western Journal of Nursing Research*, 21(6): 743–57.

Kimble, C. and Hildreth, P. (2005) 'Dualities, distributed communities of practice and knowledge management', *Journal of Knowledge Management*, 9(4): 102–13.

Kling, R. (1998) 'Technological and social access to computing, information and communication technologies', white paper for Presidential Advisory Committee on High-Performance Computing and Communications, Information Technology, and the Next Generation Internet; available at: *www.slis.indiana.edu/kling/pubs/NGI.htm* (accessed: 20 May 2002).

Koh, J. and Kim, Y. (2003) 'Sense of virtual community: a conceptual framework and empirical validation', *International Journal of Electronic Commerce*, 8(2): 75–94.

Komito, L. (1998) 'The net as a foraging society: flexible communities', *Information Society*, 14(2): 97–106.

Kvale, S. (1995) 'The social construction of validity', *Qualitative Inquiry*, 1(1): 19–40.

Kvale, S. (1996) *Interviews: An Introduction to Qualitative Research Interviewing*. Thousand Oaks, CA: Sage Publications.

Lamb, B. and Layzell, S. (1995) *Disabled in Britain. Behind Closed Doors: The Carer's Experience*. London: SCOPE.

Lazar, J. and Preece, J. (1998) 'Classification schema for online communities', in E.D. Hoadley and I. Benbasat (eds) *Proceedings of 1998 Association for Information Systems, Americas Conference*. Atlanta, GA: Association for Information Systems, pp. 84–6; available at: *www.ifsm.umbc.edu/~preece/Papers/1998_AMCIS_Paper.pdf* (accessed: 6 March 2006).

Lenhart, A., Horrigan, J., Rainie, L., Allen, K., Boyce, A., Madden, M. and O'Grady, E. (2003) 'The ever-shifting internet population: a new look at internet access and the digital divide', Pew Internet & American Life Project; available at: *www.Pewinternet.org/* (accessed: 11 May 2003).

Levy, P. (1998) *Becoming Virtual: Reality in the Digital Age*, trans. from French by R. Bononno. New York: Plenum Trade.

Lewis, O. (1969) *On Understanding Poverty: Perspectives from the Social Sciences*. New York: Basic Books.

Li, H. (2004) 'Virtual community studies: a literature review, synthesis and research agenda', in *Proceedings of the Tenth Americas Conference on Information Systems*, New York, August; available at: *e-business.fhbb.ch/eb/publications.nsf/id/345* (accessed: 17 May 2006).

Light, J.S. (2001) 'New technologies and regulation: why the future needs historians?', *Law Review*, 2: 241–4.

Lloyd, B. and Thornton, P. (1998) *Views of Older People on Getting Help When It Is Needed and on Continuing to Get Around*. York: Age Concern.

Longworth, N. (2002) 'Learning cities for a learning century: citizens and sectors – stakeholders in the lifelong learning community', in K. Appleton, C. Macpherson and D. Orr (eds) *Building Learning Communities through Education: Refereed Papers from Second International Lifelong Learning Conference*, Yeppoon, Queensland, 16–19 June. Rockhampton, QL: Central Queensland University Press, pp. 10–35.

Loos, C., Astbrink, G. and McClure, R. (1998) *REHADAT Australia: National Disability Database Linkage Project – Final Report*. Brisbane: CONROD.

Lyman, P. (1998) 'The poetics of the future: information highways, virtual communities and digital libraries', Lazerow Lecture, School of Library and Information Science, UCLA, 18 November; available at: *http://commons.somewhere.com/rre/1998/RRE.Peter.Lyman.html* (accessed: 17 April 2003).

Lyman, P. (1999) 'The social functions of digital libraries: designing information resources for virtual communities', in *Proceedings of Australian Information Online & Ondisc '99: Strategies for the Next Millennium*, Sydney, 19–21 January; available at: *www.csu.edu.au/special/online99/proceedings99/300b.htm* (accessed: 17 April 2003).

Madden, R. and Hogan, T. (1996) *The Definition of Disability in Australia: Moving Towards National Consistency*, Australian Institute of Health and Welfare; available at: *www.aihw.gov.au/publications/w_online/disdefn/disdefn.html* (accessed: 20 May 2002).

Mainelli, M. (2003) 'Risk/reward in virtual financial communities', *Information Services & Use*, 23(1): 9–18.

Marmot, M.G. (1995) 'Social differentials in mortality: the Whitehall Studies', in A.D. Lopez, G. Caselli and T. Valkonen (eds) *Adult Mortality in Developed Countries: From Description to Explanation*. Oxford: Clarendon Press.

Marmot, M.G. and Wilkinson, R.G. (1999) *Social Determinants of Health*. Oxford: Oxford University Press.

Marmot, M.G., Bosma, H., Hemingway, H., Brunner, E. and Stansfeld, S. (1997) 'Contributions to job control and other risk factors to social variations in coronary heart disease incidence', *The Lancet*, 350: 235–9.

Maslow, A.H. (1943) 'A theory of human motivation', *Psychological Review*, 50: 37–96.

Matei, S. (2005) 'From counterculture to cyberculture: virtual community discourse and the dilemma of modernity', *Journal of Computer-Mediated Communication*, 10(3); available at: *http://jcmc.indiana.edu/vol10/issue3/matei.html* (accessed: 17 May 2006).

Maxwell, J.C. (1870) *Address to the Mathematics and Physics Section*. London: British Association for the Advancement of Science.

McDonald, A. and Denning, P. (2002) 'Defining, measuring, and narrowing the digital divide – a community perspective', in G. Johanson and L. Stillman (eds) *Electronic Networking 2002 – Building Community: Conference Proceedings*. Melbourne: Monash University, Centre for Community Networking Research; available at: *www.ccnr.net/2002/* (accessed: 20 February 2004).

McEwen, B.S. (1998) 'Protective and damaging effects of stress mediators', *New England Journal of Medicine*, 338: 171–9.

Meier, A. (2002) 'EnableNet (www.enable.net.au) disability information and resource centre', *Post-Polio News: Quarterly Newsletter of Post-Polio Support Group of South Australia*, 65 (March): 8.

Merton, R.K. and Zuckerman, H.A. (1972) 'Age, aging, and age structure in science', in M.W. Riley, M. Johnson and A. Foner (eds) *A Theory of Age Stratification*, Vol. 3 of *Aging and Society*. New York: Russell Sage Foundation, pp. 292–356.

Metoyer-Duran, C. (1993) 'The information and referral process in culturally diverse communities', *Research Quarterly*, Spring: 359–71.

Midwest Institute for Telecommuting Education (2003) 'Telecommuting: a work option for persons with disabilities'; available at: *www.mite.org/telecommutdisabilities/telecommutdisabilities.html* (accessed: 20 February 2004).

Miller, W.R. and Seligman, M.E.P. (1975) 'Depression and learned helplessness in man', *Journal of Abnormal Psychology*, 84: 228–38.

Mitchell, J. (1998) *Fragmentation to Integration: National Scoping Study for the Telemedicine Industry in Australia*. Canberra: Department of Science and Industry.

Moore, N. (2000) *The Information Needs of Visually Impaired People: A Review of Research for the RNIB*. Leeds: Acumen.

Moore, N. and Steele, J. (1991) *Information-intensive Britain: A Critical Analysis of the Policy Issues*. London: Policy Studies Institute.

Morino, M. (1994) *Assessment and Evolution of Community Networking*. Washington, DC: Morino Institute.

Mossberger, K., Tolbert, C.J. and McNeal, R.S. (2007) *Digital Citizenship: The Internet, Society, and Participation*. Cambridge, MA: MIT Press.

Myers, M. (2000) 'Qualitative research and the generalizability question: standing firm with proteus', *Qualitative Report*, 4(3/4); available at: *www.nova.edu/ssss/QR/QR4-3/myers.html* (accessed: 6 August 2005).

National Office for the Information Economy (1998a) 'Towards an Australian strategy for the information economy: a preliminary statement of the government's policy approach and a basis for business and community consultation', July; available at: *www.noie.gov.au/docs/strategy/strategy.htm* (accessed: 22 March 1999).

National Office for the Information Economy (1998b) 'A strategic framework for the information economy: identifying priorities for action', December; available at: *www.noie.gov.au/docs/strategy/strategicframework.htm* (accessed: 22 March 1999).

National Office for the Information Economy (1999) 'A strategic framework for the information economy, overview: key priorities for action'; available at: *www.noie.gov.au/strategy/strategic_summaries.htm* (accessed: 1 September 1999).

Newell, C. (1998) 'Disability, disadvantage and telecommunications', in B. Langtry (ed.) *All Connected: Universal Service in Telecommunications*. Carlton, Vic.: Melbourne University Press; available at: *www.dice.org.au/online/dd&t.htm* (accessed: 4 July 2000).

Nguyen, T., Garrett, B., Downing, A., Walker, L. and Hobbs, D. (2004) 'Research into telecommunications options for people with physical disabilities', paper presented at ARATA National Conference; available at: *www.ebility/com/arataconf/abstracts/nguyen2.html* (accessed: 16 July 2004).

Nicholas, D. (1996) *Assessing Information Needs: Tools and Techniques*. London: Aslib/Association for Information Management.

Odasz, F. (undated) 'An executive overview for project planners on the hard questions for community internet empowerment'; available at: *http://lone-eagles.com/overview.htm* (accessed: 14 May 2003).

Odasz, F. (1994) 'Community economic development networks: a grassroots leadership challenge', *Internet Research*, 4(1): 2–6.

Odasz, F. (1995a) 'Community networks: an implementation planning guide', Big Sky Telegraph, Dillon, MT; available at: *telnet://bigsky.big/sky.dillon.mt.us/pub/franko/Guide* (accessed: 13 May 1999).

Odasz, F. (1995b) 'Humanizing the internet: librarians, citizens, and community networking', in *Rural Libraries and Internetworking*. Metuchen, NJ: Scarecrow Press, pp. 85–96.

Odasz, F. (1995c) 'Issues in the development of community cooperative networks', in B. Kahin and J. Keller (eds) *Public Access to the Internet*. Cambridge, MA: MIT Press, pp. 115–36.

Oliver, M. (1990) *The Politics of Disablement: A Sociological Approach*. New York: St Martin's Press.

Optus (2001) 'DDA action plan', SingTel Optus, Sydney; available at: *http://www3.optus.com.au/content/1,1463,107,00.html* (accessed: 22 June 2002).

Pantry, S. (1999) *Building Community Information Networks: Strategies and Experiences*. London: Library Association Publishing.

Paraplegic and Quadriplegic Association of Queensland (1997) *1997 Member Survey: Report*. Brisbane: I.G. Bennett and Associates, February.

Paraplegic and Quadriplegic Association of Queensland (1999) *1999 Member Survey: Report*. Brisbane: I.G. Bennett and Associates, February.

Paraplegic and Quadriplegic Association of Queensland (2001) *2001 Member Survey: Report*. Brisbane: I.G. Bennett and Associates, February.

Paraplegic and Quadriplegic Association of Queensland (2003) *2003 Member Survey: Report*. Brisbane: Simons and Associates, February.

Partridge, H., Bruce, C. and Tilley, C. (2008) 'Community information research: developing an Australian research agenda', *Libri: International Journal of Libraries and Information Services*, 58(2): 110–22.

Patton, M.Q. (1990) *Qualitative Evaluation and Research Methods*. Newbury Park, CA: Sage Publications.

Pell, S.D. (1998) 'The effects of voice recognition systems on writing styles: implications for use in the education environment', *Australian Educational Computing*, 12(2): 14–18.

Pell, S.D., Gillies, R.M. and Carss, M. (1997) 'The relationship between use of technology and employment rates for people with physical disabilities in Australia: implications for education and training programs', *Disability and Rehabilitation*, 19: 332–8.

Pell, S.D., Gillies, R.M. and Carss, M. (1999) 'Use of technology by people with physical disabilities in Australia', *Disability and Rehabilitation*, 21: 56–61.

Pendleton, V.E. and Chatman, E.A. (1998) 'Small worlds: implications for the public library', *Library Trends*, 46(4): 732–52.

Peterson, C., Maier, S.F. and Seligman, M.E.P. (1993) *Learned Helplessness: A Theory for the Age of Personal Control*. New York: Oxford University Press.

Pew Internet & American Life Project (2000) *The Internet Life Report – Tracking On-line Life: How Women Use the Internet to Cultivate Relationships with Family and Friends*. Washington, DC: Pew Research Center.

Phillips, H. (1996) *Information for Elderly People: A Vital But Missing Link in Community Care*. Plymouth: Plymouth University.

Portes, A. (1998) 'Social capital: its origin and applications in modern sociology', *Annual Review of Sociology*, 24(1): 1–24.

Preece, J. (ed.) (1993) *A Guide to Usability: Human Factors in Computing*. Wokingham: Addison-Wesley.

Preece, J. (2000) *Online Communities: Designing Usability, Supporting Sociability*. Chichester: John Wiley & Sons.

Preece, J. and Maloney-Krichmar, D. (2003) 'Online communities', in J.A. Jacko and A. Sears (eds) *Handbook of Human-Computer Interaction: Fundamentals, Evolving Technologies, and Emerging Applications*. Mahwah, NJ: Lawrence Erlbaum, pp. 596–620.

Preece, J., Maloney-Krichmar, D. and Abras, C. (2003) 'History of emergence of online communities', in B. Wellman (ed.) *Encyclopedia of Community*. Great Barrington, MA: Berkshire Publishing Group/Sage Publications.

Preece, J., Rogers, Y. and Sharp, H. (2001) *Interaction Design*. New York: John Wiley & Sons.

Preece, J., Rogers, Y., Sharp, H., Benyon, D., Holland, S. and Carey, T. (1994) *Human-Computer Interaction*. Wokingham: Addison-Wesley.

Priebe, T. (2005) 'Building integrative enterprise knowledge portals with semantic web technologies', in *Dissertations in Database and Information Systems Infix*, Vol. 92. Amsterdam: IOS Press.

Putnam, R.D. (2000) *Bowling Alone: The Decline and Revival of American Community*. New York: Simon & Schuster.

Reinharz, S. (1992) *Feminist Methods in Social Research*. Oxford: Oxford University Press.

Renninger, K.A. (2002) *Building Virtual Communities: Learning and Change in Cyberspace*. Cambridge: Cambridge University Press.

Rheingold, H. (1994a) 'A slice of life in my virtual community', in L.M. Harasim (ed.) *Global Networks: Computers and International Communication*. Cambridge, MA: MIT Press, pp. 57–80.

Rheingold, H. (1994b) *The Virtual Community: Homesteading on the Electronic Frontier*. New York: HarperPerennial.

Rheingold, H. (2002) *Smart Mobs: The Next Social Revolution*. Cambridge, MA: Basic Books.

Richards, L. and Richards, T. (1991) 'The transformation of qualitative method: computational paradigms and research processes', in N.G. Fielding and R.M. Lee (eds) *Using Computers in Qualitative Research*. Newbury Park, CA: Sage Publications, pp. 38–53.

Rideout, V. (2003) *Continentalizing Canadian Telecommunications: The Politics of Regulatory Reform*. Montreal: McGill-Queen's University Press.

Rideout, V. and Reddick, A. (2005) 'Sustaining community access to technology: who should pay and why', *Journal of Community Informatics Online*, 1(2); available at: *www.ci-journal.net/viewarticle.php?id=39* (accessed: 28 April 2006).

Rodin, J. (1986) 'Aging and health: effects of the sense of control', *Science*, 233: 1271–6.

Rodin, J. and Langer, E.J. (1977) 'Long-term effects of a control-relevant intervention with the institutionalised aged', *Journal of Personality and Social Psychology*, 35: 897–902.

Rodin, J., Timko, C. and Harris, S. (1985) 'The construct of control: biological and psychological correlates', *Annual Review of Gerontology & Geriatrics*, 5: 3–55.

Roe, P.R.W. (ed.) (2001) *Bridging the Gap? Access to Telecommunications for All People*, Commission of European Communities (COST 219); available at: *www.tiresias.org/phoneability/bridging_the_gap/index.htm* (accessed: 22 November 2003).

Rotberg, R.I. (1999) 'Social capital and political culture in Africa, America, Australasia and Europe', *Journal of Interdisciplinary History*, 29(3): 339–56.

Rothbaum, R., Weisz, J.R. and Snyder, S.S. (1982) 'Changing the world and changing the self: a two-process model of perceived control', *Journal of Personality and Social Psychology*, 42: 5–37.

Rotter, J. (1966) 'Generalized expectancies for internal versus external control of reinforcement', *Psychological Monographs*, 80(1): 1–28.

Roulstone, A. (1998) *Enabling Technology: Disabled People, Work and New Technology*. Buckingham: Open University Press.

Ryff, C.D. and Singer, B. (1998) 'The contours of positive human health', *Psychological Inquiry*, 9(1): 1–28.

Sample, I. (2005) 'The first clinical trial to implant blood vessels', *The Guardian*, 16 November.

Scherer, M.J. (2000) *Living in the State of Stuck: How Technology Impacts the Lives of People with Disabilities*, 3rd edn. Cambridge, MA: Brookline Books.

Schiller, H.I. (2005) 'The global information highway: project for an ungovernable world', in J. Brook and L.A. Boal (eds) *Resisting the Virtual Life: The Culture and Politics of Information*. San Francisco: City Lights, pp. 17–33.

Schott, G. and Hodgetts, D. (2006) 'Health and digital gaming: the benefits of a community of practice', *Journal of Health Psychology*, 11(2): 309–16.

Schuler, D. (1994) 'Community networks: building a new participatory medium', *Communications of the ACM*, 37(1): 39–51.

Schuler, D. (1995) 'Public space in cyberworld: community networks are as important to society as public libraries', *Internet World*, 6(12): 88–95; available at: *www.scn.org/ip/commnet/iwdec.html* (accessed: 21 April 1999).

Schuler, D. (1996a) 'Developing and sustaining community networks'; available at: *www.scn.org/ip/commnet/workshop.html* (accessed: 21 April 1999).

Schuler, D. (1996b) *New Community Networks – Wired for Change*. Reading, MA: Addison-Wesley.

Schuler, D. (1997) 'Let's partner as patriots: the future of democracy may lie in linking libraries with community networks', *American Libraries*, 28(8): 60–2; available at: *www.scn.org/ip/commnet/abshome.html* (accessed: 21 April 1999).

Schuler, D. (2000) 'New communities and new community networks', in M. Gurstein (ed.) *Community Infomatics: Enabling Communities with Information and Communication Technologies*. Hershey, PA: Idea Group Publishing.

Schultz, R., Heckhausen, J. and O'Brian, A.T. (1994) 'Control and the disablement process in the elderly', *Journal of Social Behavior and Personality*, 9: 139–52.

Seeman, M. (1975) 'Alienation studies', *Annual Review of Sociology*, 1: 91–123.

Seeman, M. and Lewis, S. (1995) 'Powerlessness, health and mortality: a longitudinal study of older men and mature women', *Social Science & Medicine*, 41: 517–25.

Seeman, M. and Seeman, T.E. (1983) 'Health behavior and personal autonomy', *Journal of Health & Social Behavior*, 24: 144–60.

Seeman, T.E. (1991) 'Personal control and coronary artery disease: how generalized expectancies about control may influence disease risk', *Journal of Psychosomatic Research*, 35: 661–9.

Seeman, T.E., Rodin, J. and Albert, M.A. (1993) 'Self-efficacy and cognitive performance in higher functioning older individuals: MacArthur studies of successful aging', *Journal of Aging & Health*, 5: 455–74.

Seiler, R.J., Seiler, A.M. and Ireland, J.M. (1997) 'Enhancing internet access for people with disabilities', in P.P. Maglio and R. Barrett (eds) *Proceedings of Seventh International World Wide Web Conference*, Brisbane; available at: *www.gippsnet.com.au/eiad/spathrep.htm* (accessed: 22 March 1999).

Servon, L. (2002) *Confronting the Digital Divide: Technology, Community and Public Policy.* Oxford: Blackwell.

Seymour, W. and Lupton, D. (2004) 'Holding the line online: exploring wired relationships for people with disabilities', *Disability & Society*, 19(4): 291–305; available at: *http://taylorandfrancis.metapress.com/* (accessed: 17 May 2006).

Shakespeare, T. and Watson, N. (2002) 'The social model of disability: an outdated ideology?', *Journal of Research in Social Science and Disability*, 2: 9–28; available at: *www.leeds.ac.uk/disabilitystudies/archiveuk/titles.html* (accessed: 10 May 2004).

Shearman, C. (1999) 'Local connection: making the net work for people and communities', paper presented at Community Networking Conference 'Engaging Regionalism', Ballarat, Victoria, September, unpublished.

Sheldon, A. (2003) 'Changing technology', in J. Swain, S. French, C. Barnes and C. Thomas (eds) *Disabling Barriers – Enabling Environments*. London: Sage Publications.

Shneiderman, B. (1998) *Designing the User Interface: Strategies for Effective Human-Computer Interaction*, 3rd edn. Reading, MA: Addison-Wesley.

Silver, D. (2004) 'The soil of cyberspace: historical archaeologies of the Blacksburg Electronic Village and the Seattle Community Network', in D. Schuler and P. Day (eds) *Shaping the Network Society: The New*

Role of Civil Society in Cyberspace. Cambridge, MA: MIT Press, pp. 301–24.

Smith, G. (1995) 'Virtual community in reality...', paper presented at Communities Online Conference, October; available at: *www.panizzi. shef.ac.uk/community/virtreal.htm* (accessed: 21 April 1999).

Smith, G. (2003) 'Why we need an assistive technology policy', *Link Magazine*, 12(2): 20.

Spender, L. (2000) 'Access issue won't go away', *Australian IT*, 25 February; available at: *http://wysiwyg://22/http://australianit.com.au. ..E16%252D03%252D2000%255Eopinion,00.htm* (accessed: 22 March 2000).

Sproull, L. and Kiesler, S. (1991) *Connections: New Ways of Working in the Networked Organization*. Cambridge, MA: MIT Press.

Strauss, A.L. (1995) 'Notes on the nature and development of general theories', *Qualitative Inquiry*, 1(1): 7–18.

Strauss, A.L. and Corbin, J. (1990) *Basics of Qualitative Research: Grounded Theory Procedures and Techniques*. London: Sage Publications.

Strauss, A.L. and Corbin, J. (1994) 'Grounded theory methodology: an overview', in N.K. Denzin and Y.S. Lincoln (eds) *Handbook of Qualitative Research*. Thousand Oaks, CA: Sage Publications, pp. 273–85.

Strauss, A.L. and Corbin, J. (1998) *Basics of Qualitative Research: Techniques and Procedures for Developing Grounded Theory*. Newbury Park, CA: Sage Publications.

Street, P. (1998) *Information Needs of the Elderly: The Role of the Public Library*. Liverpool: John Moores University.

Taylor, H. (2000a) 'Many people with disabilities feel isolated, left out of their communities and would like to participate more', *Harris Poll*, 34, 5 July; available at: *www.harrisinteractive.com/harris_poll/ index.asp?PID=97* (accessed: 20 February 2004).

Taylor, H. (2000b) 'How the internet is improving the lives of Americans with disabilities', *Harris Poll*, 30, 7 June; available at: *www.harrisinteractive.com/harris_poll/index.asp?PID=93* (accessed: 20 February 2004).

Technology Literacy Assessment Work Group (2003) 'Setda national leadership institute toolkit (definition of technology literacy)'; available at: *www.setda.org/NL Itoolkit/TLA/tla02.htm* (accessed: 11 February 2005).

Telstra Disability Services (1998) *Telstra's Second Disability Action Plan, 1999–2001*. Melbourne: Telstra Corporation.

Telstra Disability Services (2002) *Telstra's Third Disability Action Plan, 2002–2004*. Melbourne: Telstra Corporation; available at: *www.telstra.com.au/disability/dap_02_04.htm* (accessed: 29 June 2003).

Tester, S. (1992) *Common Knowledge: A Coordinated Approach to Information Giving*. London: Centre for Policy on Ageing.

Thurlow, C., Lengel, L.B. and Tomic, A. (2004) *Computer Mediated Communication: Social Interaction and the Internet*. Thousand Oaks, CA: Sage Publications.

Tilley, C.M., Bruce, C.S. and Hallam, G. (2007) 'Adaptive technology for people with physical disabilities using information and communications technology (ICT)', in C. Deines-Jones (ed.) *Improving Library Services to People with Disabilities*. Oxford: Chandos Publishing, pp. 65–86.

Tilley, C.M., Bruce, C.S., Hallam, G. and Hills, A.P. (2006) 'A model for the development of virtual communities for people with long-term, severe physical disabilities', *Information Research*, 11(3); available at: *http://InformationR.net/ir/11- 3/paper253.html* (accessed: 13 December 2006).

Tilley, C.M., Hills, A.P., Bruce, C.S. and Meyers, N. (2002) 'Communication, information and well-being for Australians with physical disabilities', *Disability & Rehabilitation*, 24(9): 503–10; available at: *www.tandf.co.uk/journals/* (accessed: 3 April 2005).

Tinker, A., McCreadie, C. and Salvage, A. (1993) *The Information Needs of Elderly People – An Exploratory Study*. London: Age Concern Institute of Gerontology.

Turner, N. and Pinkett, R. (2004) 'Community building and community technology: an asset-based approach', in P. Day and D. Schuler (eds) *Community Practice in the Network Society: Local Action/Global Interaction*. London: Routledge.

UNESCO (2005) 'Information for All programmes: thematic debate on information literacy', 5 April; available at: *www.unesco.org* (accessed 3 June 2005).

United Nations (1982) *World Programme of Action Concerning Disabled Persons*; available at: *www.un.org/esa/socdev/enable/diswpa00.htm* (accessed: 30 September 2007).

United Nations (1993) *Standard Rules on the Equalization of Opportunities for Persons with Disabilities*; available at: *www.un.org/documents/ga/res/48/a48r096.htm* (accessed: 30 September 2007).

United Nations (2003) 'The questionnaire on human functioning and disability statistics', Demographic and Social Statistics Division; available at: *www.un.org* (accessed: 30 September 2007).

United Nations (2006) *Demographic Yearbook*, Statistics Division; available at: *http://unstats.un.org/UNSD/demographic/products/dyb/DYB%20questionnaires/Dis_part1.pdf* (accessed: 30 September 2007).

Urquhart, C. (1997) 'Exploring analyst-client communication: using grounded theory techniques to investigate interaction in informal requirements gathering', in A.S. Lee, J. Liebenau and J.I. DeGross (eds) *Information Systems and Qualitative Research*. London: Chapman & Hall, pp. 149–81.

Urquhart, C. (2001) 'An encounter with grounded theory: tackling the practical and philosophical issues', in E.M. Trauth (ed.) *Qualitative Research in IS: Issues and Trends*. Hershey, PA: Idea Group Publishing, pp. 104–40.

US Department of Commerce (1997) *A Framework for Global Electronic Commerce*. Washington, DC: Department of Commerce; available at: *www.technology.gov/digeconomy/framewrk.htm* (accessed: 2 July 2007).

US National Telecommunications and Information Administration (1995a) *The Global Information Infrastructure: Agenda for Cooperation*. Washington, DC: NTIA; available at: *www.ntia.doc.gov/reports/giiagend.html* (accessed: 21 December 2007).

US National Telecommunications and Information Administration (1995b) 'Falling through the net: a survey of the "have-nots" in rural and urban America'. Washington, DC: NTIA; available at: *www.ntia.doc.gov/ntiahome/fallingthru.html* (accessed: 20 May 2002).

US National Telecommunications and Information Administration (1999) 'Falling through the net: defining the digital divide'. Washington, DC: NTIA; available at: *www.ntia.doc.gov/ntiahome/fttn99/contents.html* (accessed: 20 May 2002).

US National Telecommunications and Information Administration (2000) 'Falling through the net: toward digital inclusion. A report on American's access to technology tools'. Washington, DC: NTIA; available at: *www.ntia.doc.gov/ntiahome/fttn00/Falling.htm* (accessed: 20 May 2002).

US NCD (1996) *Access to the Information Superhighway and Emerging Technologies for People with Disabilities*. Washington, DC: NCD;

available at: *www.ncd.gov/newsroom/publications/1996/superhwy. htm* (accessed: 20 October 2007).

Venkatesh, M., Nosovitch, J. and Miner, W. (2004) 'Next generation community networks and user participation', in P. Day and D. Schuler (eds) *Community Practice in the Network Society: Local Action/Global Interaction*. London: Routledge.

Verbrugge, L.M. and Jette, A.M. (1994) 'The disablement process', *Social Science & Medicine*, 38(1): 1–14.

Waddell, C.D. (1998) 'Applying the ADA to the internet: a web accessibility standard', paper presented at American Bar Association National Summit on Disability Law and Policy: In Pursuit – A Blueprint for Disability Law and Policy, Washington, DC, 17–19 June; available at: *www.rit.edu/~easi/law/weblaw1.htm* (accessed: 3 May 2004).

Waddell, C.D. (1999) *Understanding the Digital Economy: Data, Tools and Research – The Growing Digital Divide in Access for People with Disabilities: Overcoming Barriers to Participation in the Digital Economy*. Washington, DC: US Department of Commerce; available at: *www.icdri.org/CynthiaW/the_digital_divide.htm* (accessed: 20 February 2004).

Warschauer, M. (2003) *Technology and Social Inclusion: Rethinking the Digital Divide*. Cambridge, MA: MIT Press.

Webb, M. (1988) 'Provision of information for people with disabilities', *ACROD Newsletter*, September: 12–13.

Wellman, B. (1982) 'Studying personal communities', in P.M.N. Lin (ed.) *Social Structure and Network Analysis*. Beverley Hills, CA: Sage Publications, pp. 61–80.

Wellman, B. (1997) 'An electronic group is virtually a social network', in S. Kiesler (ed.) *Culture of the Internet*. Mahwah, NJ: Lawrence Erlbaum, pp. 179–205.

Wellman, B. (ed.) (1999) *Networks in the Global Village: Life in Contemporary Communities*. Boulder, CO: Westview Press.

Wellman, B. (2001) 'Physical place and cyberplace: the rise of personalised networking', *International Journal of Urban and Regional Research*, 25(2): 227–52.

Wellman, B. and Gulia, M. (1999) 'Net surfers don't ride alone: virtual communities as communities', in M. Smith and P. Kullock (eds) *Communities in Cyberspace*. New York: Routledge, pp. 167–94.

Wen, X. and Fortune, N. (1999) *The Definition and Prevalence of Physical Disability in Australia*. Canberra: Australian Institute of Health and Welfare.

West, D. (2002) 'Engaging the non-user of information technology: motivations and barriers', in G. Johanson and L. Stillman (eds) *Electronic Networking 2002 – Building Community: Conference Proceedings*. Melbourne: Monash University, Centre for Community Networking Research; available at: *www.ccnr.net/2002/* (accessed: 20 February 2004).

Westbrook, L. (2001) *Identifying and Analysing User Needs: A Complete Handbook*. New York: Neal-Schuman Publishers.

Whittaker, S., Issacs, E. and O'Day, V. (1997) 'Widening the net: workshop report on the theory and practice of physical and network communities', *SIGCHI Bulletin*, 29(3): 127–37.

Whyte, W.F. (1981) *Street Corner Society: The Social Structure of an Italian Slum*, 3rd edn. Chicago: University of Chicago Press.

Williamson, K. and Stayner, R. (1980) 'Information and library needs of the aged', *Australian Library Journal*, 29: 188–95.

Williamson, K., Schauder, D. and Bow, A. (1999) 'Information seeking by blind and sight impaired citizens: an ecological study'; available at: *www.shef.ac.uk/~is/publications/infres/paper79.html* (accessed: 24 July 2000).

Williamson, K., Stockfield, L., O'Neill, F., Schauder, D. and Wright, S. (2002) 'Assisting literacy through the internet', in G. Johanson and L. Stillman (eds) *Electronic Networking 2002 – Building Community: Conference Proceedings*. Melbourne: Monash University, Centre for Community Networking Research; available at: *www.ccnr.net/2002/* (accessed: 20 February 2004).

Wilson, I. and Goggin, G. (1993) *Reforming Universal Service: The Future of Consumer Access and Equity in Australian Telecommunications*. Sydney: Consumers' Telecommunications Network.

Winter, I. (ed.) (2000) *Social Capital and Public Policy in Australia*. Melbourne: Australian Institute of Family Studies.

Wolfensberger, W. (1975) *The Origin and Nature of Our Institutional Models*. Syracuse, NY: Human Policy Press.

Wolfensberger, W. (1983) 'Social role valorization: a proposed new term for the principle of normalization', *Mental Retardation*, 21(6): 234–9.

Women with Disabilities Australia (2002) 'Submission to Regional Telecommunications Inquiry', September. Rosny Park, Tas: WWDA.

Women with Disabilities Australia (2004a) *Annual Report, September 2003 – September 2004*. Rosny Park, Tas: WWDA.

Women with Disabilities Australia (2004b) 'Development of an accessible information and referral portal for women with disabilities in Australia: project plan'. Rosny Park, Tas: WWDA, unpublished.

World Health Organization ([1980] 1997) *International Classification System of Impairments, Activities and Participation (ICIDH)*. Geneva: WHO.

World Wide Web Consortium (undated) 'Web Accessibility Initiative'; available at: *www.w3.organisation/WAI* (accessed: 24 July 2000).

Young, K.S. (2004) 'Internet addiction: a new clinical phenomenon and its consequences', *American Behavioral Scientist*, 48(4): 402–15.

Zarb, G., Arthur, S., Light, R. and Barnes, C. (1998) *Disablement and Social Exclusion*. London: Policy Studies Institute.

Zimmerman, D.E., Muraski, M., Estes, E. and Hallmark, B. (1997) 'A formative evaluation method for designing WWW sites', in *Proceedings of IEEE International Professional Communication Conference*, Salt Lake City, 22–25 October. Piscataway, NJ: IEEE, pp. 223–30.

Legislation

Australia

Disability Discrimination Act (1992); available at: *www.hreoc.gov.au/disability_rights/* (accessed: 21 March 2006).

Telecommunications Act (1997); available at: *www.austlii.edu. au/au/legis/cth/consol_act/ta1997214/index.html* (accessed: 6 September 1999).

Telecommunications (Consumer Protection and Service Standards) Act (1999); available at: *www.comlaw.gov.au/ComLaw/Management. nsf/lookupindexpagesbyid/IP2004 01807?OpenDocument* (accessed: 17 February 2008).

Telecommunications (Equipment for the Disabled) Regulations (1998); available at: *http://legislation.gov.au/ComLaw/Legislation/Legislative Instrument1.nsf/0/C56CDF B4F68D0C7ECA256F700080 C830? OpenDocument* (accessed: 12 February 2007).

Canada

Telecommunications Act (1993); available at: *http://laws. justice.gc.ca/ en/StatutoryRes* (accessed: 26 May 2007).

Europe

COST 219 bis Telecommunications Charter (1999); available at: *www.stakes.fi/cost219/charter.htm* (accessed: 17 July 2005).

United Kingdom

Data Protection and Freedom of Information Act (2003); available at: *www.jisc.ac.uk/publications/publications/pub_ib_foi.aspx* (accessed: 30 September 2007).

Disability Discrimination Act (1995); available at: *www.opsi.gov.uk/ acts/acts1995/ukpga_19950050_en_1* (accessed: 30 December 2007).

Disability Discrimination Act (2005); available at: *www.opsi.gov.uk/ Acts/acts2005/ukpga_20050013_en_1* (accessed: 30 December 2007).

Electronic Telecommunications Act (2000); available at: *www.opsi.gov.uk/acts/acts2000/ukpga_20000007_en_1* (accessed: 30 September 2007).

Privacy and Electronic Communications (EU Directive) Regulations (2003); available at: *www.opsi.gov.uk/si/si2003/20032426.htm* (accessed: 30 September 2007).

Special Education Needs and Disability Act (2001); available at: *www.opsi.gov.uk/acts/acts2001/ukpga_20010010_en_1.htm* (accessed: 30 September 2007).

Telecommunications Act (1984); available at: *www.ofcom.org.uk/ static/archive/acts/act_ownpages/about_acts.htm* (accessed: 30 September 2007).

United States

Americans with Disability Act (1990); available at: *www.eeoc.gov/ada/* (accessed: 30 September 2007).

Assistive Technology Act (2004); available at: *http://frwebgate.access. gpo.gov/cgibin/getdoc.cgi?dbname=108_cong_public_laws& docid=f:publ364.108* (accessed: 30 September 2007).

Communications Act (1996); available at: *www.fcc.gov/telecom.html* (accessed: 30 September 2007).

Technology-Related Assistance Act (1988); available at: *www.resna.org/ taproject/library/laws/techact88.htm* (accessed: 30 September 2007).

Websites

Association of Assistive Technology Act Programs: *www.ataporg.org*.

Australian Communications Authority: *www.aca.org.au*.

Australian Mobile Telecommunications Association: *www.amta.org.au*.

BITES programme (Australia): *http://bites.dest.gov.au*.

Blacksburg Electronic Village: *www.bev.net*.

Blind Citizens' Australia: *www.bca.org.au*.

BridgIT project: *www.qrwn.org.au/*.

BT Age and Disability Action: *www.btplc.com/age_disability*.

Centre of National Research on Disability and Rehabilitation Medicine, Australia (CONROD): *www.conrod.uq.edu.au*.

Disability Forum: *www.disabilityforum.org.au*.

Disability Friends Web Pals Around the World: *www.geocities.com/ dfriendswebpals/*.

Disability Lifestyles: *www.disabilitylifestyles.org.au*.

EnableNet: *www.enable.net.au*.

EQUAL Telework Project (UK): *http://content.equaltelework.org*.

Equality and Human Rights Commission (UK): *www.equalityhuman rights.com*.

European Commission Action on Telecommunications and Disability: *www.cost219.org*.

Green PC: *www.greenpc.com.au*.

Human Rights and Equal Opportunity Commission (Australia): *www. humanrights.gov.au*.

Internet Society of Australia: *www.isoc-au.org.au*.

Merc@dis (Spain): *www.mercadis.com*.

National Office for the Information Economy (Australia): *www.noie. gov.au*.

Oftel: *www.ofcom.org.uk*.

PDCA discussion list: *pdca@ozemail.com.au*.

Physical Disability Council of Australia: *www.pdca.org.au*.

REHADAT Canada: *www.nidmar.ca*.

REHADAT Germany: *www.rehadat.de/English.htm*.

Seattle Community Network: *www.scn.org/*.

Telecommunications Disability Consumer Representation (TEDICORE): *http://tedicore.ipb.icemedia.com.au*.

Telstra Consumer Consultative Council: *www.telstra.com.au/tccc/index.htm*.

Telstra Disability Services Unit: *www.telstra.com.au/disability*.

UN Online Volunteering Service: *www.onlinevolunteering.org*.

Wireless Association: *www.accesswireless.org*.

Women with Disabilities Australia: *www.wwda.org.au*.

World Wide Web Consortium: *www.w3.org/*.

Index